THE

CALCULUS OF OPERATIONS.

BY JOHN PATERSON, A. M.

ALBANY :
GRAY AND SPRAGUE.
1850.

J. MUNSELL, PRINTER,
ALBANY.

PREFACE.

The object of the present publication is partly experimental. Of the sciences denominated mathematical, geometry and trigonometry, the first in point of simplicity, are occupied primarily with the measurement of space, and afterwards incidentally with the determination of the mutual relations of various lines and angles. Arithmetic and algebra, the next in order, deal in the combination of numbers, and other ratios of a more general form, without, however, having hitherto made due inquiry into the origin and genesis of such ratios; in consequence of which omission, the operations of algebra are conducted in a sort of twilight of the understanding, the obscurity of which is increased fourfold by the frequent apparition of certain shadowy spectres, the ostensible offspring of an orthodox communion of rational deductions, but under the highly questionable guise of negative and imaginary creatures of the reason, which, like some other familiar sprites, often perform a labor of herculean dimensions at the conjurer's bidding, and then vanish, he cannot say whither. Lastly, in fluxions and mechanics, which complete the purely mathematical domain, the great problem properly consists in returning from the abstract, the ratio of unknown genesis, to the concrete, the power that generated that ratio; and thus we know this power only at second hand, that is, through the medium of ratio, itself very obscurely if at all understood, whereas such power is immediately knowable and definable as the actual generator of the very ratio in question. Now there is one feature common to all these three divisions of mathematical science : they are all constituted by the performance of operations, and exist only through the results of such operations ; and every operation involves its measure in space and time. By the calculus of operations, then, we are to give to each several form of ratio *a local habitation* as well as *a name*, by showing its actual genesis under the action of powers whose capacity and law are defined and assigned *a priori* ; and this genesis of the abstract once clearly established, a return to the concrete follows as of course. The proposed experiment is to try how far it is possible to substitute one homogeneous method, which operates on a clear stage and asks no favor, for the three comparatively darkling and defective processes of the geometrical, the algebraical, and the fluxionary methods hitherto in vogue.

A desire to contribute something towards revealing the harmony and unity which really exists among several of the chiefest and most fundamental formulæ of mathematical calculation, but which apparently stand in a somewhat isolated position with respect to each other, forms the complementary incentive to this publication.

CONTENTS.

CHAPTER I.

CLASSIFICATION AND EXPOSITION, p. 1.

CHAPTER II.

MEASUREMENT OF SPACE, AND OF FORCE OF THE FIRST ORDER, p. 8.

CHAPTER III.

THE OPERATION OF DIVISION p. 67.

CHAPTER IV.

COMPOSITION AND DECOMPOSITION OF OPERATIONS, p. 71.

CHAPTER V.

THEORY OF GENERATING POWERS, p. 79.

CHAPTER VI.

THEORY OF DESTROYING POWERS, p. 112.

CHAPTER VII.

THEORY OF REPEATING POWERS, p. 143.

CHAPTER VIII.

THE CALCULUS OF OPERATIONS, p. 165.

ADDENDA, p. 181.

RESEARCHES

IN THE

CALCULUS OF OPERATIONS.

CHAPTER I.

CLASSIFICATION AND EXPOSITION.

1. FOR the purpose of characterizing the investigations undertaken in this essay, and assigning their relative position in the general domain of science, it is convenient to arrange the infinite variety of nature under five divisions or categories, as follows :

1. SPACE, existences of extension;
2. TIME, existences of duration;
3. NOUMENA, existences of causation;
4. PHENOMENA, existences of production;
5. RATIOS, existences of intellection.

The two first categories, space and time conjoined, constitute the *containing universe;* the third and fourth, or cause and effect, comprise the *contained universe;* and the fifth category, namely, that of relations or ideas, arises from the comparison or combination and elimination of different existences of the preceding categories, and composes the *intellectual universe.*

2. SPACE is a primeval existence, infinite and eternal, and absolute in the relations of its parts, which serve to measure immediately the individual existences of production, and mediately those of causation; and from the comparison of these measures of production (phenomena), are deduced the individual existences of intellection (ratios). Space cannot be annihilated, nor altered : it would subsist nonetheless, were all its contents destroyed; and no power whatever can alter the relation of the diagonal to the side of the square.

3. TIME is also a primeval existence, eternal, and absolute in the relations of its parts, which are conjoined with those of space in the measurement of phenomena. Time cannot be arrested, nor inverted : it would continue to flow nonetheless were all events to cease, and no power whatever can change the relation between the past and the future.

Space contains all that exists simultaneously, independently of time; for, at any point of time, all the contents of the universe exist in space, even while the time is yet null. Space is neither cause nor effect, neither principle nor consequence, and is therefore unsusceptible of ordinary logical definition, which always proceeds by cause and effect, or, which is equivalent, by genus and species : it is a zero or nothing (vacuum) among phenomena; but, considered as a subject, it possesses the two attributes of magnitude and direction, attributes which are immediately available for the determination of the quantity and quality of phenomena.

Time contains all that exists successively, independently of space; for at any point of space, an event may transpire in time (such as the revolution of a point), without any change of place. Like space, time is neither cause nor effect, neither principle nor consequence, and is therefore equally unsusceptible of ordinary logical definition : it is itself a zero in extent, but is nevertheless accurately measurable in extent, by a process which determines immediately the quantity of a phenomenon, together with that of the space and time it occupies.

Space and time being severally simple or homogeneous existences, the analysis of one single definite portion of either of them establishes the true nature of the infinite remaining similar portions, and this is the reason of the simplicity and universality of geometrical and arithmetical truths; while the contents of space and time, consisting of an indefinite multiplicity of different elements or forces, endowed with different qualities or acting in different and varying directions, require multiplied observations for their determination, whereby the progress of physical science is proportionally retarded, and the universality of its facts restricted.

Space and time have neither commencement nor termination; but of their contents, many noumena or substances have both a beginning and an end, and all phenomena are of transitory existence.

4. The third category of existences comprises the NOUMENA, or efficient causes of the various phenomena or effects which make up the sensible contents of the universe. All the varied and complicated forms of existences of causation, of substance or noumena, may be conceived to arise from the act of one simple primitive noumenon developing itself in space and time according to different and oftimes interfering laws. To this primitive noumenon, or being of unfathomable origin, is attributed a perfect intelligence and an almighty power, subject only to the conditions of space and time. Regarded as a power of an infinitely high order, the acts of the primitive being may consist in the direct emanation, at pleasure, of other powers of any desired degree of inferiority, each endowed with the capacity to generate power of the next inferior order according to a predetermined law, and so on until terminating at the power of the order zero, or the phenomenon. So by development and combination, that is, the interference of different generated and generating powers, the primitive single power or noumenon finally originates the immediate efficient cause of each and every phenomenon or event in the universe; and it is the object of the following investigations to exhibit an example of such a deduction, and to show synthetically the possibility of the rational construction of a phenomenal world.

5. PHENOMENA form the fourth category, that of existences of production; and are nothing more than the revelation or mani-

fested existence of the noumena, their path or resultant in space. A phenomenon is merely the sensible resultant of interfering forces or noumena; and it is the task of analysis, in any given phenomenon, to discover the component noumena of which the phenomenon is the sensible expression and the unit measure. A resultant is always first resolvable into two components : these may each again be resolved into two still simpler components; and so on, until the ultimate elements, or generating noumena, are finally determined. A single force, existing or proceeding according to a determinate law, without encountering in its progress any opposing or combining force, would have nothing whereon to act, and therefore could produce no effect, no resultant, no phenomenon; but two encountering forces may act upon each other, and beget phenomena in space and time.

All phenomena, then, in which there occurs a uniform change in space and time, are susceptible of accurate measurement, and thus become incorporated in the domain of the exact or mathematical sciences, in which, the principles once ascertained, the consequences can be infallibly predicted : such will be the case where the phenomena result from a comparatively simple combination of noumena, as in the simpler problems of terrestrial and celestial mechanics, of optics, etc.; but where the complication of the noumena is so great as to elude reduction or isolation, as is particularly the case in questions involving the principles of vegetable and animal life, for instance, in which no standard unit of measurement can be obtained, the phenomena can only become the subject of probable knowledge, wherein the future is always afflicted with some degree of uncertainty.

As an illustration of the measurement of a simple phenomenon in space, suppose a body, placed at O, to be moved uniformly, by the exertion of a force or power of the first order (a constant velocity), from O to P. From the consideration of this operation we collect the following four fundamendal positions of mathematical science :

.O———P.

1. In *space*, the line OP is the measure of the distance between the points O and P, that is, of the linear extent lying between these two points;

2. In *time*, the line OP, having been described by the body with a uniform motion, is the measure of the time occupied in its description;

3. In *effect*, the phenomenon, which consists in the passage of the body from the point O directly to the point P, is truly measured by the same line OP ; and,

4. In *cause*, the phenomenon being here assumed to be the full and complete manifestation of its corresponding noumenon or generating cause, that cause is evidently measured by the phenomenon of which the measure is the line OP*.

6. Ratios constitute our fifth category of existence, the existences of intellection : they are obtained by the comparison,

1. Of different portions of space ;
2. Of different portions of time, when referred to their measures in space ;
3. Of different phenomena, when referred to their measures in time and space; and,
4. Of different noumena, when referred to their corresponding phenomena as their measures.

Ratios or ideas (for it might be shown that all our ideas are nothing else but relations or ratios) are freed from the element of space by the process of elimination; but the element of time is essential to their existence, and enables us always at pleasure to refer them again to space.

.O____P.

As a simple illustration, suppose a body to move uniformly from O to P : the line OP is the measure 1° of the distance OP itself, 2° of the time consumed in the transition from O to P, and 3° of the phenomenon or motion of the body. Suppose also the line O′P′ to have been described under similar con-

.O'________________________P'.

* The last position refers to the cause only as a fixed, and not as a variable one; for, if the cause varies, so also will its effect, and OP would not in that case be a general measure of the cause whose effect it measured at the time the line was described.

ditions : we have a threefold measure, just as in the former case. Now to obtain the ratio of $O'P'$ to OP, or the numerical relation of the two lines or measures, we proceed by applying OP as a unit measure say from P' towards and unto O' (which operation would evidently be equivalent to that of returning a unit mobile from P' to O'); and if we find that $P'O'$ contains x applications of PO, we conclude that,

1. The distance $O'P'$ is x times the distance OP;
2. The time occupied in $O'P'$ is x times that in OP; and,
3. The effect $O'P'$ is x times the effect OP.

Or if $OP = 1$ linear unit, $O'P' = x$ linear units.

By the return of the mobile from P' to O', the former effect, its transfer from O' to P', is neutralized; so that the line $O'P'$, considered as the measure of the phenomenon as well as of the distance itself, is now eliminated; but the ratio x of $O'P'$ to OP remains of record, and may at pleasure be taken as the ratio of the distance $\frac{O'P'}{OP}$, of the time $\frac{O'P'}{OP}$, or of the effect $\frac{O'P'}{OP}$. If $O'P'$ and OP were equal, we should obtain the ratio of equality $\frac{OP}{OP} = 1$.

By the elimination of the element of space as above, the individual effect which was measured by $O'P'$ is abstracted, as well as the time it occupied; but when once the faculty of intellection has constructed a ratio by this double process of direct and inverse operation, we can return from the abstract to the concrete by one single effort, since it is only necessary to recal (reproduce) the notion of the particular ratio, that is, the idea itself; and as the reproduction of this idea necessarily involves the element of time, it only needs to refer this element to its measure in space, in order to reconstruct the measure of the phenomenon in space. This is expressed by introducing the unit of magnitude or distance under the ratio or coefficient x, thus :

$$x \times OP = O'P', \text{ or } x\, 1_l = O'P'.$$

7. The great problem in the Calculus of Operations consists in the development of unity into multiplicity. Subject to the law of uniformity of action, the power of the nth order generates power of the (n—1)th order, which similarly generates power of the (n—2)th order, which generates power of the (n—3)th order, and so on in a descending hierarchical series to the power of the second order, which generates power of the first order, which finally generates power of the order zero, that is, the phenomenon. In order, then, that phenomena may arise, the generating powers must be reduced by interference to the first order, whence the next descending step reaches zero, or the cessation of action. It is the business of observation to ascertain the magnitude of this last step, or the ratio of the effect produced by the power of the first order, to the unit measure of space and time; which ratio is that of the phenomenon itself, and serves to mark the order of elevation of the primitive generator or noumenon which originated the immediate event observed.

In the investigations here undertaken, an event or phenomenon of the most simple character is selected, such as the motion of a material point or unit of mass, which motion is referred to an arbitrarily chosen standard unit measure of space and time; and the question opens, after recognizing the necessary conditions imposed on the admeasurement of all phenomena by the unalterable nature of the last named elements space and time, by inquiring 1° into the effect produced by the application of a single force of the first order, in the two separate cases of action in a linear and in an angular direction (the former case operating the involution of linear unity, and the latter the involution of angular and of absolute geometrical and phenomenal unity); and 2° into the effect produced by the interference of two forces of the first order, both in the case where the two forces are of translation (parallelogram of forces), and in that where they are of rotation (principle of the lever).

CHAPTER II.

ON THE MEASUREMENT OF SPACE, AND OF THE EFFECT OF FORCE OF THE FIRST ORDER.

8. There are three species of magnitude, namely, linear, superficial, and solid; respectively constituting the straight line, plane, and volume; and involving successively one, two, and lastly the three dimensions of space. A line in general may be described or generated by the motion of a point; and the simplest case of motion is that which is uniform in velocity and direction, and is therefore measured by the straight line. A more complex case of motion will be that of a line in space; and if the generating line is straight, and moves on two parallel straight directing lines, the surface generated will be a plane, which will be the measure of the motion of the line; and if one of the directrices be reduced to a point, the line can no more move parallel to itself, but will describe a plane angle, which is the element of surface reduced to its simplest form. A third case of motion will be that of a surface in space; and when that surface is a plane, and moves in the direction of its perpendicular, the volume generated will be the measure of the motion of the surface. In this wise, a volume in space serves as the measure of a phenomenon (the solid content of a body, for example); and this measure of three dimensions may, by what precedes, be reduced first to two dimensions, and finally to one, the straight line; that is, the volume is a function of the line. So also the plane and the plane angle, shown to be generated by the straight line, are functions of the same.

Corresponding to the three different species of magnitude, which compose and fill up universal space, there will be three different units of magnitude : the unit of length, the unit of surface, and the unit of volume. Let the movable body, material point, or unit of mass be denoted by 1_{μ}, and describe the distance or straight line OP [fig. 1] by a uniform movement. We take the line OP as unit of distance, or linear unit 1_l; and as it is also a measure of the time occupied by this movement, it may be taken as unit of time, or temporal unit 1_t. Next let the line OP $= 1_l$ [fig. 2] move parallel to itself, through the distance OO′ = OP : it will describe the square OPO′P′ constructed on the line OP, which square may be taken as the unit of surface, and denoted by 1_l^2; and as the movement is to be uniform as before, it occupies precisely a second unit of time 1_t^2, where the index 2 refers to succession in time, the preceding unit measure 1_t^1 having disappeared, and the second or immediately succeeding unit measure 1_t^2 taking its place; while in the expression 1_l^2, the index refers to simultaneity, both the line OP $= 1_l^1$ and the square OPO′P′ $= 1_l^2$ existing at the same time. Lastly, let the surface OPO′P′ move perpendicular to itself, through a distance OO″ = OO′ = OP $= 1_l$, in the unit of time : it will describe a cube OPO′P′O″P″O‴P‴ constructed on the line OP, which cube may be taken as the unit of volume, and denoted by 1_l^3; and, by what precedes, the index 3 in the expression 1_t^3 refers to the third succeeding unit measure of time; while in the expression 1_l^3 it denotes the simultaneous existence of the line 1_l^1, the surface 1_l^2, and the volume 1_l^3. Thus when the straight line is assumed as the element of magnitude, the remaining two species may be deduced as functions of it; and in time, the successive units are functions of the primitive unit. All therefore depends upon the determination of this unique and simple element, the straight line which measures the distance between two points.

9. Through any point of space as origin of measurement, three mutually perpendicular straight lines may be drawn : any definite portion of each line in this position *is equal to its own length in its own direction*, and *to zero in the direction of each of the two coexistent perpendicular lines*. These three mutually perpendicular lines form the system of coordinate axes, or axes of measurement in space; and if planes be passed through each pair of lines, they will be coordinate planes.

Three conditions are requisite for the determination of a point in space, and these conditions may be, first, its respective distances to the three rectangular planes of measurement, that is, its rectangular coordinates; or, secondly, its distance (radius vector) from the origin of measurement, and the angles formed by the radius vector with any two of the three axes, that is to say, the polar coordinates of the point. In the first case, that of rectangular coordinates, the distance of a point to a plane is equal to its distance measured on the axis perpendicular to that plane; so that the respective distances of the point to any two of the three rectangular planes may be measured on the axes contained in the third perpendicular plane. In the case of polar coordinates, the angle with any one of the axes is measured in the plane of intersection of the radius vector and that axis. In either case, therefore, the question reduces itself to the determination of a point in a plane; and thus, although the ultimate elements of position are the three perpendicular directions in space, the determination of any two of them is effected independently of the third, and we are then only concerned with operations in one single plane.

10. Considering any one of the four right angles about the point O [fig. 3] in this plane, then, the lines OX and OY are the primary and secondary axes. Any line ON in the primary direction OX is equal to its own magnitude in that direction, and to zero in the secondary direction OY, or its primary measure is ON and its secondary measure is zero; and any line ON′ in the secondary direction OY is equal to its own magnitude in that direction, and to zero in the primary direction OX, or its primary measure is zero and its secondary measure is ON′.

Two conditions are requisite for the determination of the point M, and these may be either, first, its distances MN′ and MN to the axes OY and OX, and which are measured on the axes by ON and ON′ its rectangular coordinates; or, secondly, its distance OM to the origin O, and the angle XOM or YOM with one of the axes, being its polar coordinates.

The angle MOX has a determinate relation with the lines ON′ and ON, and increases from zero at A to a right angle AA′, while ON′ increases from zero at O to the length OA′, and ON decreases from the length OA to zero at O. The angle MOX is determined, for the radius OM, by either of the lines ON or ON′, and therefore has two linear measures; while the lines ON and ON′ are both determined by the angle MOX to the radius OM, and therefore have but one angular measure. If OA′ = OA be called a linear unit, the right angle, which is an angular unit, will be measured by the linear unit; and in general any angle has two linear measures, a primary and a secondary, which reduce to one in the case of the right angle.

Any line OM [fig. 4] inclined to the primary and secondary axes, has two linear measures; the primary measure ON is the magnitude of OM in the primary direction OX, and the secondary measure ON′ is the magnitude of OM in the secondary direction OY. Both these measures are necessary for the determination of the line OM; and a line has in general two measures, a primary and a secondary, which reduce to one when the line corresponds in direction with the primary or secondary axis. The intrinsic attributes of a line are thus three in number : its own measure in its own direction, its primary measure in an arbitrary primary direction, and its secondary measure in the secondary or perpendicular direction; and any two of these three measures suffice for the complete determination of the line.

Considering finally the system of four right angles about a point O [fig. 5], the primary and secondary axes being X′X and Y′Y: all that has been said in relation to the measurement of a line OM applies indeterminately in either of these four right angles. Having the primary and secondary measures of a line OM, it is yet necessary for the determination of the point M in our plane, to know on which pair of semiaxes, OX and OY, OX′ and OY, OX′ and OY′, OX and OY′, the primary and secondary measures of the line OM are counted, for the point M may be situated in either of the four right angles. An entire axis X′X or Y′Y constitutes the element of linear direction without regard to any origin; and a semiaxis OX or OX′, OY or OY′, constitutes the element of linear direction referred to the origin O. We therefore complete our classification of the linear elements of direction, by denominating OX as the positive primary direction, OY the positive secondary direction, OX′ the negative primary direction, and OY′ the negative secondary direction. The complete catalogue of requisitions for the determination of a point M in a plane, therefore, embraces a knowledge of the primary and secondary measures of its distance OM from the origin O, together with that of the positive or negative character of each measure. The line OM, having the primary and secondary measures ON and OP, will be determinately located by affixing to each of these measures a conventional mark, intimating whether the measure is in the positive or negative direction of its axis at the origin. I choose the characters $\|_1$ and $\|_2$ to indicate direction on the respective axes X′X and Y′Y, without regard to origin; and observing that each two complementary semiaxes OX and OX′, OY and OY′, have mutually the relation of opposition of direction, I select the character + to represent the principle of agreement, and the character — to represent the principle of opposition, and finally the signs for OX and OY are respectively $+\|_1$ and $+\|_2$, and those for OX′ and OY′ are $-\|_1$ and $-\|_2$. Collecting all together, we have for the coordination of a point M situate in either of the four right angles about the point O, in terms of the distance OM, severally the measures with their indications of direction :

For M′, positive primary and positive secondary, $+\|_1 ON'$ and $+\|_2 OP'$;
for M″, negative primary and positive secondary, $-\|_1 ON''$ & $+\|_2 OP''$;
for M‴, negative primary and negative secondary, $-\|_1 ON'''$ & $-\|_2 OP'''$;
for M^{iv}, positive primary and negative secondary, $+\|_1 ON^{iv}$ & $-\|_2 OP^{iv}$.

Each pair of measures also evidently determines the respective corresponding angle of the lines OM′, OM″, OM‴, OM^{iv}, with the positive primary axis OX; and conversely each arc described from OX by the respective radii OM′, OM″, OM‴, OM^{iv}, will also severally determine both the primary and secondary measures of its corresponding line, and the particular directions of these measures.

11. Having located our origin and axes of measurement, two data are requisite for the determination of a point in a plane, to wit, its two coordinates, linear or polar; for the distance OP [fig. 6] refers to any point whatever on the line L, and OQ refers to any point on the line L′ : so that both OP and OQ are requisite data for the point M. In polar coordinates, the data are the radius vector OM, and the angle MOX. In the first question, it is the

magnitude and position of the line OM that is sought; and in the second question, in which the line OM and the angle MOX are given, OP and OQ are the terms sought.

To solve the first question, we must find the relation between OM and OP, OQ ; and since two conditions are to be fulfilled, namely, the measurement of OP and of OQ, two operations are consequently required, and OM will therefore be expressed as a function of these two operations, or as a power or ratio of the second order.

In the triangle ABC [fig. 7], produce the side BA, making AB′ equal to BC, when of course A′B′ will be equal to AB. Let the line A′B move parallel to itself through the distance BC, and the line A′B′ move similarly through the distance B′C′ = AB : we shall have the square A′BCD = $(\text{line BC})^2$, and the square A′B′C′D′ = $(\text{line AB})^2$. Next let the line AC move parallel to itself through the distance AC′ = AC, and it will give the square ABC″C′= $(\text{line AC})^2$. Now BC = AB′= C″D′, and AB = B′C′ =C′D′=C″D ; and therefore the triangles ABC, C′B′A′, C′D′C″ and C″DC are all equal : that is, $(AB)^2+(BC)^2=(AC)^2$. In fig. 6, then, if we make OM = r, OP = x, OQ = y, we have

$$r^2 = x^2+ y^2, \quad \text{or } r = \sqrt{(x^2+ y^2)}$$

expressed as a function of the second order.

By our second question, we are led into the examination of ratio as it follows :

The ratio of a line OM to a linear unit 1_l, is the number of times that 1_l will be counted when applied as a measure of OM, both in one same direction; or, in general, the number of times that any magnitude contains a unit measure of its own species : or, again, arithmetical ratio is the number of times that a line OM is equal in magnitude to a given linear unit 1_l, and is entirely independent of the positions and directions of the lines compared.

Let 1_l be the linear unit, and [fig. 8] OM = $a.1_l$; then -----
$\frac{ON}{OM} = \cos\theta$, and $\frac{ON'}{OM} = \sin\theta$, θ being the angle XOL. The distances of the point M to the rectangular axes OY and OX are respectively MN′ = ON = $a \cos\theta\, 1_l$, and
MN = ON′ = $a \sin\theta\, 1_l$. Refer now the points N

and N′ to the rectangular axes OL and ZZ′ : the distance of the point N to the axis Z′Z is NQ = OR, and that of the point N′ to the same axis is N′Q′ = OR′; and the sum of OR and OR′ is equal to OM. Now

$$\frac{\text{OR}}{\text{ON}} = \frac{\text{ON}}{\text{OM}} = \cos\theta, \text{ and OR} = \text{ON}\cos\theta = a\cos^2\theta\, 1_\iota; \text{ and}$$

$$\frac{\text{OR}'}{\text{ON}'} = \frac{\text{ON}'}{\text{OM}} = \sin\theta, \text{ and OR}' = \text{ON}'\sin\theta = a\sin^2\theta\, 1_\iota; \text{ and}$$

finally OR + OR′ = OM, or $a(\cos^2\theta + \sin^2\theta)1_\iota = a.1_\iota$: therefore $\cos^2\theta + \sin^2\theta = 1$, a relation strictly numerical. The ratios $a.1$, $a\cos\theta$ and $a\sin\theta$ are entirely independent of the place and direction of the lines from which they are deduced; and $a\cos\theta\, 1_\iota$ and $a\sin\theta\, 1_\iota$ express lines which are absolutely indeterminate in their location or in their position with respect to $a.1_\iota$, their magnitude alone being indicated in these expressions. Thus $\cos\theta\, 1_\iota$ expresses the geometrical magnitude of the *primary measure* of a linear unit 1_ι forming an acute angle with a primary axis, and $\sin\theta\, 1_\iota$ expresses the geometrical magnitude of the *positive secondary measure* of 1_ι; but the magnitudes alone of the lines are embraced in these expressions, and not their relative positions or their directions. The line OM, and its relative measures ON and ON′, are then subject to the condition of numerical unity expressed by the equation $\cos^2\theta + \sin^2\theta = 1$; but position is not at all implied in the expression.

12. The linear unit is arbitrary, and also indeterminate; for linear extent in space is infinite, so that there is no absolute linear unit except infinity. The angular unit may also be arbitrarily chosen, but cannot be indeterminate; for although a plane is infinite in all directions about one same point therein, yet all this infinite extent is embraced within the compass of four right angles about this point. The absolute whole or infinity of space is measured by four right angles; and the angular magnitude of any angle being independent of its radius of reference, the entire four right angles about a point, or the circumference of a circle to any given radius, forms an absolute angular or circular unit, or the *absolute geometrical unit.*

13. All physical operations are actions performed in space and time, by active on passive (or more properly reactive) bodies, the former transferring the latter from one point of space to another in a term of time; and the distance between these two points is evidently a geometrical measure of the action performed, or of the effect of the force operating the change of place of the passive body, and is for us the only known representative and measure of the force itself.

14. The mental operations of addition and substraction represent physical actions of a mutually opposite nature, performed by active on passive bodies, as thus : Let O [fig. 9] be the position of a pile consisting of an indefinite number N of oranges b, and P that of a basket already containing or not m oranges. I wish to add n oranges to the m oranges contained in the basket. I transfer n oranges from the pile to the basket, and I write the result

$$y = 0 + mb + nb,$$

the empty basket being zero. I afterwards wish to subtract p oranges from those contained in the basket. To do this, I return p oranges from the basket to the pile, and write the result

$$y' = 0 + mb + nb - pb.$$

The *opposite nature* of the actions performed on the oranges, or passive bodies, in adding and subtracting them *to* and *from*, may here evidently be geometrically interpreted by the *opposition of the directions* OP and PO in which the bodies added and subtracted were in each case carried. The notation $+ b$ directs the transport of b TO the given point P, and $- b$ directs the transport of b FROM the point P, or in the opposite direction. From this example, the geometrical interpretation of the qualities of agreement and opposition, expressed by the characters + and −, follows easily.

15. Multiplication by an abstract number is an abridged method of performing a series of additions. Thus, the multiplication of m bodies b by the number n, is a process equivalent to the operation of adding together n parcels of m bodies each; but when the multiplier n is 1, the process reduces to one single addition of m bodies b, *to* the point P for instance, if we are at liberty to regard this multiplying unit as a concrete number. Multiplication by unity being equivalent to one single addition, in order to multiply

b by 1, I add b to the point P, by transferring it from O through the distance OP, which may be adopted as linear unit OP = 1; and then this multiplier 1, or the linear distance OP, will be the *measure of the mechanical effect* (change of place) produced on the passive body by the active power or force which operates the multiplication $1.b$, and thus we have a geometrical interpretation of the operation of multiplying by a unit.

16. Abstract numbers, or numerical ratios, are representatives of the relations between the magnitudes of certain portions of space; and in order to return from these relations to the representation of the magnitudes themselves, it is evidently necessary to refer each particular numerical ratio to its corresponding unit of magnitude. In adding together two numbers m and n, it is not the numbers themselves on which we directly operate, they being representatives of mere relations only, and not of any thing which may submit to modification; but the magnitudes from which those relations were deduced are tangible subjects for the application of force, which, by changing their positions in space with respect to each other, annihilate the former relations, and generate new ones. If m and n be added and give the sum p, it is not that the relations m and n have been operated on and converted into the relation p; but m and n represented certain relations which existed between things submitted to a particular arrangement, and this arrangement being altered, the relations m and n cease to exist, and their place is supplied by the new relation p. Thus m may indicate certain magnitudes μ arranged in one locality, and n certain similar magnitudes arranged in another locality; placing both $m\mu$ and $n\mu$ in one same locality, the arrangement of the magnitudes is altered, the relations m and n no more have place, but are succeeded by the new relation p. The general or abstract relations m and n being entirely independent of their sources of deduction, are afterwards applicable as coefficients to other species of magnitude, and thereby become divested of indeterminacy, and particularized as relations actually existing between the new magnitudes to which they are referred.

17. In operating a product between two factors m and n, the multiplicand is passive, and the multiplier active; the former indicating a number m of passive magnitudes μ, and the latter a

number n of active magnitudes λ, that is, of lines regarded as the measures of the forces which operate the product. Attaching to each factor its appropriate magnitude, the notation $m\mu.n\lambda$ comes to say that each of the m passive magnitudes μ is acted upon by each of the n active magnitudes λ; so that if we denote the unit of passivity by 1_μ, and the unit of activity by 1_λ, we may allow 1_μ to represent any geometrical magnitude whatever, a surface, a line, or even a point (it being in effect the measure of the unit of mass or of inertia); but we are restricted to interpret 1_λ as representing the distance through which 1_μ is transferred by the force operating the multiplication, in a portion of time considered as unity for the sake of homogeneity, and which force is denoted and measured by the factor 1_λ itself. Thus [fig. 10], if $m = 2$ and $n = 3$, the notation $2 . 1_\mu . 3 . 1_\lambda$ signifies that 2 passive magnitudes 1_μ are transferred by the active factor $1_\lambda = \text{OP}'$ through 3 distances 1_λ, or from O to P‴; the result affording the new relation or ratio 6.

Let the multiplicand be $1_\iota = \text{OA}$ [fig. 11], and the multiplier $1_\lambda = \text{OP}$. I take the product $1_\iota . 1_\lambda$, and the line OA is moved parallel to itself on OP into the position PB, describing the surface OABP, or the rectangle constructed on 1_ι and 1_λ; so that if $1_\lambda = 1_\iota$, the expression 1_ι^2 represents the square of a linear unit; and in general the expression $a1_\iota . b1_{\iota'}$ will represent the rectangle constructed on the lines $a1_\iota$ and $b1_{\iota'}$.

Let the multiplicand be $1_\iota . 1_{\iota'} = \text{OAPB}$, and the multiplier $1_\lambda = \text{OQ}$ be taken perpendicular to the plane of $1_\iota . 1_{\iota'}$. I take the product $1_\iota . 1_{\iota'} . 1_\lambda$, and the surface OAPB is moved parallel to itself on OQ into the position QA′P′B′, describing thus a volume OAPBQA′P′B′, or the parallelopipedon constructed on 1_ι, $1_{\iota'}$ and 1_λ; so that if $1_\iota = 1_{\iota'} = 1_\lambda$, the expression 1_ι^3 represents the cube of a linear unit; and in general the expression $a1_\iota . b1_{\iota'} . c1_{\iota''}$ will represent the rectangular parallelopipedon constructed on the lines $a1_\iota$, $b1_{\iota'}$ and $c1_{\iota''}$.

If we take severally for multiplicand the three lines, to wit, $a1_\iota$, $a\cos\theta 1_\iota$ and $a\sin\theta 1_\iota$, which are in magnitude the three sides of a rightangled triangle, and for their respective multipliers the lines $a'1_\lambda$, $a'\cos\theta 1_\lambda$ and $a'\sin\theta 1_\lambda$, each in perpendicularity to its multiplicand, the products $aa'1_\iota . 1_\lambda$, $aa'\cos^2\theta 1_\iota . 1_\lambda$ and $aa'\sin^2\theta 1_\iota . 1_\lambda$

will represent the three rectangular parallelograms generated by the lines $a1_{\iota}$, $a\cos\theta 1_{\iota}$ and $a\sin\theta 1_{\iota}$, in moving each parallel to itself on the length of its respective multiplier; and in virtue of the relation $\sin^2\theta + \cos^2\theta = 1$ [n° 11], we have the geometrical equality $a a'(\cos^2\theta + \sin^2\theta)1_{\iota} . 1_{\lambda} = a a' 1_{\iota} . 1_{\lambda}$, which reduces to $a^2(\cos^2\theta + \sin^2\theta)1_{\iota}^2 = a^2 1_{\iota}^2$ when $a = a$ and $1_{\lambda} = 1_{\iota}$.

When the multiplier is a linear factor, or a force of translation, the multiplication of a point generates a straight line, or the element of length; the multiplication of a straight line generates an area, or the element of surface; and the multiplication of a surface generates a solid, or the element of volume : these generations being merely forms of space, and not at all mistaken for any of its contents, but possessing with material magnitude only the common attribute of dimension.

If the multiplier be an angular factor, or a force of rotation, and the multiplicand a fixed point in a movable radius, the point will describe an arc of circle.

18. The numerical value of any power n of a unit 1 is also 1; that is, $1^n = 1$. The numerical unit is absolute, but abstract, being the ratio of two equal magnitudes $\frac{a}{a} = 1$.

The linear unit 1_{ι} or 1_{λ} is arbitrary, being any line at pleasure [fig. 12], $OP = 1_{\lambda}$; but having the numerical value 1, the numerical value of its nth power 1_{λ}^n must be $1^n = 1$, whatever be the linear value of that power; so that if we legitimately determine that the nth power of the linear unit OP is OP′, the numerical value of OP′ will also be 1, for $OP' = (OP)^n = 1_{\lambda}^n = 1^n = 1$; and this can evidently be the case, inasmuch as the linear unit being entirely arbitrary, its nth power may also be a unit. Conversely, if OP′ be first chosen a linear unit 1_{λ}, and its nth root be shown to be OP, the latter will also be a unit, for

$$OP = [OP']^{\frac{1}{n}} = 1_{\lambda}^{\frac{1}{n}} = 1^{\frac{1}{n}} = 1.$$

The circumference of a circle is an absolute geometrical unit 1_{0}, being the measure of four right angles, or the sum or one entire whole [fig. 13] composed of all the angles AOM which exist about the point O. If AM be chosen a circular unit 1_{θ}, and its nth power be found to be AA′A″A‴A, we should have $1_{\theta}^n = 1_{0}$, an absolute geometrical unit; and conversely AM would in this case be the nth root of AA′A″A‴A, or $1_\theta = 1_0^{\frac{1}{n}}$, or the nth root of an absolute geometrical unit.

Let the multiplicand 1_μ be the unit measure of a passive magnitude, conceived under the form of a material point deposited at [fig. 14] O. I multiply 1_μ successively by the linear factors OP′, P′P″, P″P‴, P‴P^{iv}, all chosen in the same direction, and the results are

$$OP'.1_\mu,\ (OP')(P'P'')1_\mu = (OP'')1_\mu,\ (OP'')(P''P''')1_\mu = (OP''')1_\mu,$$
$$\text{and } (OP''')(P'''P^{iv})1_\mu = (OP^{iv})1_\mu;$$

1_μ being successively transferred from O to P′, to P″, to P‴, and to P^{iv}. Make $OP' = P'P'' = P''P''' = P'''P^{iv} = 1_\lambda$, and the results are $OP' = 1_\lambda . 1_\mu$, $OP'' = 1_\lambda^2 . 1_\mu$, $OP''' = 1_\lambda^3 . 1_\mu$, and $OP^{iv} = 1_\lambda^4 . 1_\mu$. Now the multiplier being a linear unit, its numerical value is 1; and all its successive powers will also be linear units, and have the numerical value 1; so that we may write $1_\lambda = 1_1$, $1_\lambda^1 = 1_2$, $1_\lambda^3 = 1_3$, $1_\lambda^4 = 1_4$; each being numerically a unit or 1, although the linear value from the origin O is different for each different power. If, then, after first obtaining $OP'.1_\mu = 1_\lambda . 1_\mu$, we find a series of n geometrical factors whose continued product shall restore 1_μ to P′, the linear value of this continued product (P′P″)(P″P‴) . . . ., from the origin P′, will be equal to that of OP′, that is to say, $(P'P'')(P''P''') \ldots . 1_\mu = OP'.1_\mu$; and as $OP' = 1_\lambda = 1$, we must have $(P'P'')(P''P''') \ldots . = 1$; and consequently if the factors are each equal to $1_{\lambda'}$, we have $1_{\lambda'}^n = 1_\lambda = 1$; the power coinciding with its root in numerical value and linear distance from the origin, as well as in position, all which requisitions are essential to the condition of absolute unity. Such a series of factors will be the n arcs forming the circumference of the circle whose radius is OP′.

19. The multiplicand being always 1_μ, let the linear multiplier be denoted by $\alpha = OP' = P'P'' = P''P''' = P'''P^{iv}$ [fig. 14]. 1_μ being first at O, I multiply it by α, and it is transferred to P′, the operation being expressed by $\alpha . 1_\mu$, and giving $\alpha = OP'$; multiplying again by α, and 1_μ is transferred to P″, the expression being $\alpha^2 1_\mu$, giving $\alpha^2 = OP'' = 2(OP')$; a third multiplication carries 1_μ to P‴, and gives the expression $\alpha^3 1_\mu$, and $\alpha^3 = OP''' = 3(OP')$; and the fourth multiplication carries 1_μ to P^{iv}, giving $\alpha^4 1_\mu$ for the ex-

pression of the result of the four successive multiplications of 1_μ by the linear unit α=OP′, and α^4=OP^{iv}= 4(OP′). Thus the successive powers of a linear unit are formed by successively adding the linear value of the unit; and the nth power of a linear unit 1_λ is a linear unit 1_λ^n of n times the magnitude of the linear unit taken to form the involution, or $1_\lambda^n = n.1_\lambda$ in linear magnitude; and, in general, the continued product of any number of geometrical factors is equal to their sum in linear value.

From the linear power OP^{iv}=α^4, we may by inspection deduce the following results :

$$\text{OP}'\times\text{P}'\text{P}^{iv} = \alpha\,.\alpha^3 = \alpha^4 = 1; \qquad \alpha^3 = \alpha^{-1} = \text{OP}''' = \frac{\text{OP}^{iv}}{\text{OP}'};$$

$$\text{OP}''\times\text{P}''\text{P}^{iv} = \alpha^2.\alpha^2 = \alpha^4 = 1; \qquad \alpha^2 = \alpha^{-2} = \text{OP}'' = \frac{\text{OP}^{iv}}{\text{OP}''};$$

$$\text{OP}'''\times\text{P}'''\text{P}^{iv} = \alpha^3.\alpha = \alpha^4 = 1. \qquad \alpha = \alpha^{-3} = \text{OP}' = \frac{\text{OP}^{iv}}{\text{OP}'''}.$$

$$\alpha = \tfrac{1}{4}.\text{OP}^{iv} = 1^{\frac{1}{4}}; \quad \alpha^2 = \tfrac{1}{2}.\text{OP}^{iv} = 1^{\frac{1}{2}}; \quad \alpha^3 = \tfrac{3}{4}.\text{OP}^{iv} = 1^{\frac{3}{4}}.$$

So that were OP^{iv} an absolute unit, OP′, OP″, OP‴ would be the three imaginary fourth roots of unity, the real root being OP^{iv} itself; OP′ and P′P^{iv}, OP″ and P″P^{iv}, OP‴ and P‴P^{iv} would be pairs of roots complementary to unity; and OP′ and $\frac{\text{OP}^{iv}}{\text{OP}'}$, OP″ and $\frac{\text{OP}^{iv}}{\text{OP}''}$, OP‴ and $\frac{\text{OP}^{iv}}{\text{OP}'''}$ would be reciprocal roots of unity; and OP′ the primitive fourth root of unity, its successive powers giving all the other roots in their order of magnitude.

20. Let [fig. 15] the radius OP=1_λ, and quadrantal arc PP′=α. The multiplicand or unit of passivity 1_μ being in deposit at O, I multiply it first by 1_λ, which transfers it to P, giving $1_\lambda.1_\mu$=OP.1_μ; and since $1_\lambda.1_\mu$ is next to be our passive multiplicand, I reduce its notation to simple unity thus, $1_\lambda.1_\mu=1.1_\mu=1_\mu$, the location of 1_μ remaining still at P. I now multiply 1_μ by the circular unit----- PP′=α, and it is transferred to P′, the notation being PP′1_μ=$\alpha 1_\mu$, or as well OP′1_μ=$1_1.1_\mu$, since OP′ is the linear measure of the right angle POP′ or the arc PP′ [n° 10]. I again multiply 1_μ by α, and it is transferred to P″, being expressed by $\alpha^2 1_\mu$= PP′P″1_μ or $1_2.1_\mu$=OP″1_μ : a third multiplication by α transfers 1_μ to P‴

and gives the expression $\alpha^3 1_\mu = PP'P''P''' 1_\mu$ or $1_3.1_\mu$; and finally the fourth multiplication of 1_μ by α restores 1_μ to its primitive position at P, and furnishes the final result

$$\alpha^4.1_\mu = PP'P''P'''P.1_\mu = 1_0.1_\mu = 1.1_\mu = 1_\mu,$$

for the circumference is an absolute geometrical unit $1_0 = 1$; or as well $1_4.1_\mu = OP.1_\mu = 1_\lambda.1_\mu = 1_\mu$, fulfilling at the same time the condition of numerical unity, and that of geometrical unity both in magnitude and position. We may immediately transfer by inspection the notations of our preceding linear example to the present angular or circular one, and examine the results in detail; observing that we can at the same time attend to the angular or circular values from P, and the linear values from the origin O.

We have $OP = 1$; $PP' = \alpha$, and $OP' = 1_1$; $PP'P'' = \alpha^2$, and $OP'' = 1_2$; $PP'P''P''' = \alpha^3$, and $OP''' = 1_3$; and $PP'P''P'''P = \alpha^4 = 1_0$, and $OP = 1_4 = 1$. Then,

$$PP' \times P'P''P'''P = \alpha.\alpha^3 = \alpha^4 = 1_0; \quad \alpha^3 = \alpha^{-1} = PP'P''P''' = \frac{PP'P''P'''P}{PP'};$$

$$PP'P'' \times P''P'''P = \alpha^2.\alpha^2 = \alpha^4 = 1_0; \quad \alpha^2 = \alpha^{-2} = PP'P'' = \frac{PP'P''P'''P}{PP'P''};$$

$$PP'P''P''' \times P'''P = \alpha^3.\alpha = \alpha^4 = 1_0; \quad \alpha = \alpha^{-3} = PP' = \frac{PP'P''P'''P}{PP'P''P'''}.$$

Also, inversely, $\alpha = PP' = \frac{1}{4}.PP'P''P'''P = 1_0^{\frac{1}{4}}$;

$\alpha^2 = PP'P'' = \frac{1}{2}.PP'P''P'''P = 1_0^{\frac{1}{2}}$;

$\alpha^3 = PP'P''P''' = \frac{3}{4}.PP'P''P'''P = 1_0^{\frac{3}{4}}$.

We conclude that $\alpha = PP'$, $\alpha^2 = PP'P'''$, $\alpha^3 = PP'P''P'''$ and $\alpha^4 = PP'P''P'''P = 1_0$ are the four fourth roots of unity, α being itself the primitive fourth root; that

α and α^{-1}, or PP′ and P′P,
α^2 and α^{-2}, or PP′P″ and P″P′P,
α^3 and α^{-3}, or PP′P″P‴ and P‴P″P′P, and
α^4 and α^{-4}, or PP′P″P‴P and PP‴P″P′P are the four pairs of reciprocal fourth roots of unity; and that

α^1 and α^3, or PP′ and P′P″P‴P,
α^2 and α^2, or PP′P″ and P″P‴P,
α^3 and α^1, or PP′P″P‴ and P‴P, and
α^4 and α^0, or PP′P″P‴ and P or PP are the four pairs of fourth roots complementary to unity.

Having multiplied $1_\mu = OP.1_\mu$ by $\alpha = PP'$, it becomes $\alpha 1_\mu = OP' 1_\mu$; now being multiplied by $\alpha^3 = P'P''P'''P$, it is transferred at once through the arc $P'P''P'''P$ to P, becoming $\alpha.\alpha^3.1_\mu = 1_0.1_\mu = OP.1_\mu$; but if $\alpha.1_\mu = OP'.1_\mu$ be multiplied by α^{-1}, it is retrograded through $P'P$ to P, equally becoming $\alpha.\alpha^{-1}.1_\mu = 1_0.1_\mu = OP.1_\mu$. Multiplication by the reciprocal α^{-1} of a factor α being equivalent to division by this same factor α, we see in this example the relation between the operations of geometrical multiplication and division, the latter being the inverse of the former. A reciprocal factor α^{-1} is then to be counted in a direction opposite to that of the factor α itself. If 1_μ in OP be multiplied by $\alpha^{-3} = PP'''P''P'$, it becomes $\alpha^{-3}.1_\mu = OP'.1_\mu$; and it may hence be restored to OP either by means of the inverse factor α^{-1} through $P'P$, or by means of the direct factor α^3 through $P'P''P'''P$, becoming $\alpha^{-3}.\alpha^{-1}.1_\mu = \alpha^{-4}.1_\mu = 1_0.1_\mu$ in the first case, and $\alpha^{-3}.\alpha^3.1_\mu = 1^0.1_\mu$ in the second. The sum of the effects of any two circular factors which are complementary to the circumference, is equivalent to the effect unity; and, in general, the continued product of any number n of arcs or angles is equal to their sum, which becomes an absolute unit when these arcs or angles complete the circumference or four right angles.

We have seen that $\alpha = PP'$ is the primitive fourth root of unity, its successive powers yielding all the other roots in their order of geometrical magnitude. Let now 1_μ be successively multiplied by $\alpha^2 = PP'P''$, and the results are $\alpha^2.1_\mu = OP''.1_\mu$, $\alpha^4.1_\mu = OP.1_\mu$; and by $\alpha^3 = PP'P''$, the results are $\alpha^3.1_\mu = OP'''.1_\mu$, $\alpha^2.1_\mu = OP''.1_\mu$, $\alpha.1_\mu = OP'.1_\mu$, $\alpha^4.1_\mu = OP.1_\mu$: this last multiplication by α^3 transferring 1_μ first from P through $PP'P''P'''$ to P''', secondly from P''' through $P'''PP'P''$ to P'', thirdly from P'' through $P''P'''PP'$ to P', and fourthly from P' through $P'P''P'''P$ to P. The successive powers of each of the imaginary roots of unity give all the other roots, but those of the primitive root alone give them in their regular succession. Finally multiplication by $\alpha^4 = 1_0 = PP$ always carries the multiplicand from P through the entire circumference $PP'P''P'''P$; and the inverse factor $\alpha^{-4} = 1 \div 1_0 = 1^0 = 1_0$ transfers 1_μ in the opposite angular direction from P, through $PP'''P''P'P$ to P again.

When the multiplier is a linear unit 1_λ, the successive results $1_\lambda.1_\mu$, $1_\lambda^2.1_\mu$, $1_\lambda^3.1_\mu$, ... , $1_\lambda^n.1_\mu$, have each the same arithmetical value 1.1_μ, but different geometrical values from the origin; for although 1^n_λ is always a linear unit, it is a different one for every different value of n, and no two different powers 1^n_λ and $1^{n'}_\lambda$ will render $1^n_\lambda = 1^{n'}_\lambda$ in position as well as in number and magnitude; or, in other words, no two different powers of a linear unit will refer 1_μ to one same position P. But when the circumference $PP = 1_0$ is the multiplier, the successive results $1_0.1_\mu$, $1^2_0.1_\mu$, $1^3_0.1_\mu$, ..., $1^n_0.1_\mu$, have all a coincident geometrical as well as arithmetical value 1.1_μ; for each successive multiplication by 1_0 transfers 1_μ from the point P, through the circumference, to the point P again : $1^n_0.1_\mu = 1.1_\mu$, or $1^n_0 = 1$, the condition of absolute unity. If the multiplier be the nth part of the circumference, that is, if $1_\theta = \frac{1}{n}.PP'P''P'''P$, we see that $1^n_\theta.1_\mu$ transfers 1_μ, by n successive equal steps, through the circumference from P to P again, and gives $1^n_\theta.1_\mu = 1_0.1_\mu$; so that the circumference $PP = 1_0$ being an absolute geometrical unit, its nth part is its nth root, or the primitive nth root of unity, the one which by its successive powers will give each of the other $(n-1)$ roots, and repeat them indefinitely for values of the exponent greater than n, yielding always also $1^n_\theta = 1^{2n}_\theta = 1^{3n}_\theta = 1^{4n}_\theta = 1^{n'n}_\theta = 1_0 = 1$ an absolute unit. And when the multiplier is the nth part of any number m of circumferences, or $1_\theta = \frac{4\,m}{n}$ right angles, it is equally evident that we have $1^n_\theta = 1^m_0 = 1_0 = 1$ an absolute unit.

21. In the preceding paragraph, we have given [fig. 15] the following four pairs of equivalent expressions for the results of the four successive multiplications of 1_μ by the primitive fourth root of unity, to wit :

$$PP'.1_\mu = \alpha.1_\mu, \text{ or } OP'.1_\mu = 1_1.1_\mu;$$
$$PP'P''.1_\mu = \alpha^2.1_\mu, \text{ or } OP''.1_\mu = 1_3.1_\mu;$$
$$PP'P''P'''.1_\mu = \alpha^3.1_\mu, \text{ or } OP'''.1_\mu = 1_3.1_\mu; \text{ and}$$
$$PP'P''P'''P.1_\mu = \alpha^4.1_\mu, \text{ or } OP.1_\mu = 1_4.1_\mu.$$

Now the linear units $OP' = 1_1$, $OP'' = 1_2$, $OP''' = 1_3$ and $OP = 1_4$, are all equal in magnitude, and each is a linear measure of its corresponding right angle; and it only remains to attach respectively the significations of direction to these four units 1_1, 1_2, 1_3 and 1_4, to qualify them as linear measures of the successive circular units PP′, PP′P″, PP′P″P‴ and PP [n° 10]; and thus in all cases to admit of the substitution of the linear units 1_1, 1_2, 1_3 and 1_4 respectively for their corresponding equivalent circular units α, α^2, α^3 and 1_o; for in any case a multiplication by the circular factor α' would bring its equivalent linear result $\alpha'.1_\mu = 1'.1_\mu$; and therefore we may write $1_1 = \alpha$, $1_1^2 = 1_2 = \alpha^2$, $1_1^3 = 1_3 = \alpha^3$ and $1_1^4 = 1_4 = \alpha^4 = 1_o$, and inversely $1_1 = 1_o^{\frac{1}{4}} = 1_2^{\frac{1}{2}}$, $1_2 = 1_o^{\frac{1}{2}}$, etc. Relying upon the notations for direction established in n° 10, we see that in taking the direction OP for that of the positive primary semiaxis OX, we have immediately

$1_4 = \mathrm{OP} = +\|_1.1_l$, writing the linear unit instead of radius OP;
$1_1 = \mathrm{OP}' = +\|_2.1_l$;
$1_2 = \mathrm{OP}'' = -\|_1.1_l$, and
$1_3 = \mathrm{OP}''' = -\|_2.1_l$. These notations may be simplified by means of the relation $1_1 = 1_2^{\frac{1}{2}}$, that is $+\|_2.1_l = +\surd(-\|_1.1_l)$, which evidently points to its opposite 1_3 or $-\surd(-\|_1.1_l)$ as the expression for its complementary semiaxis; for on examining the four notations $+\|_1.1_l$, $-\|_1 1_l$, $+\surd(-\|_1.1_l)$, $-\surd(-\|_1.1_l)$, it is visible that we may dispense with the marks $\|_1$, $\|_2$ for the general elements of direction without regard to origin, and convene to understand that the notations $+1_l$, $+\surd-1_l$, -1_l and $-\surd-1_l$ severally represent a linear unit on 1° the positive primary, 2° the positive secondary, 3° the negative primary, and 4° the negative secondary semiaxis, all commencing at the same point as origin.

It is well understood that each of the foregoing separate acts of multiplication is performed in an equal unit interval of time 1_t; and now by eliminating the linear unit between each of the four expressions $+\surd-1_l$, -1_l, $-\surd-1_l$, $+1_l$, and 1_l itself, by division [n° 6], we complete the genesis of the remarkable unit ratios $+\surd-1$, -1, $-\surd-1$ and $+1$, whose practical signification has long been known, but whose theoretical construction is alone possible by the method of the Calculus of Operations.

In all this genesis we recognize the concurrence of the four first categories of existence [n° 1] : 1° Category of extension, the space in which the operations are performed, expressed in its twofold linear and angular unit measures [n° 10] the radii vectores OP, etc. and the arcs PP′, etc.; 2° Category of duration, the time occupied in the performance of the operations, expressed by its unit measure 1_t; 3° Category of causation, the two interfering noumena or forces of the first order, the multiplier and multiplicand expressed by their respective unit measures 1_θ and 1_μ, which perform the operations and eliminate each other by their mutual interference; 4° Category of production, the phenomenon, which consists in the actual transportation of the passive body 1_μ, by the active power 1_θ, through the distances PP′, etc., in equal intervals of time 1_t, the angular measures of the successive stages of the phenomenon being expressed by 1_θ^1, 1_θ^2, 1_θ^3 and 1_θ^4, and the linear measures of the same stages by $+\sqrt{-1}_l$, -1_l, $-\sqrt{-1}_l$ and $+1_l$; and finally the fifth category, that of intellection, the ratio or pure idea, here expressed severally by the symbols $+\sqrt{-1}$, -1, $-\sqrt{-1}$ and $+1$, which serve as invariable coefficients in all space and time, arises from the elimination of the unit of space as above, that of the time always commencing with the mental reproduction of the ratio itself [n° 6].

22. Since the coefficient $+\sqrt{-1}$ is truly the ratio of the linear measure of a right angle $\frac{1}{2}\pi$ compared to the linear unit 1_l which measures the angle 0π or 2π, we return to the linear measure of the right angle by restoring the linear unit to that coefficient; and then this linear measure $+\sqrt{-1}.1_l$ of the right angle may replace the circular measure 1_θ of that angle, when the latter is regarded as the unit measure of the rotatory force of the first order which operates the revolution of the material point 1_μ upon the radius [fig. 15] OP $= 1_l$ about the point O; and hence we may write $+\sqrt{-1}.1_\theta$ for $\alpha =$ PP′ in the notation of the successive multiplications by angular unity. The first multiplicand is $OP.1_\mu = 1_l.1_\mu$, and the first multiplication gives $+\sqrt{-1}.1_\theta.1_\mu = OP'.1_\mu$; in the second multiplication, the multiplicand is $+\sqrt{-1}.1_l.1_\mu$, and the product is $(+\sqrt{-1}.1_\theta)^2 1_\mu = OP''.1_\mu = -1.1_l.1_\mu$; in the third multiplication, the multiplicand is $-1.1_l.1_\mu$, and the multiplier being always $+\sqrt{-1}.1_\theta$, gives the product $(+\sqrt{-1}.1_\theta)^3 1_\mu = OP'''.1_\mu = -\sqrt{-1}.1_l.1_\mu$; in its turn $-\sqrt{-1}.1_l.1_\mu$ becomes the multiplicand, and gives us the final result $(+\sqrt{-1}.1_\theta)^4 1_\mu = OP.1_\mu = +1.1_l.1_\mu$, the complete unit of periodical effect, or *unit of periodicity.*

Thus the four coefficients $+1$, -1, $+\sqrt{-1}$, $-\sqrt{-1}$, are each susceptible of an active and a passive application. For instance, the multiplier -1.1_θ, which is the same as $(+\surd-1.1_\theta)^2$ or 1_θ^2 or α^2, corresponds to the angle or arc π, through which it transfers the multiplicand 1_μ from its position $+1.1_\iota$ at P, by one single step. In operating the product $(-1.1_\theta)(+1)1_\iota.1_\mu$, the multiplier -1.1_θ acts not at all on the coefficient $+1$ of the multiplicand, but only on the passive line and point $1_\iota.1_\mu$, by revolving them from the position OP into the new position OP″, thereby creating the new relation -1.1_ι, the relation $+1.1_\iota$ having now ceased to exist. The expression $-1.1_\iota.1_\mu$ in its turn being taken for multiplicand, if we take for multiplier the term $+\surd-1.1_\theta$, which is the same as 1_θ or α or $\frac{1}{2}\pi$, the operation of the product $(+\surd-1.1_\theta)(-1)1_\iota.1_\mu$ rotates the passive line and point $1_\iota.1_\mu$ into the position OP‴, and gives the new relation $-\surd-1.1_\iota$, the former one -1.1_ι having ceased to exist. And so for either of the four coefficients in its application to a unit of activity or of passivity : when it governs the former, the unit is a right angle, or sum of two, three or four right angles; and when it governs the latter, the unit is in general the line 1_ι measured on one of the four semiaxes. The two complete sets of factors, with their proper coefficients, are as they follow [fig. 15] :

ACTIVE FACTORS.

$$+\surd-1.1_\theta = PP' = \tfrac{1}{2}\pi;$$
$$-1.1_\theta = PP'P'' = \pi;$$
$$-\surd-1.1_\theta = PP'P''P''' = \tfrac{3}{2}\pi;$$
$$+1.1_\theta = PP'P''P'''P = 2\pi.$$

PASSIVE FACTORS.

$+\surd-1.1_\iota$ = OP′, on the positive secondary axis OY;
-1.1_ι = OP″, on the negative primary axis OX′;
$-\surd-1.1_\iota$ = OP‴ on the negative secondary axis OY′;
$+1.1_\iota$ = OP, on the positive primary axis OX.

From the notations of n° 20, we deduce these transformations :

$$\alpha = +\surd-1.1_\theta = (+1.1_\theta)^{\frac{1}{4}} = (-1.1_\theta)^{\frac{1}{2}};$$
$$\alpha^2 = -1.1_\theta = (+\surd-1.1_\theta)^2 = (+1.1_\theta)^{\frac{1}{2}};$$
$$\alpha^3 = -\surd-1.1_\theta = (+\surd-1.1_\theta)^3 = (-1.1_\theta)^{-\frac{1}{2}};$$
$$\alpha^4 = +1.1_\theta = (+\surd-1.1_\theta)^4 = (-1.1_\theta)^2 = 1_0 = 1.$$

Also we see that $+\sqrt{-1}.1_\theta$ and $(+\sqrt{-1}.1_\theta)^{-1}$,
-1.1_θ and $(-1.1_\theta)^{-1}$,
$-\sqrt{-1}.1_\theta$ and $(-\sqrt{-1}.1_\theta)^{-1}$,
$+1.1_\theta$ and $(+1.1_\theta)^{-1}$, are the four pairs of reciprocal fourth roots of unity; and that
$+\sqrt{-1}.1_\theta$ and $-\sqrt{-1}.1_\theta$,
-1.1_θ and -1.1_θ,
$-\sqrt{-1}.1_\theta$ and $+\sqrt{-1}.1_\theta$,
$+1.1_\theta$ and $+1.1_\theta$, are the four pairs of fourth roots complementary to unity, all in terms of the right angle expressed by its appropriate linear unit measure on the rectangular system of axes.

23. While the four symbolical coefficients $+1$, $+\sqrt{-1}$, -1 and $-\sqrt{-1}$ severally indicate the performance of an operation or action, together with its direction in space, the tense of that operation or action is in reality aoristical, and may therefore be changed at will from the past to the future, or the contrary; and [n° 16], moreover, since a ratio or coefficient may in general be applied to govern other species of measures of magnitude than that from which it was originally deduced, it may be transferred from a unit measure of activity 1_λ or 1_θ, to one of passivity 1_ι, etc. Now from their deduction, to wit,

$$\frac{+1_\lambda}{1_\lambda} = +1 = \frac{OP}{OP}, \qquad \frac{+\sqrt{-1}_\lambda}{1_\lambda} = +\sqrt{-1} = \frac{OP'}{OP},$$

$$\frac{-1_\lambda}{1_\lambda} = -1 = \frac{OP''}{OP}, \qquad \frac{-\sqrt{-1}_\lambda}{1_\lambda} = -\sqrt{-1} = \frac{OP'''}{OP},$$

these coefficients imply the result of an operation achieved in a unit of time, as specified by the unit measure of that operation; but the unit of activity 1_θ once eliminated, nothing forbids us to replace it by the linear unit of passivity 1_ι, or by either the linear or angular unit of activity 1_λ or 1_θ. By the first option, we make the notations $+1.a1_\iota$, $+\sqrt{-1}.a1_\iota$, $-1.a1_\iota$, $-\sqrt{-1}\,a1_\iota$, respectively say that an action measured by the line $a1_\iota$ *has been* performed in the direction indicated by the particular coefficient considered, since the unit of passivity 1_ι can only appropriately be employed to signify the measure of the result of an operation fully achieved. The second option empowers us either : 1° By choosing the linear unit 1_λ, to command the transfer of the material unit 1_μ, by means of the expressions $+1.x1_\lambda$, $+\sqrt{-1}.x1_\lambda$, $-1.x1_\lambda$, $-\sqrt{-1}.x1_\lambda$, through a distance equal to $x1_\lambda$ in the particular direction indicated by the coefficient considered ; or 2° By choosing the circular unit 1_θ, to command the rotation of either one of the loaded radii $+1.1_r.1_\mu$, $+\sqrt{-1}.1_r.1_\mu$, $-1.1_r.1_\mu$, $-\sqrt{-1}.1_r.1_\mu$, by means of the expressions $+1.1_\theta$, $+\sqrt{-1}.1_\theta$, -1.1_θ, $-\sqrt{-1}.1_\theta$, through an angle equal to that indicated by the particular coefficient considered; for instance, if the loaded radius be $+1.1_r.1_\mu$, and the expression -1.1_θ be particularized, the product $(+1.1_\theta)(-1.1_r.1_\mu)$ commands the rotation of the radius, from its position on the primary positive axis, through the angle π indicated by the coefficient -1, into the opposite position on the negative primary axis, in which position it is expressed by the new relation $-1.1_r.1_\mu$, whereby we are authorised to say (by attending only to the coefficients) that $(-1)\times(+1) = -1$, or that the product of unlike signs is negative. Now the above commands necessarily refer to the future tense, to an action yet *to be* achieved, and they are therefore appropriately imposed upon the unit of activity, which is of itself susceptible of a prospective interpretation.

24. In the equality $a+b-c = d$, where a, b, c and d are pure numerical ratios, the signs $+$ and $-$ indicate the performance of operations of a known nature on certain things whose number alone is in each term specified by the numerical coefficient. The agent or performer of these operations, and the tense of their performance, are alike indeterminate, as are also the species of the things themselves; and convenience alone might authorise us so to generalize the interpretation of the formula, as to enable it to comprehend within itself the elements of its own existence. The result d certainly does not exist independently of the operations $+$ and $-$; that is to say, a things μ must be added to b things μ, and c things μ subtracted from their sum, leaving d things μ, before we can deduce the relation d; but these three operations $+a$, $+b$ and $-c$ may have a simultaneous and self-existent reality and interpretation, on the hypothesis that the measure of the effect of a force stands for the force itself; since

then, taking instead of the thing μ the linear unit 1_ι, $a1_\iota+b1_\iota$ may represent the sum of the effects of two positive forces, and $-c1_\iota$ the effect of a negative force, whence $(a+b-c)1_\iota=d1_\iota$. And finally the whole interpretation becomes indispensably necessary for the management of a point considered as having or taking various positions with respect to the origin to which it is referred; it being obviously impossible that one same formula could represent this point as occupying successively two different positions without passing through the intermediate space, a circumstance which requires that the formula should command the point.

25. By any means capable to produce a uniform motion (such, for instance, as the generation of velocity by impulsion, abstraction being made of the centrifugal force when the motion is circular), imagine the body or material point 1_μ to be carried from [fig. 15] O to P in the unit of time, and let it be there at first arrested in its course as by a fixed obstacle : the distance $OP=1_\lambda$ will be the unit measure of the operation. Next let the point 1_μ begin anew from P by the operation of a new impulsion, and be now carried the distance $2\pi 1_\iota$ in the first unit of time after leaving P; and let the movement continue this time unarrested but uniform, that is, $2\pi 1_\iota$ in the second, third, etc. unit of time after leaving P. If this motion have place in the continuation of the direction OP, the record of the successive distances after leaving O will be 1_ι, $(1+2\pi)1_\iota$, $(1+4\pi)1_\iota$, etc.; and these distances will be the true measures of the velocity and time consumed in their generation, and of the number and magnitude of the operations performed on 1_μ; but if the direction of the second impulsion be angular instead of linear, and the moving point 1_μ be constrained to remain attached to the extremity of the radius OP rotating freely about the point O, then, although 1_μ describes the distance $2\pi 1_\iota$ in the first unit of time after leaving P, as in the former case, the measure of this operation (albeit the circumference is a unit of space embraced within absolutely definite natural limits, while the boundaries of the linear unit are entirely arbitrary or artificial) cannot be added to that of the movement from OP, since the distance from O is the same as before. Nevertheless a measurable operation has been performed, and the measure of that operation is a definite

unit of space $1_0.1_l = 2\pi.1_l$. The movement continuing, the distance $2\pi.1_l = 1_0.1_l$ is described in the second unit of time after leaving P, and so on indefinitely. Now these successively completed operations cannot be measured by distance from the new origin P, for the moving point always returns to P : therefore the record must be kept by a different notation; to do which, we avail ourselves of the use of exponents instead of the coefficients proper to linear motion, and write 1_0^1, 1_0^2, 1_0^3, etc. in lieu of 2π, 4π, 6π, etc. By this distinction, the number of operations is recorded, the relation of the moving point 1_μ to the origin O is restored at the end of each operation, and the condition of numerical unity $1^n = 1$ is fulfilled.

If the radius rotate through one right angle, or the moving point describe the arc $\frac{1}{2}\pi 1_l$ in the unit of time, since the arc is measured by its sine which is now $OP' = 1_l$, this line, marked so as to define its position with regard to OP its equal in magnitude, will be the measure of the operation : then if the unit right angle be written 1_θ, the radius OP' may be written $1_1.1_l$, or $1_1.1_\lambda$ to indicate that it is the measure of an operation. In the next unit of time the position of the radius becomes OP'', which is now the linear measure of the whole operation from P, and is written $1_2.1_\lambda$, the circular measure of the same operation being $1_\theta^2 = \pi\, 1_l$. The third unit of time brings us to the position $OP''' = 1_3.1_\lambda$, corresponding to $1_\theta^3 = \frac{3}{2}\pi.1_l$ on the arc; and now the fourth unit of time restores $OP = 1_4.1_\lambda = 1_0.1_\lambda$, corresponding to $1_\theta^4 = 2\pi.1_l$ the circumference or absolute unit measure of space. Now [n° 10] the signs + and — have at first no other signification than that of simple agreement and opposition of direction; so that if $OP = 1_4.1_\lambda = 1_0.1_\lambda$ be written $+1_\lambda$, the notation for $OP'' = 1_2.1_\lambda$ will be -1_λ. Also from the relation between the arcs $\pi 1_l$ and $\frac{1}{2}\pi 1_l$, or 1_θ^2 and 1_θ, to which correspond the radii $1_2.1_\lambda$ and $1_1.1_\lambda$, we have $1_\theta = \sqrt{(1_\theta^2)}$, and therefore $1_1.1_\lambda = \sqrt{(1_2.1_\lambda)} = \sqrt{(-1_\lambda)}$ as a corresponding notation for the linear measure OP'; which last notation obviously refers to $-\sqrt{(-1_\lambda)}$ as the notation for its opposite direction $OP''' = 1_3.1_\lambda$, the linear measure of the arc $\frac{3}{2}\pi 1_l$ or 1_θ^3, all the linear expressions being truly linear measures of the angular effects expressed by the powers of the corresponding circular units. By taking the ratio of each of the complex linear units $+1_\lambda$, -1_λ, $\sqrt{-1_\lambda}$ and $=\sqrt{-1_\lambda}$, to the simple linear unit 1_λ, we get the four signs $+1$, -1, $+\sqrt{-1}$ and $-\sqrt{-1}$, which have now become converted from simple indications of direction in space [n_o 10], into coefficients implying both the direction and the unit measure of an operation in space and time.

If the radius OP were rotated through the semicircumference in a first unit of time, we should have immediately the result $OP''=-1.1_\lambda$, and the restored result $OP=+1.1_\lambda$ in the second unit of time; and therefore if we take $-1.1_\theta=$ arc $PP'P''=\pi.1_t$, we see that the product $(-1.1_\theta)(+1.1_t)=-1.1_t$, and that the product $(-1.1_\theta)(-1.1_t)=+1.1_t$, which instances explain the algebraical operation of multiplying a quantity by -1. If the radius complete a revolution in the unit of time, then, accordingly as that revolution begins at P or P″, we show that the product $(+1.1_\theta)(+1.1_t=+1.1_t$, or the product $(+1.1_\theta)(-1.1_t)=-1.1_t$, and these instances explain the algebraical operation of multiplying a quantity by $+1$. We have here the ground of the common rule that the product of like signs $+\times+$ or $-\times-$ is positive, and that the product of unlike signs $+\times-$ or $-\times+$ is negative.

If we recal the fact that the characters + and — were at first brought into use as signs of command to perform respectively the operations of addition and subtraction, that is, to execute actions whose measures are distinctly indicated by the opposition of the directions of the actions themselves in space, as *to* and *from* the point P for instance [n° 14], the reason for adopting them as marks of direction [n° 10] is obvious, the *to* and *from* being properly *to the right* and *to the left* of the origin O; and when we further observe that multiplication by $+1.1_\lambda$ and -1.1_λ is respectively equivalent to one addition and one subtraction, that is, to one act of transportation *to the right* and one *to the left* of the starting point O (the succession of which actions necessarily obliges the operator to wheel half round as on the centre O), the appositeness and significancy of the whole notation, as it has finally perfected itself, are rendered strikingly manifest. A remarkable conclusion from the interpretation of the subsequently introduced sign $\sqrt{-1}$, is that the action which it commands is entirely indifferent in its consequences with regard to that commanded by the sign $+1$, while its repetition tells upon the latter to a complete reversal.

26. The result of the multiplication of a point by a geometrical factor being a line straight or circular, according as the multiplier is the measure of a force of translation or of rotation, it becomes necessary to refer the generated line to the system of rectangular axes of measurement, for any angle of the generated line with the primary axis; for we have hitherto considered only right angles.

I first consider the case of one single right angle XOY [fig. 16]. If 1_μ is placed at N′, and multiplied by N′M in the primary direction OX, it is transferred to M, the primary measure being ON and the secondary measure zero; both measures being the same as if the movable point 1_μ had been situated at O, and multiplied by ON. Similarly if 1_μ were placed at N or O, and multiplied by NM or ON′, the primary measure would be zero and the secondary measure ON′.

Next let 1_μ at O be multiplied by OM, and it is transferred to M; and the primary measure of OM is ON, and its secondary measure is ON′. More generally we may say that ON and ON′ are the primary and secondary measures of the point M, when it is unnecessary to specify the force which has transferred 1_μ to M.

Again, suppose 1_μ placed at A on the radius OA. If multiplied by the arc AM, 1_μ is transferred to M, and has the primary and secondary measures ON and ON′. Now it has been agreed that the lines ON and ON′ are the primary and secondary measures of the arc AM [n° 10], and reciprocally that the arc AM is the circular measure of the lines ON and ON′, and so of the point M on OM. We may therefore say that ON and ON′ are the primary and secondary measures of the circular factor AM; and reciprocally that the arc AM is the circular measure of the linear factors ON and ON′, or of the linear factor OM, or of the point M.

We lastly remark that the linear factor OM, or the point M, has the measure OM in its own direction OL, which we term the absolute measure of the point M. And the linear factors ON and ON′, or the points N and N′, referred to the line OL as a primary axis, have respectively for primary measures the lines OR and OR′, whose sum is equal to the absolute measure OM of the point M; and for secondary measures the lines OQ and OQ′, equal and in opposite directions zero. Thus the absolute measure of the line OM is equal to the sum of the primary measures (taken on OM as primary axis) of its own primary and secondary measures taken on any rectangular axes OX, OY.

The linear factor OM, or the measure of the point M, is then finally represented either by the system of its primary and secondary measures, the rectangular coordinates ON and ON′; or by its circular measure, the arc AM to the radius OA. Either of these systems of measures determine OM, and consequently M.

27. If 1_μ at O [fig. 17] be multiplied by the linear factor OM, it is transferred to M; and ON is the distance 1_μ has been moved in the direction OA, or is the measure of the effect of the factor OM in the direction OA, ON′ being at the same time the measure of the effect of the same factor OM in the perpendicular direction OA′. Indeed, if a material body move from O to M, it has evidently travelled from the line OA′ to the line NT, and from the line OA to the line N′T′, at one and the same time; and the distances between OA′ and NT, and between OA and N′T′, are severally equal to the lines ON and ON′, or such is the effect simultaneously accomplished in these directions. If, when at O, 1_μ be multiplied by ON, the distance 1_μ is moved in the direction OM is OR, or OR is the effect of the factor ON in the direction OM; and if, still at O, 1_μ were multiplied by ON′, the measure of the effect of the factor ON′, counted also in the direction OM, will be OR′; OR and OR′ being respectively the measures of the factors ON and ON′, taken on the axis OM, and the sum of OR and OR′ being equal to OM. Let now, at O, 1_μ be multiplied simultaneously by ON and ON′ in their proper directions : by virtue of the principle of passivity, 1_μ must yield obedience to each factor in its direction, by describing a line OM equal to the factor ON in its direction, and to the factor ON′ in its direction.

In this example, ON′ has the measure zero in the direction of ON, and reciprocally ON has the measure zero in the direction of ON′; so that the effect of ON in its direction is neither increased nor diminished by that of ON′, and reciprocally the effect of ON′ is undisturbed by ON.

When the angle NON′ is acute [fig. 18], ON′ has the positive primary measure OQ, which is to be added to that of ON, and we then get the equivalent factors OP and OP′ for the true primary and secondary measures of the point M, or of the resultant of the factors ON and ON′.

When the angle NON′ is obtuse [fig. 19], ON′ has the negative primary measure OQ, which is to be subtracted (or algebraically added) to the primary measure of ON, and we then get the equivalent factors OP and OP′ for the true primary and secondary measures of the point M, or of the resultant of the factors ON and ON′.

28. Let the radius [fig. 20] $OM = 1_\iota$, and angle $AOM = \theta$: then we know the ratios $\frac{ON}{OM} = \cos\theta$ and $\frac{ON'}{OM} = \sin\theta$; and therefore that $ON = \cos\theta.1_\iota$ and $ON' = \sin\theta.1_\iota$ in magnitude, but the positions are entirely undetermined by the expressions. Now since the linear unit is arbitrary, we may substitute therefor in ON, ON′ and OM, the respective linear units $+1.1_\lambda$, $+\sqrt{-1}.1_\lambda$ 1_ι, mutually equal and indeterminate in magnitude, but the two first determinate in the directions OA and OA′; and then we have

$ON = \cos\theta(+1.1_\lambda) = +1.\cos\theta.1_\lambda$, and

$ON' = \sin\theta(+\sqrt{-1}.1_\lambda) = +\sqrt{-1}.\sin\theta.1_\lambda$, in magnitude and position; while $OM = 1_\iota$, expressed in magnitude only.

Now suppose the multiplicand point 1_μ at O : I multiply it simultaneously by the two linear factors $+\sqrt{-1}.\sin\theta.1_\lambda$ and $+1.\cos\theta.1_\lambda$, that is to say, I multiply 1_μ at O by the compound factor $(+1.\cos\theta+\sqrt{-1}.\sin\theta)1_\lambda$, and, by virtue of n° 27, 1_μ is transferred from O to the point M, in which position it has for primary and secondary measures the lines $+1.\cos\theta.1_\iota = ON$ and $+\sqrt{-1}.\sin\theta.1_\iota = ON'$, the passive measures of the active factors which generated OM. Thus the absolute measure of the resultant line $OM = 1_\lambda$ is equal to the sum of the primary and secondary measures of its components $+1.\cos\theta.1_\lambda$ and $+\sqrt{-1}.\sin\theta.1_\lambda$; that is, the expression $(+1.\cos\theta+\sqrt{-1}.\sin\theta)1_\lambda$ is a compound linear unit factor equivalent to the simple factor $OM = 1_\lambda$ in magnitude, and forming the angle θ with the positive primary semiaxis; or, again, it is equivalent to the circular factor $\theta 1_\lambda$ in magnitude, this arc having the identical linear measure $(+1\cos\theta+\sqrt{-1}\sin\theta)1_\iota$.

29. Take now the general case of the system of four right angles [fig. 5]. Let the radius $OA = 1_\iota = 1_\lambda$, and the arcs $AM' = \theta'$,

$AM''=\theta''$, $AM'''=\theta'''$, $AM^{iv}=\theta^{iv}$. Comparing n°s 10, 26 and 28, we construct the following expressions as lineo-angular measures of the several linear factors OM', OM'', OM''' and OM^{iv}, or of the circular factors AM', AM'', AM''' and AM^{iv} :

For the point M',

$$(+1.\cos\theta'+\sqrt{-1}.\sin\theta')1_\lambda = +1.ON'+\sqrt{-1}.OP' = OM' \text{ or } AM';$$

for the point M'',

$$(-1.\cos\theta''+\sqrt{-1}.\sin\theta'')1_\lambda = -1.ON''+\sqrt{-1}.OP'' = OM'' \text{ or } AM'';$$

for the point M''',

$$(-1.\cos\theta'''-\sqrt{-1}.\sin\theta''')1_\lambda = -1.ON'''-\sqrt{-1}.OP''' = OM''' \text{ or } AM''';$$

and for the point M^{iv},

$$(+1.\cos\theta^{iv}-\sqrt{-1}.\sin\theta^{iv})1_\lambda = +1.ON^{iv}-\sqrt{-1}.OP^{iv} = OM^{iv} \text{ or } AM^{iv};$$

that is to say, the material unit 1_μ will be transferred from O to one of the points M by a corresponding linear factor, or from A to such point M by the corresponding circular factor, always in a unit of time 1_t. This is the complete system of coordination of measures of magnitude, direction and action, for the four semiaxes OX, OY, OX′ and OY′.

30. Let [fig. 21] $PM=\theta$, and $PP'P''P'''M'=2\pi-\theta$; then the lineo-angular measure of $OM = (+1.\cos\theta+\sqrt{-1}.\sin\theta)1_t$, and that of $OM' = (+1.\cos\theta-\sqrt{-1}.\sin\theta)1_t$. Now the arc $(2\pi-\theta)1_t$ is the complement of $\theta.1_t$ to the circumference, and the lineo-angular measures of OM and OM′ are also respectively the lineo-angular measures of these arcs $\theta 1_t$ and $(2\pi-\theta)1_t$. Taking then the multiplicand point 1_μ at O, I effect the first multiplication $OP.1_\mu = 1_r.1_\mu$. Let now $1_r.1_\mu$ be the multiplicand, and I effect a second multiplication by the arc $\theta.1_\lambda$ expressed by its lineo-angular measure, and $(+1.\cos\theta+\sqrt{-1}.\sin\theta)1_\lambda.1_\mu = OM.1_\mu$ is the result. From the position in M, one single multiplication by the arc complementary of $\theta 1_\lambda$ to $2\pi 1_\lambda$ will carry 1_μ to P, through MP′P″P‴P. The lineo-angular measure of this complementary arc being $(+1.\cos\theta-\sqrt{-1}.\sin\theta)1_\lambda$, I effect the multiplication---- $(+1.\cos\theta-\sqrt{-1}.\sin\theta)1_\lambda.(+1.\cos\theta+\sqrt{-1}.\sin\theta)1_r.1_\mu$, and it reduces to $(+1.\cos^2\theta+1.\sin^2\theta)1_r.1_\mu = +1.1_r.1_\mu = OP.1_\mu$, because $(+1.\cos^2\theta+1.\sin^2\theta)1_r = +1.(\cos^2\theta+\sin^2\theta)1_r = +1.1.1_r$ by n° 11.

Thus the two expressions, namely, $(+1.\cos\theta+\sqrt{-1}.\sin\theta)$ and $(+1.\cos\theta-\sqrt{-1}.\sin\theta)$, are respectively the complex ratios of the inclined radii OM and OM′ to the horizontal radius OP (the angles of inclination being θ and $-\theta$), and at the same time are coefficients of factors that are mutually complementary to unity. The first is the lineo-angular measure of the radius $OM=1_r$, or as well of the arc $PM=\theta 1_r$, and therefore may represent this arc as a multiplier to the multiplicand $1_r.1_\mu=OP.1_\mu$, transferring 1.1_μ into the position OM, so that $(+1.\cos\theta+\sqrt{-1}.\sin\theta)1_r.1_\mu=OM.1_\mu$; and the second is the lineo-angular measure of the line OM′, or of the arc $PP'P''P'''M'=MP'P''P'''P=(2\pi-\theta)1_r$ complementary of $\theta.1_r$ to the circumference, and therefore may be taken as a multiplier to the multiplicand $(+1.\cos\theta+\sqrt{-1}.\sin\theta)1_r.1_\mu$, to transfer 1_μ from M through MP′P″P‴P to P, so that $(+1.\cos\theta-\sqrt{-1}.\sin\theta)1_\lambda.(+1.\cos\theta+\sqrt{-1}.\sin\theta)1_r.1_\mu=OP.1_\mu$, or $+1(\cos^2\theta+\sin^2\theta)1_r.1_\mu=+1.1_r.1_\mu$, or $+1.1=+1$, thus fulfilling the condition of numerical and geometrical and dynamical unity, or of absolute unity.

By varying the order of application of the two complementary coefficients $(+1.\cos\theta+\sqrt{-1}.\sin\theta)$ and $(+1.\cos\theta-\sqrt{-1}.\sin\theta)$, we may achieve the absolute unit in two different ways, a direct and an inverse circulation from P through the circumference; and similarly each factor with its reciprocal will furnish two variations which bring the result unity, giving in all six combinations, as may be seen in the table opposite. For instance [fig. 22], we reach the point M from P, directly through PM by means of the factor $(+1.\cos\theta+\sqrt{-1}.\sin\theta)1_\lambda$, or inversely through PP‴P″P′M by its reciprocal $\frac{1}{+1.\cos\theta+\sqrt{-1}.\sin\theta}.1_\lambda$; and we reach P from M, directly through MP′P″P‴P by means of the factor --------- $(+1.\cos\theta-\sqrt{-1}\sin\theta)1_\lambda$, or inversely through MP by its reciprocal $\frac{1}{+1.\cos-\sqrt{-1}.\sin\theta}.1_\lambda$. The product of $(+1.\cos\theta+\sqrt{-1}.\sin\theta)1_\iota$ by its complementary factor $(+1.\cos\theta-\sqrt{-1}.\sin\theta)1_\lambda$ is equal in effect to the product of the same factor $(+1.\cos\theta+\sqrt{-1}.\sin\theta)1_\iota$ by its reciprocal $\frac{1}{+1.\cos\theta+\sqrt{-1}.\sin\theta}.1_\lambda$, but the two effects are had by traversing in the opposite directions PP′ and PP‴.

TABLE A.

EXHIBITING THE SIX COMBINATIONS OF TWO FACTORS COMPLEMENTARY TO UNITY (Fig. 22).

Initial position.	Multiplicand.	Multiplier.	Product.	Circuit.	Final position.
I. 1. OP, 2. OM,	1_μ, $(+1\cos\theta+\sqrt{-1}\sin\theta)1_\mu$,	$(+1\cos\theta+\sqrt{-1}\sin\theta)$, $(+1\cos\theta-\sqrt{-1}\sin\theta)$,	$(+1\cos\theta+\sqrt{-1}\sin\theta)1_\mu$, $+1.1_\mu$,	PM, MP'P''P'''P,	OM; OP.
II. 1. OP, 2. OM',	1_μ, $(+1\cos\theta-\sqrt{-1}\sin\theta)1_\mu$,	$(+1\cos\theta-\sqrt{-1}\sin\theta)$, $(+1\cos\theta+\sqrt{-1}\sin\theta)$,	$(+1\cos\theta-\sqrt{-1}\sin\theta)1_\mu$, $+1.1_\mu$,	PP'P''P'''M', M'P,	OM'; OP.
III. 1. OP, 2. OM,	1_μ, $(+1\cos\theta+\sqrt{-1}\sin\theta)1_\mu$,	$(+1\cos\theta+\sqrt{-1}\sin\theta)$, $(+1\cos\theta+\sqrt{-1}\sin\theta)^{-1}$,	$(+1\cos\theta+\sqrt{-1}\sin\theta)1_\mu$, $+1.1_\mu$,	PM, MP,	OM; OP.
IV. 1. OP, 2. OM',	1_μ, $(+1\cos\theta+\sqrt{-1}\sin\theta)^{-1}1_\mu$,	$(+1\cos\theta+\sqrt{-1}\sin\theta)^{-1}$, $(+1\cos\theta+\sqrt{-1}\sin\theta)$,	$(+1\cos\theta+\sqrt{-1}\sin\theta)^{-1}1_\mu$, $+1.1_\mu$,	PM', M'P,	OM'; OP.
V. 1. OP, 2. OM',	1_μ, $(+1\cos\theta-\sqrt{-1}\sin\theta)1_\mu$,	$(+1\cos\theta-\sqrt{-1}\sin\theta)$, $(+1\cos\theta-\sqrt{-1}\sin\theta)^{-1}$,	$(+1\cos\theta-\sqrt{-1}\sin\theta)1_\mu$, $+1.1_\mu$,	PP'P''P'''M', M'P'''P''P'P,	OM'; OP.
VI. 1. OP, 2. OM,	1_μ, $(+1\cos\theta-\sqrt{-1}\sin\theta)^{-1}1_\mu$,	$(+1\cos\theta-\sqrt{-1}\sin\theta)^{-1}$, $(+1\cos\theta-\sqrt{-1}\sin\theta)$,	$(+1\cos\theta-\sqrt{-1}\sin\theta)^{-1}1_\mu$, $+1.1_\mu$,	PP'''P''P'M, MP'P''P'''P,	OM; OP.

[*To face page* 36.]

31. By compounding the two elementary factors or ratios --- $+1.\cos\theta+\sqrt{-1}.\sin\theta$ and $+1.\cos\theta-\sqrt{-1}.\sin\theta$ (the linear units being omitted but understood), we get the well known équality $+1(\cos^2\theta+\sin^2\theta) = +1.1$, or equation of numerical, geometrical and dynamical unity, from which we deduce by division this other equality $\cos^2\theta+\sin^2\theta = 1$, or equation of numerical unity. Conversely, if we multiply this last equality by $+1$ to render it a function of general unity, we ought to be able to decompose the compound ratio $+1.\cos^2\theta+1.\sin^2\theta$ into its primitive elements. In attempting the decomposition by division, both the divisor and quotient are to be sought from the dividend. Because $(+1)^2=+1$, the first term of both divisor and quotient must be $+1.\cos\theta$; but although $\sin\theta$ must obviously enter the second term, its coefficient is not so readily perceived : it is some unknown function of general unity $\phi\,(+1)$. We then proceed as usual, and determine the form of the function by equating the remainder of the division to zero, as followeth :

$$\begin{array}{l|l}
+1\cos\theta+\phi(+1)\sin\theta & +1\cos^2\theta+1\sin^2\theta \\
+1\cos\theta-\phi(+1)\sin\theta; & \underline{+1\cos^2\theta+1\,\phi(+1)\cos\theta\,\sin\theta} \\
 & \text{----}\ -1\,\phi(+1)\cos\theta\,\sin\theta+1\sin^2\theta \\
 & \quad\ \underline{-1\,\phi(+1)\cos\theta\,\sin\theta-(\phi(+1))^2\sin^2\theta} \\
 & \text{----}\ (\phi(+1))^2\sin^2\theta+1\sin^2\theta = 0; \\
 & \qquad\qquad (\phi(+1))^2 = -1; \\
 & \qquad\qquad \phi(+1) = \sqrt{(-1)}.
\end{array}$$

32. The two complementary ratios $+1.\cos\theta+\sqrt{-1}.\sin\theta$ and $+1.\cos\theta-\sqrt{-1}.\sin\theta$ may also be applied as binomial coefficients; in which case the factors $+1.\cos\theta.1_\lambda$ and $+\sqrt{-1}.\sin\theta.1_\lambda$ would respectively transfer 1_μ and $1'_\mu$ from O to P and Q [fig. 22′], thereby generating the lines $OP = +1.\cos\theta.1_l$ = projection of OM on OA, and $OQ = +\sqrt{-1}.\sin\theta.1_l$ = projection of OM on OA′; while the lineo-angular measures of the terms of the second factor will be $OP = +1.\cos\theta.1_\lambda$ and $OQ = -\sqrt{-1}.\sin\theta.1_\lambda$. Then operating the product of the multiplicand $+1.\cos\theta.1_l+\sqrt{-}\sin\theta.1_l$ and multiplier $+1.1_\theta.\cos\theta-\sqrt{-1}.1_\theta.\sin\theta$ by terms, the first partial product $(+1.1_\theta)(+1.1_l)\cos^2\theta$ revolves OP through the four right angles to OA again by means of $+1.1_\theta$ [n° 22], and reduces $OP = \cos\theta.1_l$ to $ON = \cos^2\theta.1_l$ = projection of OP on OM; the

second partial product $(+1.1_\theta)(+\sqrt{-1}.1_\iota)\cos\theta\sin\theta$ revolves OQ through the four right angles to OA′ again by means of $+1.1_\theta$, and reduces $OQ=\sin\theta.1_\iota$ to $OR=\cos\theta\sin\theta.1_\iota$; the third partial product $(-\sqrt{-1}.1_\theta)(+1.1_\iota)\sin\theta\cos\theta$ revolves OP through three right angles to OA‴ by means of $-\sqrt{-1}.1_\theta$, and reduces $OP=\cos\theta.1_\iota$ to $OR'=\sin\theta\cos\theta.1_\iota$; and the fourth partial product $(-\sqrt{-1}.1_\theta)(+\sqrt{-1}.1_\iota)\sin^2\theta$ revolves OQ through three right angles to OA by means of $-\sqrt{-1}.1_\theta$, and reduces $OQ=\sin\theta.1_\iota$ to $ON'=\sin^2\theta.1_\iota$ = projection of OQ on OM; and finally we have $OQ-OQ'=0.1_\iota$, and $ON+ON'=OA=+1.1_\iota$. Thus, as it ought to be, the product of the two pairs of components is equal to the product of their resultants.

It will be seen, in passing, that figs. 7, 8 and 22′ respectively correspond to a geometrical, an arithmetical, and an algebraical demonstration of the forty-seventh proposition of the first book of Euclid.

33. Suppose now that we choose the angle θ equal to the nth part of four right angles. The factor $(+1.\cos\theta+\sqrt{-1}.\sin\theta)1_r$ expresses the radius [fig. 23] $OM=1_r$, or the arc $PM=\theta.1_r$, in terms of its primary and secondary measures, and is the measure of the angular effect of the arc $\theta.1_\lambda$ on the radius OM; and since we here suppose $\theta=\frac{2\pi}{n}$, it follows that n successive multiplications of $1_r.1_\mu=OP.1_\mu$ by the factor $(+1.\cos\theta+\sqrt{-1}.\sin\theta)1_\lambda$ will transfer $1_r.1_\mu$, by n successive steps in angular direction PP′, from OP to OP again; that is, we shall have

$$(+1.\cos\theta+\sqrt{-1}.\sin\theta)^n.1_\lambda.1_\mu=+1.1_\iota.1_\mu=+1.1_\mu,$$

or the accomplishment of the effect unity. Then $(+1.\cos\theta+\sqrt{-1}.\sin\theta)1_\iota=(+1.1_\lambda)^{\frac{1}{n}}$, and is therefore the primitive nth root of unity; and its complementary factor to unity, $(+1.\cos\theta-\sqrt{-1}.\sin\theta)1_\lambda$, is equal to the product of the $(n-1)$ remaining nth roots of unity. We may, therefore, by expounding n in the expression $+1.\cos\frac{2\pi}{n}+\sqrt{-1}.\sin\frac{2\pi}{n}$ successively by the numbers 1, 2, 3, 4, ..., obtain the primitive first, second, third, fourth, ..., root of unity, and its complementary factor to unity from the expression $+.1\cos\frac{2\pi}{n}-\sqrt{-1}.\sin\frac{2\pi}{n}$. But we will first show some of the relations of the different roots of unity.

34. We take for example that of the fourth roots of unity, as exhibited in the linear and the angular form, and, laying aside the multiplicand 1_μ, attend only to the multipliers.

Let [fig. 24] O1 be the linear multiplier, and OP′ be supposed the absolute geometrical unit; then O1 $= \alpha$ will be the primitive fourth root of unity, and its successive powers furnish the following table exhibiting the genesis of each root distinctly :

Linear factor.	First root.	Second root.	Third root.	Fourth root.	Circular factor.
O to 1	α^1				$\frac{1}{2}\pi = PP'$;
O to 2	α^2	β^1			$1\pi = PP'P''$;
O to 3	α^3		γ^1		$\frac{3}{2}\pi = PP'P''P'''$;
O to P′	α^4	β^2		$1^1 = 1$	$2\pi = PP$.
O to 5	$\alpha^5 = \alpha^1$				
6	$\alpha^6 = \alpha^2$	β^3	γ^2		
7	$\alpha^7 = \alpha^3$				
O to P″	$\alpha^8 = \alpha^4$	β^4		$1^2 = 1$	$4\pi = PPP$.
9	$\alpha^9 = \alpha^1$		γ^3		
10	$\alpha^{10} = \alpha^2$	$\beta^5 = \beta^1$			
11	$\alpha^{11} = \alpha^3$				
O toP‴	$\alpha^{12} = \alpha^4$	$\beta^6 = \beta^2$	γ^4	$1^3 = 1$	$6\pi = PPPP$.
13	$\alpha^{13} = \alpha^1$				
14	$\alpha^{14} = \alpha^2$	$\beta^7 = \beta^3$			
15	$\alpha^{15} = \alpha^3$		$\gamma^5 = \gamma^1$		
O to P^{iv}	$\alpha^{16} = \alpha^4$	$\beta^8 = \beta^4$		$1^4 = 1$	$8\pi = PPPPP$.

From this table we collect the following, for immediate reference to the circular system of roots :

$$\alpha = (1_0^1)^{\frac{1}{4}} = \tfrac{1}{4}.2\pi.1_r = \tfrac{1}{2}\pi.1_r;$$
$$\beta = (1_0^2)^{\frac{1}{4}} = \tfrac{1}{4}.4\pi.1_r = 1\pi.1_r;$$
$$\gamma = (1_0^3)^{\frac{1}{4}} = \tfrac{1}{4}.6\pi.1_r = \tfrac{3}{2}\pi.1_r;$$
$$1_0 = (1_0^4)^{\frac{1}{4}} = \tfrac{1}{4}.8\pi.1_r = 2\pi.1_r.$$

Thus we see that the primitive root α is alone the true fourth root of 1; the second root β being really the fourth root of 1^1, the third root γ being the fourth root of 1^3, and the fourth or numerical root 1 being in fact the fourth root of 1^4.

To each of the four pretended absolute linear units OP′, OP″, OP‴ and OP^{iv}, corresponds a real absolute circular unit $2\pi.1_r$,

$4\pi.1_r$, $6\pi.1_r$ or $8\pi.1_r$. Therefore, instead of obtaining the roots β, γ and 1 by the successive multiplication of the primitive root α, we may get each of them by the division of its proper arc, in the manner the primitive root is obtained from $2\pi.1_r$; for if

$\alpha = \frac{1}{2}\pi.1_r$ be the primitive fourth root of the absolute unit $2\pi.1_r$,
$\beta = 1\pi.1_r$ is the primitive fourth root of the absolute unit $4\pi.1_r$,
$\gamma = \frac{3}{2}\pi.1_r$ is the similar root of the absolute unit $6\pi.1_r$, and
$1_0 = 2\pi.1_r$ is the primitive fourth root of the absolute unit $8\pi.1_r$.

We arrange the several pairs of complementary fourth roots as followeth :

$\alpha^1 = \alpha = \frac{1}{4}.1.2\pi.1_r = \frac{1}{2}\pi.1_r$, and $\alpha^3 = \gamma = \frac{1}{4}.3.2\pi.1_r = \frac{3}{2}\pi.1_r$;
$\alpha^2 = \beta = \frac{1}{4}.2.2\pi.1_r = 1\pi.1_r$, and $\alpha^2 = \beta = \frac{1}{4}.2.4\pi.1_r = 1\pi.1_r$;
$\alpha^3 = \gamma = \frac{1}{4}.3.2\pi.1_r = \frac{3}{2}\pi.1_r$, and $\alpha^1 = \alpha = \frac{1}{4}.1.2\pi.1_r = \frac{1}{2}\pi.1_r$;
$\alpha^4 = 1^1 = \frac{1}{4}.4.2\pi.1_r = 2\pi.1_r$, and $\alpha^0 = 1^0 = \frac{1}{4}.0.2\pi.1_r = 0\pi.1_r$.

By setting aside the numerical complementary roots $1^0 = 0\pi.1_r$ and $1^1 = 2\pi.1_r$, which will be the same for all values of n whatever, we see that it is only necessary to continue the terms of the series up to the semicircumference or 1π, the remaining half of the series between 1π and 2π being complementary to the first half. Thus,

$\alpha = \frac{1}{2}\pi.1_r$ has for complement $\alpha^3 = \frac{3}{2}\pi.1_r$; and
$\alpha^2 = 1\pi.1_r$ has for complement $\alpha^2 = 1\pi.1_r$.

35. Recal we now again, that similarly as a *passive* line or arc (measure of magnitude merely) is known by its primary and secondary measures, so is an *active* line (measure of action), or continued product of geometrical factors, or the nth power or root of a geometrical unit, known by the system of its primary and secondary measures.

The expression $(+1.\cos\theta + \sqrt{-1}.\sin\theta)1_r$ is, as we have seen, the lineo-angular measure of the radius $OM = 1_r$ [fig. 23], and is at the same time the lineo-angular measure of the arc $PM = \theta.1_r$, and thus represents this arc as a geometrical factor. When ---- $\theta = \frac{2\pi}{n}$, this measure becomes $(\pm 1.\cos\frac{2\pi}{n} \pm \sqrt{-1}.\sin\frac{2\pi}{n})1_r$; the upper or lower sign of the cosine having place accordingly as the arc is comprised between $\frac{3}{2}\pi$ and $\frac{1}{2}\pi$, or between $\frac{1}{2}\pi$ and $\frac{3}{2}\pi$; and the upper or lower sign of the sine having place accordingly as the same arc is comprised between 0 and π, or between π and 2π, as is seen by reference to fig. 5.

The expression $\pm 1.\cos\frac{2\pi}{n} \pm\sqrt{-1}.\sin\frac{2\pi}{n}$ is then the coefficieut of the lineo-angular measure of the arc $\theta.1_r$ equal to the nth part of the circumference, and of the radius 1_r forming the angle θ with the positive primary semiaxis; and therefore [n° 33] affords the equation $(\pm 1.\cos\frac{2\pi}{n} \pm\sqrt{-1}.\sin\frac{2\pi}{n})1_l = (+1_0)^{\frac{1}{n}}1_l = \frac{1}{n}.2\pi.1_l$, for the primitive root of 1. The $n-1$ remaining nth roots of 1 being really the respective primitive roots of 1^2, 1^3, 1^4, ..., 1^n, where the successive powers of unity correspond to the successive arcs 2.2π, 3.2π, 4.2π, ..., $n.2\pi$, we have for these $n-1$ roots the $n-1$ equations,

$$\pm 1.\cos 2.\frac{2\pi}{n} \pm\sqrt{-1}.\sin 2.\frac{2\pi}{n} = (+1^2)^{\frac{1}{n}} = \frac{1}{n}.2.2\pi;$$

$$\pm 1.\cos 3.\frac{2\pi}{n} \pm\sqrt{-1}.\sin 3.\frac{2\pi}{n} = (+1^3)^{\frac{1}{n}} = \frac{1}{n}.3.2\pi;$$

$$\pm 1.\cos 4.\frac{2\pi}{n} \pm\sqrt{-1}.\sin 4.\frac{2\pi}{n} = (+1^4)^{\frac{1}{n}} = \frac{1}{n}.4.2\pi;$$

- - - - - - - - - - - -

$$\pm 1.\cos n.\frac{2\pi}{n} \pm\sqrt{-1}.\sin n.\frac{2\pi}{n} = (+1^n)^{\frac{1}{n}} = \frac{1}{n}.n.2\pi,$$

the linear unit being omitted as understood, and the double signs to be determined as before stated. By setting aside the nth equation, which is always that of the pair of complementary numerical roots 1^0 and 1^1 for any value of n, and observing that each root comprehended between 0π and 1π, and the sign of whose sine therefore is $+\sqrt{-1}$, has its complementary root comprehended between 1π and 2π, the sign of its sine consequently being $-\sqrt{-1}$, we can reduce the number of equations for the determination of the $n-1$ algebraical nth roots of unity to $\frac{1}{2}n$ or $\frac{1}{2}(n-1)$, accordingly as n is an even or an odd number; but for the first five values of n (beginning with zero), the formulæ complete for all the roots are:

$1^0\ n=0,\quad +1.\cos\frac{1}{0}.0\pi + \sqrt{-1}.\sin\frac{1}{0}.0\pi = (+1^0)^{\frac{1}{0}} = +1^0.$

$2^0\ n=1,\quad +1.\cos\frac{1}{1}.2\pi + \sqrt{-1}.\sin\frac{1}{1}.2\pi = (+1^1)^{\frac{1}{1}} = +1^1.$

$3^0\ n=2,\quad -1.\cos\frac{1}{2}.2\pi + \sqrt{-1}.\sin\frac{1}{2}.2\pi = (+1^1)^{\frac{1}{2}} = -1;$

$\qquad +1.\cos\frac{1}{2}.4\pi - \sqrt{-1}.\sin\frac{1}{2}.4\pi = (+1^2)^{\frac{1}{2}} = +1.$

$4^0\ n=3,\quad ----\cos\frac{1}{3}.2\pi\ ----\sin\frac{1}{3}.2\pi = (+1^1)^{\frac{1}{3}}$

$= -1.\cos 120^\circ + \sqrt{-1}.\sin 120^\circ = -\frac{1}{2} + \frac{1}{2}\sqrt{-1}.\sqrt{3};$

$----\cos\frac{1}{3}.4\pi\ ----\sin\frac{1}{3}.4\pi = (+1^2)^{\frac{1}{3}}$

$= -1.\cos 240^\circ - \sqrt{-1}.\sin 240^\circ = -\frac{1}{2} - \frac{1}{2}\sqrt{-1}.\sqrt{3};$

$----\cos\frac{1}{3}\ 6\pi\ ----\sin\frac{1}{3}.6\pi = (+1^3)^{\frac{1}{3}}$

$= +1.\cos 360^\circ + \sqrt{-1}.\sin 360^\circ = +1.$

$5^0\ n=4,\quad ----\cos\frac{1}{4}.2\pi\ ----\sin\frac{1}{4}.2\pi = (+1^1)^{\frac{1}{4}}$

$= +1.\cos\ 90^\circ + \sqrt{-1}.\sin\ 90^\circ = +\sqrt{-1};$

$----\cos\frac{1}{4}4\pi\ ----\sin\frac{1}{4}.4\pi = (+1^2)^{\frac{1}{4}}$

$= -1.\cos 180^\circ + \sqrt{-1}.\sin 180^\circ = -1;$

$----\cos\frac{1}{4}.6\pi\ ----\sin\frac{1}{4}.6\pi = (+1^3)^{\frac{1}{4}}$

$= -1.\cos 270^\circ - \sqrt{-1}.\sin 270^\circ = -\sqrt{-1};$

$----\cos\frac{1}{4}.8\pi\ ----\sin\frac{1}{4}.8\pi = (+1^4)^{\frac{1}{4}}$

$= +1.\cos 360^\circ - \sqrt{-1}.\sin 360^\circ = +1.$

35. Thus by the division of the circumference into n equal parts, we obtain first the primitive nth root of unity; and by subsequently adding successively the circumference to the previous dividend, and dividing each sum into n equal parts, we get the remaining $n-1$ nth roots. So by subdividing the nth part of the circumference into p equal parts, we shall obtain first the primitive pth root of the primitive nth root of unity; and by subsequently adding successively the circumference to the previous dividend, and dividing each sum into p equal parts, we will get the $p-1$ remaining pth roots of the primitive nth root. To obtain the pth roots of the $n-1$ remaining nth roots of 1, we begin successively with twice, thrice, ... , n times the nth part of the circumference, from which we get the primitive pth root as above, and then proceed as before for the $p-1$ others; and so on until we

have obtained all the pth roots of all the nth roots of unity, as here shortly exemplified :

1^0 $n = 2$ and $p = 2$.

1. *Square roots of the primitive square root of unity.*

$\frac{1}{2}\cdot\frac{1}{2}\cdot 2\pi=\frac{1}{2}\pi$: $+1\cos 90^\circ+\sqrt{-1}\sin 90^\circ = +1.0+\sqrt{-1}.1$;
$\frac{1}{2}(\frac{1}{2}.2+2)\pi=\frac{3}{2}\pi$: $-1\cos 270^\circ-\sqrt{-1}\sin 270^\circ = -1.0-\sqrt{-1}.1$.

2. *Square roots of the second square root.*

$\frac{1}{2}\cdot\frac{2}{2}\cdot 2\pi=\pi$: $-1\cos 180^\circ+\sqrt{-1}\sin 180^\circ = -1.1+\sqrt{-1}.0$;
$\frac{1}{2}(\frac{2}{2}.2+2)\pi=2\pi$: $+1\cos 360^\circ-\sqrt{-1}\sin 360^\circ = +1.1-\sqrt{-1}.0$.

2^0 $n = 2$ and $p = 3$.

1. *Cube roots of the primitive square root of unity.*

$\frac{1}{3}.\frac{1}{2}.2\pi=\frac{1}{3}\pi$: $+1\cos 60^\circ+\sqrt{-1}\sin 60^\circ = +1.\frac{1}{2}+\sqrt{-1}.\frac{1}{2}\sqrt{3}$;
$\frac{1}{3}(\frac{1}{2}.2+2)\pi=\pi$: $-1\cos 180^\circ+\sqrt{-1}\sin 180^\circ = -1.1+\sqrt{-1}.0$;
$\frac{1}{3}(\frac{1}{2}.2+4)\pi=\frac{5}{3}\pi$: $+1\cos 300^\circ-\sqrt{-1}\sin 300^\circ = +1.\frac{1}{2}-\sqrt{-1}.\frac{1}{2}\sqrt{3}$.

2. *Cube roots of the second square root.*

$\frac{1}{3}.\frac{2}{2}.2\pi=\frac{2}{3}\pi$: $-1\cos 120^\circ+\sqrt{-1}\sin 120^\circ = -1.\frac{1}{2}+\sqrt{-1}.\frac{1}{2}\sqrt{3}$;
$\frac{1}{3}(\frac{2}{2}.2+2)\pi=\frac{4}{3}\pi$: $-1\cos 240^\circ-\sqrt{-1}\sin 140^\circ = -1.\frac{1}{2}-\sqrt{-1}.\frac{1}{2}\sqrt{3}$;
$\frac{1}{3}(\frac{2}{3}.2+4)\pi=2\pi$: $+1\cos 360^\circ-\sqrt{-1}\sin 360^\circ = +1.1-\sqrt{-1}.0$.

3^0 $n = 3$ and $p = 2$.

1. *Square roots of the primitive cube root of unity.*

$\frac{1}{2}.\frac{1}{3}.2\pi=\frac{1}{3}\pi$: $+1\cos 60^\circ+\sqrt{-1}\sin 60^\circ = +1.\frac{1}{2}+\sqrt{-1}.\frac{1}{2}\sqrt{3}$;
$\frac{1}{2}(\frac{1}{3}.2+2)\pi=\frac{4}{3}\pi$: $-1\cos 240^\circ-\sqrt{-1}\sin 240^\circ = -1.\frac{1}{2}-\sqrt{-1}.\frac{1}{2}\sqrt{3}$.

2. *Square roots of the second cube root.*

$\frac{1}{2}.\frac{2}{3}.2\pi=\frac{2}{3}\pi$: $-1\cos 120^\circ+\sqrt{-1}\sin 120^\circ = -1.\frac{1}{2}+\sqrt{-1}.\frac{1}{2}\sqrt{3}$;
$\frac{1}{2}(\frac{2}{3}.2+2)\pi=\frac{5}{3}\pi$: $+1\cos 300^\circ-\sqrt{-1}\sin 300^\circ = +1.\frac{1}{2}-\sqrt{-1}.\frac{1}{2}\sqrt{3}$.

3. *Square roots of the third cube root.*

$\frac{1}{2}.\frac{3}{3}.2\pi=\pi$: $-1\cos 180^\circ+\sqrt{-1}\sin 180^\circ = -1.1+\sqrt{-1}.0$;
$\frac{1}{2}(\frac{3}{3}.2+2)\pi=2\pi$: $+1\cos 360^\circ-\sqrt{-1}\sin 360^\circ = +1.1-\sqrt{-1}.0$.

Tablets 2^0 and 3^0 each exhibit the six 6th roots of unity.

4° $n - 4$ and $p = 3$.

1. *Cube roots of the primitive biquadrate root of unity.*

$\frac{1}{3}.\frac{1}{4}.2\pi=\frac{1}{6}\pi$: $+1\cos 30°+\sqrt{-1}\sin 30° = +1.\frac{1}{2}\sqrt{3}+\sqrt{-1}.\frac{1}{2}$;
$\frac{1}{3}(\frac{1}{4}.2+2)\pi=\frac{5}{6}\pi$: $-1\cos 150°+\sqrt{-1}\sin 150° = -1.\frac{1}{2}\sqrt{3}+\sqrt{-1}.\frac{1}{2}$;
$\frac{1}{3}(\frac{1}{4}.2+4)\pi=\frac{9}{6}\pi$: $-1\cos 270°-\sqrt{-1}\sin 270° = -1.0-\sqrt{-1}.1$.

2. *Cube roots of the second biquadrate root.*

$\frac{1}{3}.\frac{2}{4}.2\pi=\frac{2}{6}\pi$: $+1\cos 60°+\sqrt{-1}\sin 60° = +1.\frac{1}{2}+\sqrt{-1}.\frac{1}{2}\sqrt{3}$;
$\frac{1}{3}(\frac{2}{4}.2+2)\pi=\frac{6}{6}\pi$: $-1\cos 180°+\sqrt{-1}\sin 180° = -1.1+\sqrt{-1}.0$;
$\frac{1}{3}(\frac{2}{4}.2+4)\pi=\frac{10}{6}\pi$: $+1\cos 300°-\sqrt{-1}\sin 300° = +1.\frac{1}{2}-\sqrt{-1}.\frac{1}{2}\sqrt{3}$.

3. *Cube roots of the third biquadrate root.*

$\frac{1}{3}.\frac{3}{4}.2\pi=\frac{3}{6}\pi$: $+1\cos 90°+\sqrt{-1}\sin 90° = +1.0+\sqrt{-1}.1$;
$\frac{1}{3}(\frac{3}{4}.2+2)\pi=\frac{7}{6}\pi$: $-1\cos 210°-\sqrt{-1}\sin 210° = -1.\frac{1}{2}\sqrt{3}-\sqrt{-1}.\frac{1}{2}$;
$\frac{1}{3}(\frac{3}{4}.2+4)\pi=\frac{11}{6}\pi$: $+1\cos 330°-\sqrt{-1}\sin 330° = +1.\frac{1}{2}\sqrt{3}-\sqrt{-1}.\frac{1}{2}$.

4. *Cube roots of the fourth biquadrate root.*

$\frac{1}{3}.\frac{4}{4}.2\pi=\frac{4}{6}\pi$: $-1\cos 120°+\sqrt{-1}\sin 120° = -1.\frac{1}{2}+\sqrt{-1}.\frac{1}{2}\sqrt{3}$;
$\frac{1}{3}(\frac{4}{4}.2+2)\pi=\frac{8}{6}\pi$: $-1\cos 240°-\sqrt{-1}\sin 240° = -1.\frac{1}{2}-\sqrt{-1}.\frac{1}{2}\sqrt{3}$;
$\frac{1}{3}(\frac{4}{4}.2+4)\pi=\frac{12}{6}\pi$: $+1\cos 360°-\sqrt{-1}\sin 360° = +1.1-\sqrt{-1}.0$.

This last tablet comprises 1° the square root of $+1$ and of -1; 2° the four biquadrate roots of $+1$; 3° the three cube roots of $+\sqrt{-1}$, of -1, of $-\sqrt{-1}$ and of $+1$; and 4° the twelve 12th roots of $+1$.

36. It is shown abundantly by the preceding investigations into the nature of the roots of unity, that the nth power of a geometrical unit is a similar unit equal in magnitude to n times its root; that is, $1_\lambda^n=n.1_\lambda$ or $1_\theta^n=n.1_\theta$, or $1_l^n=n.1_l$; the suffixes λ and θ indicating the unit to be the measure of a cause, and l that of an effect; of the velocity, or of the distance generated by that velocity in the unit of time 1_t.

As the unit multiplier is arbitrary, let it be [fig. 25] the arc AP $= \theta$, and let $n = 7$: we shall have

$$(AP)^7 = 7\,(AP) = AP',$$

$\theta^7 = 7\,\theta = \theta'$. Writing 1_θ for θ (since the arc must be held to the condition unity), this equality will be

$1^7_\theta = 7.1_\theta = \theta'$. But instead of θ, we might take the thousandth part of AP for multiplying unit δ, and then we should have

$$\delta^{1000} = 1000.\delta = \theta.$$

Recollecting that the two symbols of perpendicularity $\pm\sqrt{-1}$ have the value ± 0 in the direction OA to which they are perpendicular, we shall understand the equalities (e, according to custom, denoting the base of napierian logarithms)

$$e^{+\sqrt{-1}} = e^{-\sqrt{-1}} = e^0 = 1,$$

and therefore $e^{+\sqrt{-1}}.1_l = e^{-\sqrt{-1}}.1_l = e^0.1_l = 1.1_l = +1.1_l =$ OA.

Also since the arc is always perpendicular to the radius, the two expressions $+\sqrt{-1}.\delta$ and $+\sqrt{-1}.\theta$ indicate the arcs in their position as well as magnitude, so that the preceding equalities determine the following :

$$e^{+\sqrt{-1}.1000\delta} = e^{+\sqrt{-1}.\theta} = +1^\theta = +1.\theta, \text{ and}$$

$e^{+\sqrt{-1}.\theta}.1_l = +1.\theta.1_l =$ OP (for, just as in rectilinear multiplication $1^n.1_l = n.1_l$, so in angular or circular multiplication $1^\theta.1_l = \theta.1_l$); and if the arc be negative, or counted in the opposite direction, we shall have

$$e^{-\sqrt{-1}.\theta}.1_l = +1(-\theta)1_l = -1.\theta.1_l = \text{OQ}.$$

Thus by virtue of the equality $\sqrt{-1} = 0$ in the primary direction, the expression $e^{\sqrt{-1}}$ is equal to $e^0 = 1$, and is therefore the coefficient of a linear unit, or of the radius 1_r in a primary direction, giving always $e^{\sqrt{-1}}.1_r = 1.1_r$; and by virtue of the value $\sqrt{-1} = 1$ in the secondary or perpendicular direction, the expression $\sqrt{-1}.\delta$ represents the infinitesimal arc δ (an arc so small as to be equal to its sine) placed perpendicular to the radius; so that $e^{\sqrt{-1}.\delta}$ signifies a numerical unit $e^{\sqrt{-1}} = e^0$ involved to the infinitesimal power δ, whence $e^{\sqrt{-1}.\delta}.1_\lambda$ will be the sine of (and equal to) this small arc δ, and is indeed the same thing as $d\theta$ the differential of the arc θ; and therefore $e^{\sqrt{-1}.1000.\delta}.1_\lambda = e^{\sqrt{-1}.\theta}.1_\lambda$ signifies this infinitesimal unit sine or arc involved to the finite power θ, and is the same thing as the integral $\int d\theta = \theta$ with the linear unit in evidence, the arbitrary constant being zero. As the symbol $-\sqrt{-1}$ has also the value zero in the primary direction, the same reasoning applies to show that $e^{-\sqrt{-1}}.1_r = 1.1_r$, but we shall have $e^{-\sqrt{-1}.\theta}.1_\lambda = -\theta.1_\lambda$. The characters δ and θ stand for pure abstract numbers, namely, the ratios of the respective arcs to the radius, the unit arc being equal in length to the radius. Hence the so-called imaginary exponentials $e^{+\sqrt{-1}.\theta}$ and $e^{-\sqrt{-1}.\theta}$ are angular coefficients, implying the position of the radius in terms of the arc which measures its inclination to the primary axis, and indicating that arc as the measure of an operation, to wit, that of transferring the unit of passivity 1_μ from A to P or Q by circular multiplication, expressed in full by

$$e^{+\sqrt{-1}.\theta}.1_\lambda.1_r.1_\mu = +\theta.1_r.1_\mu \text{ and } e^{-\sqrt{-1}.\theta}.1_\lambda.1_r.1_\mu = -\theta.1_r.1_\mu.$$

The units 1_λ and 1_μ, as well as the radius 1_r, are commonly omitted; but when all the significant elements of the notation are duly attended to, we see that while $e^{+\sqrt{-1}}.1_r$ signifies the radius on the primary axis, the very similar expression $e^{+\sqrt{-1}.1}.1_\lambda.1_r$ signifies the radius inclined to that axis at the angle of 57° 17′ 44,8″.

If we now compare the two pairs of equalities [fig. 26]

$$OM = (+1\cos\theta + \sqrt{-1}\sin\theta\,)1_r,$$
$$OM' = (+1\cos\theta' - \sqrt{-1}\sin\theta')1_r, \text{ and}$$
$$OM = e^{+\sqrt{-1}\theta}.1_r,$$
$$OM' = e^{-\sqrt{-1}\theta'}.1_r,$$ we see that the first pair express the positions of the radii in terms of the sines and cosines, which are themselves measures of the corresponding arcs; and the last pair express those positions directly in terms of the arcs which are their own measures in their own positions.

Since we have $e^{+\sqrt{-1}.\theta} = +1.\cos\theta + \sqrt{-1}.\sin\theta$, and
$e^{-\sqrt{-1}.\theta} = +1.\cos\theta - \sqrt{-1}.\sin\theta$, we get by addition $e^{+\sqrt{-1}.\theta} + e^{-\sqrt{-1}.\theta} = +1.2\cos\theta$, and by subtraction
$e^{+\sqrt{-1}.\theta} - e^{-\sqrt{-1}.\theta} = +\sqrt{-1}.2\sin\theta$; so that

$$\cos\theta = \frac{e^{+\sqrt{-1}.\theta} + e^{-\sqrt{-1}.\theta}}{+1.2}, \text{ and } \sin\theta = \frac{e^{+\sqrt{-1}.\theta} - e^{-\sqrt{-1}.\theta}}{+\sqrt{-1}.2},$$

in ratio of magnitude without regard to position [fig. 27].

By substituting for θ in the equation

$$e^{+\sqrt{-1}.\theta}.1_r = +1.\cos\theta + \sqrt{-1}.\sin\theta)1_r = OM \text{ [fig. 28]},$$

we deduce
$$e^{+\sqrt{-1}.\frac{1}{2}\pi}.1_r = +\sqrt{-1}.1_r = OB,$$
$$e^{+\sqrt{-1}.\pi}.1_r = -1.1_r = OA',$$
$$e^{+\sqrt{-1}.3.\frac{1}{2}\pi}.1_r = -\sqrt{-1}.1_r = OB', \text{ and}$$
$$e^{+\sqrt{-1}.2\pi}.1_r = +1.1_r = OA.$$

37. In any exponential equality $a^x.1_l = \text{N}.1_l$, the exponent x denotes the number of times (whole or fractional) the passive unit 1_l must be multiplied by the base a, so as to produce the concrete number $\text{N}.1_l$. In the equality $e^{+\sqrt{-1}}.1_l = e^0.1_l = 1_l$, the exponent $\sqrt{-1}$, by its value 0, shows that no multiplication or operation has been yet performed on the linear unit, which is therefore expressed as unaffected by any coefficient; but in the equality last deduced on the preceding page, namely, $e^{+\sqrt{-1}.2\pi}.1_l = +1.1_l$, the efficient factor 2π of the exponent (which shows that the circular unit $e^{+\sqrt{-1}.1}.1_\lambda$, = arc 1 = radius 1, has been raised to the power denoted by the number 2π, and so become an arc equal to 2π times the arc 1 or radius) indicates that the passive radius 1_l has undergone a complete unit of operation, and has again become *one* with its former condition; while the coefficient factor $+\sqrt{-1}$ indicates that the direction of the force of the first order which performed the operation was constantly perpendicular to the revolving radius; and the result of the operation is truly recorded on the second side of the equality by the coefficient $+1$ of absolute unity, that is, one complete operation has now been performed on the linear unit 1_l, and is expressed by its coefficient. The exponent $+\sqrt{-1}.2\pi$ is therefore the logarithm of $+1$; and in general any line $a.1_l$ on the positive primary axis, being properly expressed by $+1.a.1_l$, will be given by the exponential $e^{+\sqrt{-1}.2\pi+n}$ (n being the logarithm of a), and consequently its logarithm is $+\sqrt{-1}.2\pi+n$; and the same line on the negative primary axis will be $-1.a.1_l = e^{+\sqrt{-1}.\pi+n}.1_l$, and have $+\sqrt{-1}.\pi + n$ for its its logarithm.

From the two equations

$+\sqrt{-1}.\theta = \log(+1.\cos\theta+\sqrt{-1}.\sin\theta)$ and

$-\sqrt{-1}.\theta = \log(+1.\cos\theta-\sqrt{-1}.\sin\theta)$, obtained from the exponentials $e^{+\sqrt{-1}.\theta}$ and $e^{-\sqrt{-1}.\theta}$, we deduce two different logarithms for one same unit measure $1^{\frac{1}{4}}.1_\theta$ of angular operation:

1° $+\sqrt{-1}.\tfrac{1}{2}\pi = \log+\sqrt{-1}$,
$+\sqrt{-1}.1\pi = \log-1$,
$+\sqrt{-1}.\tfrac{3}{2}\pi = \log-\sqrt{-1}$, and
$+\sqrt{-1}.2\pi = \log+1$; and

2° $-\sqrt{-1}.\tfrac{1}{2}\pi = \log-\sqrt{-1}$,
$-\sqrt{-1}.1\pi = \log-1$,
$-\sqrt{-1}.\tfrac{3}{2}\pi = \log+\sqrt{-1}$, and
$-\sqrt{-1}.2\pi = \log+1$.

The difference in the manner of obtaining the two classes of results will explain the anomaly. The result $-\sqrt{-1}.1_l$, for instance, may be had either by proceeding in the positive angular direction as above explained at length, when $+\sqrt{-1}.\frac{3}{2}\pi$ is its logarithm; or by proceeding in the negative angular direction, which will give $-\sqrt{-1}.\frac{1}{2}\pi$ for the logarithm of the same result $-\sqrt{-1}.1_l$, and so for the other instances deduced from the second equation.

We here consider a logarithm as noting the number and direction of the successive equal operations or multiplications which must be performed on the radius as unit of passivity or multiplicand, in order to produce a given result or power of unity; and we have found that while 0 is the logarithm of the unit radius undisturbed, that of one complete unit of operation $+1.1_\lambda$ is $+\sqrt{-1}.2\pi$. From this we infer that the logarithm of a half unit of operation, that is, of $(+1)^{\frac{1}{2}}1_r = -1.1_r$, is $+\sqrt{-1}.\pi$; that of a quarter unit of operation, or of $(+)^{\frac{1}{4}}1_r = +\sqrt{-1}.1_r$, is ---- $+\sqrt{-1}.\frac{1}{2}\pi$, etc. Commencing with the primitive fourth root of unity, the series of ascending powers $1^{\frac{1}{4}}$, $1^{\frac{1}{2}}$, 1^1, 1^2, 1^3, etc., when both the multiplying and the multiplied unit are expressed, becomes $1_0^{\frac{1}{4}}.1_r$, $1_0^{\frac{1}{2}}.1_r$, $1_0^1.1_r$, $1_0^2.1_r$, $1_0^3.1_r$, etc. (1_0 being the multiplying circumference and 1_r the multiplicand radius); and this last is the same as the series $+\sqrt{-1}.1_r$, -1.1_r, $+1.1_r$, $(+1)^2 1_r$, $(+1)^3 1_r$, etc., of which the logarithms are $\frac{1}{2}\pi$, 1π, 2π, 4π, 6π, etc., each multiplied by the coefficient $+\sqrt{-1}$. The direction of the operation of multiplication is positive, and therefore these logarithms have a positive coefficient; but if the operation be one of division, which is the reverse of multiplication and therefore negative, its logarithm should have a negative coefficient. Now the series of negative powers of unity, which may commence with the third 4th root, is, when the terms are referred to their generation by division,

$$1_r \div 1_0^{\frac{1}{4}} = 1^{-\frac{1}{4}}.1_r = -\sqrt{-1}.1_r,$$
$$1_r \div 1_0^{\frac{1}{2}} = 1^{-\frac{1}{2}}.1_r = -1.1_r,$$
$$1_r \div 1_0^{1} = 1^{-1}.1_r = +1.1_r,$$
$$1_r \div 1_0^{2} = 1^{-2}.1_r = (+1)^2 1_r,$$
$$1_r \div 1_0^{3} = 1^{-3}.1_r = (+1)^3 1_r, \text{ etc.;}$$

and by counting the angles in the negative direction, the corresponding logarithms are found to be $\frac{1}{2}\pi$, 1π, 2π, 4π, 6π, etc., each multiplied by the negative coefficient $-\sqrt{-1}$.

38. The equation $b^2x^2 \pm a^2y^2 = a^2b^2$ represents an ellipse or a hyperbola, accordingly as the upper or lower sign of the second term of the lefthand member is adopted. If we make $x = a.\cos\theta$ and $y = b.\sin\theta$, these equations become

$$a^2b^2\cos^2\theta \pm a^2b^2\sin^2\theta = a^2b^2 1, \text{ or}$$

$\cos^2\theta \pm \sin^2\theta = 1$; where, accordingly as the upper or lower sign is used, the sines and cosines are the ordinary ones of the circle, which have zero and unity for their inferior and superior limits; or those deduced from the equilateral hyperbola, in which the inferior limit of the cosines is unity, that of the sines being zero as before, while the superior limit of both is infinity. The original equations, resolved for y, become

[a] $$y = \frac{b}{a}(x^2-a^2)^{\frac{1}{2}}, \text{ for the hyperbola; and}$$

[b] $$y = \frac{b}{a}(a^2-x^2)^{\frac{1}{2}}, \text{ or}$$

[c] $$y = \frac{b}{a}(x^2-a^2)^{\frac{1}{2}} \times (\pm\sqrt{-1}), \text{ for the ellipse.}$$

This last result is commonly announced by saying that the substitution of $b\sqrt{-1}$ for b in the equation of the ellipse converts it into that of the hyperbola, but we see that the requisite operation consists in multiplying the ordinate of the ellipse by either of the imaginary fourth roots of unity; and since

$$a^2b^2\left(\frac{x^2}{a^2}+\frac{y^2}{b^2}\right) = a^2b^2\left(\frac{x}{a}+\sqrt{-1}.\frac{y}{b}\right)\left(\frac{x}{a}-\sqrt{-1}.\frac{y}{b}\right) = a^2b^2 1, \quad \text{or}$$

[d] $$a^2b^2(\cos^2\theta+\sin^2\theta) = a^2b^2(\cos\theta+\sqrt{-1}.\sin)(\cos\theta-\sqrt{-1}.\sin\theta),$$

that ordinate is already implicitly under the sign of perpendicularity in the original equation, as it is yet in equation [b]; while the actual introduction of that sign (which might be written immediately after the semiconjugate axis b) into equation [c] effects the rotation of the ordinate through a right angle upon the primary axis, and gives the equation the form [a] of the ordinate of the hyperbola. Substituting now respectively the hyperbolical and circular sines and cosines in equations [a], [b] and [c], we get $\text{h}\sin\theta = (\text{h}\cos^2\theta-1)^{\frac{1}{2}}$ for the hyperbola, and

$\sin\theta = (1-\cos^2\theta)^{\frac{1}{2}} = (\cos^2\theta-1)^{\frac{1}{2}}\times(\pm\sqrt{-1})$ for the ellipse.

Then if we substitute this last value of $\sin\theta$ in the decomposed equation [d], it will be equivalent to multiplying the ordinates $\pm\sqrt{-1}.\sin\theta$ by $+\sqrt{-1}$, and will transform the equation into

$a^2b^2(\cos\theta-\sin\theta)(\cos\theta+\sin\theta) = a^2b^2(\cos^2\theta-\sin^2\theta)$, which is the form for the hyperbola, nothing more being necessary than to render the sines and cosines hyperbolical.

The sines in the righthand member of equation [d] have the requisite position to merge the product of the factors into the sum of two squares equal to unity, to fulfil the conditions of the ellipse; and by multiplying both sines $+\sqrt{-1}.\sin\theta$ and $-\sqrt{-1}.\sin\theta$, as they stand in the righthand member of the same equation [d], by either $+\sqrt{-1}$ or $-\sqrt{-1}$, they are rotated respectively through one or three right angles (accordingly as $+\sqrt{-1}$ or $-\sqrt{-1}$ is the multiplier), and become $-1.\sin\theta$ and $+1.\sin\theta$ or $+1.\sin\theta$ and $-1.\sin\theta$ on the primary axis, in which position the product of the factors merges into the difference of two squares equal to unity, to fulfil the conditions of the hyperbola.

39. When $x = a\cos\theta$ and $y = b\sin\theta$, the equation

$$b^2x^2+a^2y^2 = a^2b^2 \text{ or}$$

$$a^2b^2\cos^2\theta+a^2b^2\sin^2\theta = a^2b^21 \text{ or}$$

[a] $\cos^2\theta+\sin^2\theta = 1$, which is that of the ellipse when the sine and cosine are both confined between the limits zero and unity, yields the hyperbola when either the cosine or sine surpasses the last limit, provided the other variable (sine or cosine) be determined so as to satisfy the equation. Taking the cosine as the leading variable, when it is zero, the sine is 1; and when it increases from zero to unity, the sine decreases from 1 to 0. When $\cos\theta$ is made to surpass unity, the square of the sine, being always equal to $1-\cos^2\theta$, becomes a negative quantity, and consequently the sine itself becomes imaginary; but the square of the sine, being now negative, should be written accordingly, and this converts equation [a] into

[b] $\cos^2\theta-\sin^2\theta = 1$, in which, for all values of $\cos\theta$ greater than unity, we have real values for $\sin\theta$; and the construction of these values, according to equation [b], gives us the primitive hyperbola on the positive primary axis.

In equation [a], while the cosine *increases* from 0 to 1, the arc of the circle *decreases* from $\frac{1}{2}\pi$ to 0. In equation [b], the cosine increases from unity to infinity, and the sine increases from zero towards the same limit, but always so that the difference of the squares remains equal to unity; and now the arc *increases* with the *increase* of the cosine, and is therefore that of the equilateral hyperbola (or inverted circle), and corresponds to the imaginary arc of the circle.

Now if in equation [b] we make $\cos\theta$ less than unity, we shall have $-\sin^2\theta = 1-\cos^2\theta$, or $\sin^2\theta = -(1-\cos^2\theta)$, that is, the square of the sine equal to a negative quantity, and consequently the sine itself imaginary; but since the difference of the squares $\cos^2\theta-\sin^2\theta$ is negative when $\cos\theta$ is less and $\sin\theta$ greater than unity, equation [b] may be converted into

$$\cos^2\theta-\sin^2\theta = -1 \text{ or}$$

[c] $\sin^2\theta-\cos^2\theta = 1$, in which, for all values of $\sin\theta$ greater than unity, we have real values for $\cos\theta$, the construction of which values gives us the conjugate hyperbola on the positive secondary axis.

By setting out from equation [b] with the negative instead of the positive cosine, we shall construct the opposite hyperbola on the negative primary axis; and similarly by setting out from the equation [c] with the negative instead of the positive sine, we shall construct the opposite conjugate hyperbola on the negative secondary axis. To each positive and each negative cosine and sine, both in the circle and equilateral hyperbola, corresponds respectively a positive and a negative sine and cosine, which furnish two opposite branches to each curve; and thus by the analysis of the equation [a], we obtain the system of four equilateral mutually conjugate hyperbolæ, and their inscribed circle; and by substituting $x\div a$ for $\cos\theta$ and $y\div b$ for $\sin\theta$, we may in any case convert the circle or equilateral hyperbola into the ellipse or the general hyperbola expressed by the equations

$$b^2x\pm a^2y^2 = a^2b^2.$$

Thus the circle may be transformed into the equilateral hyperbola in either of two ways: 1° By changing the sign of one of the terms in the lefthand member of the equation $\cos^2\theta+\sin^2\theta = 1$, which change alters the limits of the variables; or 2° By changing the limits of one of the variables, which, in its turn, necessitates a change in the sign of the other term, to fulfil the condition of equality to positive unity.

When the equations $\cos^2\theta \pm \sin^2\theta = 1$ are each regarded as generated by the multiplication of a single pair of factors, they decompose [n° 31] into

$$(\cos\theta+\surd-1.\sin\theta)(\cos\theta-\surd-1.\sin\theta) = 1 \text{ for the circle, and}$$

$$(\cos\theta+1.\sin\theta)(\cos\theta-1.\sin\theta) = 1 \text{ for the equilateral hyperbola;}$$

where the first exhibits the imaginary sign in the *generating factors* of the ellipse, while the factors are real for the hyperbola. But when viewed as the sum of two squares, the equations are

$$((+1)^{\frac{1}{2}}\cos\theta)^2+((+1)^{\frac{1}{2}}\sin\theta)^2 = 1 \text{ for the circle, and}$$

$$((+1)^{\frac{1}{2}}\cos\theta)^2+((-1)^{\frac{1}{2}}\sin\theta)^2 = 1 \text{ for the equilateral hyperbola;}$$

where the imaginary sign appears in the decomposition of the result or *generated ratio* of the hyperbola, that of the ellipse remaining real.

The equation $\cos^2\theta+\sin^2\theta = 1$ being formed, I multiply 1_μ first by $\cos^2\theta.1_\lambda$, which transfers it on the positive primary axis to a distance equal to $\cos^2\theta.1_\iota$ from the origin; and next by $\sin^2\theta.1_\lambda$, which brings it to the distance $+1.1_\iota$ from the origin. If now $\cos\theta$ be made to surpass unity, the multiplication of 1_μ by $\cos^2\theta.1_\lambda$ carries that mobile to a point on the positive primary axis, to the right of that measured by $+1.1_\iota$; and then from this point, the square of the perpendicular line $\sin\theta.1_\lambda = +\surd-1(1-\cos^2\theta)^{\frac{1}{2}}1_\lambda$, that is, $\sin^2\theta.1_\lambda = -1(1-\cos^2\theta)1_\lambda$, will return 1_μ to the point whose distance from the origin is $+1.1_\iota$, and give the result unity. In the equation $\cos^2\theta-\sin^2\theta = 1$, the inferior limit of $\cos\theta$ is unity; but if the cosine be made less than unity, the product $\cos^2\theta.1_\lambda.1_\mu$ transfers 1_μ from the point measured by $+1.1_\iota$, *towards* the origin; from which position it will be restored to the point $+1.1_\iota$ by the product $\sin^2\theta.1_\lambda.1_\mu = -1(1-\cos^2\theta)1_\lambda.1_\mu$ (that is, the square of the perpendicular sine $+\surd-1(1-\cos^2\theta)^{\frac{1}{2}}.1_\lambda$), which must now be applied in the *opposite* direction to that in the former instance, so as to produce the result unity, and also in accordance with the law that a negative factor must carry the mobile in the direction opposite to that in which the corresponding positive factor carries it [n° 25]. And in a similar manner may the operation be shown in the equation $\sin^2\vartheta - \cos^2\vartheta = 1$, when the sine is reduced below the limit unity.

By making $\sin\theta = 0$ in the equation $(\cos^2\theta - \sin^2\theta)1_\iota = 1.1_\iota$, we get $\cos\theta.1_\iota = \pm 1.1_\iota$ for the abscissæ of the vertices of the two opposite hyperbolæ on the primary axis; and by making $\cos\theta = 0$, we get $\sin\theta.1_\iota = \pm\sqrt{-1}.1_\iota$ for the abscissæ of the vertices of the two opposite hyperbolæ on the secondary axis. In a similar manner, by making $\cos\theta = 0$ in the equation $(\sin^2\theta - \cos^2\theta)1_\iota = 1.1_\iota$, we get $\sin\theta.1_\iota = \pm 1.1_\iota$ for the abscissæ of the vertices of the two opposite hyperbolæ on the secondary axis; and $\sin\theta = 0$ gives $\cos\theta.1_\iota = \pm\sqrt{-1}.1_\iota$ for the abscissæ of the vertices of the two opposite hyperbolæ on the primary axis. But the form of these equations is such that they do not yield a positive result when $\cos\theta$ in the first, and $\sin\theta$ in the second, are made less than unity; and therefore the square root of negative unity appears in the abscissæ of the conjugate hyperbola whose axis forms a right angle with that of its primitive. So in the equation of the circle $(\sin^2\theta + \cos^2\theta)1_\iota = 1.1_\iota$, if we give to $\sin\theta$ or $\cos\theta$ a value greater than unity, the value of the cosine or sine becomes imaginary, and points to the primitive and its conjugate hyperbola, whose arcs are competent to yield the values thus attributed to the sine and cosine.

40. Having sufficiently investigated the measures of a single linear and angular force of the first order, it remains to attempt a brief consideration upon the measure of two interfering forces of the same kind.

A force is known to us by the unit measure of the quantity and quality of its effect in space and time; that is, by the length and direction of the path of the body or point moved during a unit of time. In combining the effects of interfering forces, therefore, we must give to each force its full effect in the direction in which it acts; and this evidently requires that the measure of the combined effect of the two forces in the unit of time shall be equal to the *sum* of the measures of their effects in the unit of time, if the forces act in the same direction, and to the *difference* of their measures if the forces act in opposite directions.

Let the lines OP and O′P′ [fig. 29] be the unit measures of two forces of the first order. If these two forces are simultaneously applied to the unit mobile 1_μ placed at the origin O of either of the three figures 30, 31 and 32, the effect of each force must be measured in the direction in which it acts. Before adopting the conventional system of rectangular coordinates of measurement with one same point as origin, we are held only to the conditions of *magnitude* and *direction;* and any line parallel to OP, and equal to it in magnitude, such as QR in either of the three figures, evidently fulfils these conditions for the force OP, and similarly the line PR fulfils the same conditions for the force OQ. Then if the mobile 1_μ trace the diagonal OR of the parallelogram OPQR, it will simultaneously obey the action of the two forces, and reach the same point R in the unit of time that it would have reached by the successive application of the forces in two distinct units of time.

Now let the forces be referred to rectangular axes OX and OY.

1° If the two component forces are inclined to each other at an acute angle, suppose them so placed that each makes acute angles with the positive axes of x and y [fig. 33] : then the effects of the forces are positive on each of these axes, and must be added; that is, OP′+OQ″=OR′ and OQ′+OP″=OR″, and the diagonal of the parallelogram on OR′ and OR″ will be identical with that of the parallelogram on OP and OQ the original components.

2° If the components form a right angle, let them be taken on the axes themselves, and the diagonal OR is given without further construction [fig. 34].

3° If the components form an obtuse angle with each other, let them be so placed that the first forms acute angles with the positive axes of x and y, and the other an obtuse angle with the positive axis of x and an acute angle with the positive axis of y [fig. 35]: then both effects are positive on the axis of y, and must be added together; but on the axis of x, the first effect is positive and the other negative, which last must therefore be subtracted from the first; that is, OQ′+OP″ = OR″ and OP′−OQ″ = OR′, and the diagonal OR of the parallelogram on OR′ and OR″ will be identical with that of the parallelogram on OP and OQ the original components.

Inversely [fig. 36], if OR be the unit measure of a single force of the first order, it may be resolved into either of the three pairs of components OP and OQ, OP′ and OQ′, or OP″ and OQ″, forming respectively an acute, a right and an obtuse angle together, since OR is equally the diagonal of the parallelograms OPQR, OP′Q′R and OP″Q″R; and, moreover, the effect of OR in the directions OX and OY is equal in each case to the algebraical sum of the effects of the two components.

The two forces P and Q are given in terms of their respective unit measures involving direction; but the linear measure OP, in either of the three figures 37, 38 or 39, convenes to any of its parallels between the parallels OQ and PR, and the measure OQ similarly convenes to its parallels between OP and QR; so that magnitude and direction alone do not fix the origin of measurement, which is here in fact placed under the control of the second force, and the path of the mobile (the diagonal OR) completely fulfils the condition that each force must have its full effect in its own direction.

41. The question of the parallelogram of forces may yet be instructively investigated as it follows:

1° Suppose the line OR [fig. 40] to be the measure of the effect of the single force R, acting on the material unit 1_μ in the direction OR. The same effect OR, in the direction OX, will be measured by OP, and by OQ in the perpendicular direction OY; and these two last measures may be those of two other forces P and Q, acting respectively in the directions OP and OQ. Now OP, measured in the direction OR, is equal to OP′; and OQ in that direction equals OQ′, and OP′+OQ′ = OR : therefore OR is the effect of the forces P and Q, acting in the directions OX and OY, but measured in the direction OR. As the directions OX and OY are mutually perpendicular, the forces P and Q will neither oppose nor conspire (since the direction OP, for instance, is not confined to the line OP, but answers to any line parallel thereto), and the point is free to move on the line which shall measure the full effect of each force in its own direction, that is, the diagonal OR.

2° Let OR be placed [fig. 41] perpendicularly to the primary axis OX, on which its measure will consequently be zero. The components P and Q remaining precisely as before, we see that their measures OP′ and OQ′ on the primary axis oppose and therefore destroy each other; which establishes the conclusion, that when the direction of a force makes an obtuse angle with the axis to which it is referred, it destroys a portion of the effect of another force whose direction makes an acute angle with the same axis, both effects being measured on that axis. From the same construction, we see also that the measures OP″ and OQ″ of P and Q on the secondary axis OY conspire, and therefore increase each other; which establishes the conclusion, that when the directions of two forces make acute angles with the axis to which they are referred, their effects, measured on that axis, are to be added together.

3° Let [fig. 42] P and Q form an acute and an obtuse angle with the positive primary axis, and acute angles with the positive secondary. The measure of P on the primary axis must be diminished by that of Q, giving OP′—OQ′=OR′; and the measure of P on the secondary axis must be increased by that of Q, giving OP″+OQ″ = OR″; and OR′, OR″ determine the resultant OR, the diagonal of the parallelogram OPQR.

4° Let [fig. 43] P and Q form acute angles with both the positive axes. The measures of P and Q on each axis respectively must be added together, which will give OP′+OQ′ = OR′ and OP″+OQ″ = OR″; and OR′, OR″ determine the resultant OR, the diagonal of the parallelogram OPQR.

42. As the measure of a force of translation is the rectilinear distance which it causes the mobile to describe in the unit of time, so the measure of a force of rotation will be the length of the circular arc which it causes the mobile to describe in the unit of time. It will [fig. 44] require a greater force to transfer the material unit 1_μ through the arc P′M′ than through the arc PM in the unit of time 1_t, in the exact proportion of the arcs P′M′ to PM, which is that of their radii OP′ to OP, or $r' : r$. If F′ and F be the greater and the lesser force, the arc P′M′ will be the unit measure of F′, and PM that of F, and we have the proportion

$$F' : F :: \text{arc } P'M' : \text{arc } PM :: r' : r, \text{ which gives}$$

$$F' = \frac{r'}{r}.F.$$

The *origin* of the force forms none of the data of the question :

all that is requisite is that the direction of the action shall be perpendicular to the radius, and this condition might even be fulfilled by the application of a force of rotation at the centre O itself; or, again, the origins of the forces may move for cause shown [n° 40], since the points of application to the respective mobiles are insured by the intervention of the radii.

In all the five figures 44, 45, 46, 47, 48, let the several radii OP, OP′, and arcs PM, P′M′, of the same name, be equal :

1° In fig. 45, OP=r; and if F′ be applied at P, it will transfer the material unit through the arc PM′ (=arc P′M′ of 44) in the unit of time.

2° In fig. 46, OP′=r'; and if F be applied at P′, it will transfer the material unit through the arc P′M (=arc PM of 44) in the unit of time.

3° In fig. 47, if F′ be applied at P, and connected so as to act perpendicularly and without hindrance upon the material unit 1_μ placed at P′, it will transfer that mobile through P′M′ in the unit of time.

4° In fig. 48, if F be applied at P′, and connected as above with 1_μ placed at P, it will transfer that mobile through PM in the unit of time : the distance through which the material unit is carried in the unit of time, being always the measure of the force which effects the transportation.

5° In fig. 44, let the radius OP′ be rigid and movable about the centre O. The force F′, applied at P and moving in the arc PM, and acting in the arc P′M′; and the force F, applied at P′ and moving in the arc P′M′, and acting in the arc PM, would each transfer a like material unit through the same angular extent in the same time; and if the angle of any two rigid radii ON, OP′ be rendered invariable, and F′ be applied at N, its effect in the arc P′M′ will be the same as before; so that if the direction of one of the forces was reversed, they would equilibrate each other*.

* In instances 3° and 4°, the origins of the forces F′ and F remain fixed at P and P′, and the distances of their points of application change during the motion through the angle MOP′; while in 5° the origins change, and the distances of the points of application remain unchanged. This transposition of conditions is sanctioned by the consideration that the forces F′ and F are destitute of mass; so that it requires no additional expendi-

43. The following positions are gathered from the preceding investigations :

1° That the straight line is the ultimate, simple, and unique element of magnitude, the various other species being expressible as functions of it : that the straight line is produced, described, or generated by the motion of a unit of body or material point, and its measure is obtained by an equivalent operation; so that this measure at once necessarily expresses the distance between the points of origin and termination (extension), the time consumed in the transition (duration), the phenomenon of motion (production), and the force or power that effected the description or operation of measurement (causation).

2° That angular magnitude, which is the element of surface, is generated by the revolution of a straight line, and is primarily measured by the arc described; and, therefore, the arc being determinable in terms of the radius, the angle itself becomes expressible as a function of the straight line, which, in any position of its revolution, must consequently imply the measure of its distance from the origin of its motion : and the determination of this measure in terms of the rectangular coordinates to which the operations are referred, has led first to the establishment of the simple relations $+\sqrt{-1}$, -1, $-\sqrt{-1}$, $+1$, and finally to the deduction of the more remarkable ones $e^{\sqrt{-1}} = \cos\theta \pm \sqrt{-1}.\sin\theta$.

3° That these relations or ratios, obtained by the comparison of different angular with linear magnitudes, and subsequent elimination of the linear units or elements of magnitude, are true abstractions (existences of intellection), expressing the relations of the measures of the operations performed in producing them, and universally available again to represent the results of those operations when the linear unit is restored.

4° That the primitive fourth root of unity $+\sqrt{-1}$, of which we have seen the remaining three to be functions, signifies this relation, that a line having its own value or measure in its own direction, has no value or measure in the direction perpendicular thereto; that is to say, the term $+\sqrt{-1}.1_{\iota}$ has, at one and the

ture of power on the part of either force F′ or F, beyond that consumed in transferring the unit of mass 1_{μ}, to transfer at the same time the origin of the force F or F′.

same time, *two different values*, that of unity in the direction OB, and of zero in the direction OA [fig. 49].

5° The arithmetical symbols 1, 2, 3, etc. or a, b, c, etc. express particular or general ratios of quantity; while the algebraical symbols $+1$, -1, etc. express ratios of quality.

44. In order to place in as clear a light as possible the analogy between the elementary operations of addition and subtraction, and of positive and negative multiplication, one more argument is yet here adduced, which it is hoped will not incur the charge of being a useless repetition.

If we subtract 1_l from $+1.1_l$, the result is $0.1_l=0$, and a second subtraction gives $0.1_l-1_l = -1.1_l$; that is, two negative operations are requisite to convert the ratio $+1$ into the ratio -1, the first negative operation having given the neutral ratio 0. And on the contrary, if we add 1_l to -1.1_l, the result is $0.1_l=0$, and the second addition gives $0.1_l+1_l=+1.1_l$; that is, two positive operations are requisite to convert the ratio -1 into the ratio $+1$, the first operation giving the neutral ratio 0 as before. Now when $+1.1_l$ is multiplied by $+\sqrt{-1}.1_\lambda$, it becomes $+\sqrt{-1}.1_l=0.1_l$, the neutral value of 1_l on the primary axis; and the second multiplication by $+\sqrt{-1}.1_\lambda$ gives the negative value -1.1_l, agreeing with that produced by two subtractions. Multiplication of this last result by $+\sqrt{-1}.1_\lambda$ gives $-\sqrt{-1}.1_l=0.1_l$ on the primary axis, the same as produced by adding $+1.1_l$ to -1.1_l; and the second multiplication by $+\sqrt{-1}.1_\lambda$ gives us $+1.1_l$, agreeing with two additions of positive unity to -1.1_l.

.P′ ____ .O ____ .P

The subtraction of 1_μ from P is measured by the negatively directed movement on the line PO, and therefore cancels the measure of the operation of adding 1_μ to P from O (where $OP=1_l$, and is traversed in the unit of time 1_t); and the second subtraction of 1_μ from O gives for measure the negative result $OP'=-1.1_l$, always in the unit of time 1_t.

.O ____ .P ____ .P′

If the direction were to perform two additions, there would be two ways of executing the operation : 1° By transferring two burthens 1_μ and $1'_\mu$ from O to P at one step; or 2° By transferring one burthen 1_μ first from O to P, and then from P to P′ at a second step; but in either case the actual measure of the resultant effect will be $2\times OP = OP' = 2.1_l$. Now positive multiplication is an abridged method of performing a series of additions : consequently negative multiplication is an abridged method of performing a series of subtractions; and it has been shown in n° 20 that one multiplication by -1.1_λ is equivalent to two multiplications by $+\sqrt{-1}.1_\lambda$ or $-\sqrt{-1}.1_l$, and therefore abridges the two subtractions of 1_l into one negative multiplication, that is, converts the ratio $+1$ into -1.

45. In performing the operation of division, which is properly an inverse multiplication, the quotient, or ratio of the direct to the inverse path of the material unit, and not the resultant effect of the two opposite motions, is taken as the measure of the operation, the general explanation of which must be deferred to the succeeding chapters; but for the case of a monomial, the peculiar operations which produce the differential coefficient, the integral, and the logarithm of a given function, may be appropriately shown in this place, for the purpose of exhibiting their several relations to the operations of multiplication and division.

When the passive unit 1_μ is multiplied n times successively by the linear factor $x.1_\lambda$, the result is $x^n.n.1_\lambda.1_\mu$, and its ratio to the linear unit 1_λ or 1_l is nx^n, which is n times the nth power of x, or x times the differential coefficient or derivative function of x^n. This ratio nx^n has been obtained by making the multiplying unit 1_λ (that is, the velocity, or force of the first order which effects the operation) *constant*, and prolonging the operation through n successive intervals of time each $x1_t$; but we may condition the velocity (or linear unit) to *increase* from zero at the beginning, to the value $n1_\lambda$ at the end of the unit of time 1_t, when, as will hereafter be shown, the distance $x^n.1_l$ will be generated in one single interval of time $x1_t$; while the unit measure of the velocity generated in the same time, by the same force or power which generates the distance, will be $nx^n.1_\lambda\div x=nx^{n-1}.1_\lambda$, which velocity will generate the distance $nx^n.1_l$ in the succeeding time $x.1_t$. It is the business of the integral calculus to find the distance generated in the time $x1_t$, from the unit measure of the velocity generated in that time; and this distance is found by dividing the unit measure $nx^{n-1}.1_\lambda$ of the velocity generated in the time $x.1_t$, by the velocity $n.1_\lambda$ generated in the unit of time 1_t, and multiplying the quotient by $x1_t = x1_\lambda = x1_l$, which givès $x^n 1_l$ as the integral of the differential $nx^{n-1}.1_\lambda$, and would therefore give $\frac{x^{n+1}}{n+1}.1_l$ for integral of $x^n.1_l$, etc.

In the operation of multiplication, the multiplying unit 1_λ exists in its full magnitude at the commencement, and the ratio nx^n is generated in the time $nx1_t$; while in that kind of operation which yields the differential coefficient, the multiplying unit is itself generated during the time $x1_t$; and, with its final value $nx^{n-1}.1_\lambda$, now made constant, this generated factor will generate the ratio nx^n in the time $x1_t$, the same as that generated by n multiplications in the time $nx1_t$. This sufficiently shews the analogy between the operations of multiplication and differentiation, so far as concerns only a single term; and we have but to observe that division of the product $nx^n.1_l$, and of the *complete* differential $nx^{n-1}.x.1_l$, by the linear factor $n1_\lambda$, equally give the algebraical ratio x^n, in order to perceive the analogy between the operations of division and integration in the like case of a single term.

46. We pass, then, from the function fx to its complete differential by introducing 1_λ^n the unit of velocity in place of 1_l the unit of distance (that is, by writing $n.1_\lambda$ for $1_\lambda^n = 1_l$ in the function); and subsequent division by the time $x1_t$, that *has been* occupied by the appropriate force in the generation of the distance $fx.1_l$, and that *would be* occupied by the generated velocity in the generation of n times the distance $fx.1_l$, gives the unit measure, the differential coefficient proper of the function; from which, inversely, we return to the integral or primitive function by dividing by the generated velocity (that is, by writing $1_\lambda^n = 1_l$ for $n1_\lambda$ in the differential), and multiplying by the time $x1_t$ occupied by the force in generating the velocity*.

Exemplify the function $x^n.1_l$ for different values of n :

1° If $n = 2$, then $x^2.1_l = x^2.1_\lambda^2 = x^2.2.1_\lambda = 2x^2.1_\lambda$ is the complete differential of the ratio of the second order x^2; and dividing by

* When the primitive function is given to find its derivative, multiply by the space and divide by the time; and, conversely, when the derivative function is given to find its primitive, divide by the space and multiply by the time.

the time $x.1_t$, which *has been* occupied by the force or power of the second order in generating the distance $x^2.1_l$, and is equal to the time that *would be* occupied by the simultaneously generated velocity in generating the distance $2x^2.1_l$, we get $2x$ for the unit measure, the differential coefficient proper of the function $x^2.1_l$, or of the ratio of the second order x^2. Inversely, if the differential or derivative function $2x.1_l$ be given, we obtain for the integral or primitive function $2x.1_l \div 2.1_l \times x1._t = x^2.1_t = x^2.1_l$.

2^0 If $n = 1$, then $x^1.1_l = x^1.1_\lambda^1 = x.1.1_\lambda = 1x1_l$ is the complete differential of the ratio of the first order x; and $1x1_l$ divided by the time $x1_t$, gives the unit measure 1 as the differential coefficient of the function x, to which of course corresponds the integral $1_l \div 1_l \times x1_t = x1_t = x1_l$. Thus if the unit of velocity be linear, the product $x1_l.1_\mu$ will carry the passive unit 1_μ through the distance $x1_l$ in the time $x1_t$ uniformly; but if instead of the linear velocity 1_l we take the uniform circular velocity 1_θ, the product $x1_\theta.1_\mu$ carries the passive unit 1_μ through the arc AM $= x1_\theta$ [fig. 50] (if $1_\theta = 1_r$ the radius), in which position it will have for measure the line OP$=\sin x1_r$. If the passive unit 1_μ be now multiplied by that angular unit which has for measure the linear unit, namely, the arc 90^0 whose sine is 1_r, it is submitted to a uniform angular velocity, and will be transferred through x right angles in the time $x1_t$, and therefore through one right angle in the time 1_t, which gives for measure OP$' = \sin(x+\frac{1}{2}\pi)1_r = \cos x1_r$. A second multiplication by the unit of angular velocity will give the measure OP$'' = \sin(x+\pi)1_r = -\sin x1_r$; a third multiplication will give the measure OP$''' = \sin(x+\frac{3}{2}\pi)1_r = -\cos x1_r$; and a fourth, the measure OP $= \sin(x+2\pi)1_r = +\sin x1_r$, the same with which we first set out. Thus a contant velocity, operating in a circular direction, generates the infinite series of periodical ratios $\sin x$, $\cos x$, $-\sin x$, $-\cos x$, $+\sin x$, etc. (when the sine is taken as measure of the arc), where each term is the differential coefficient of the preceding, and consequently the integral of the succeeding one.

The same arc [fig. 50] AM has also for measure OQ $= \cos x1_r$. Introducing the angular unit by its measure the cosine of 90^0, the multiplicand 1_μ is advanced from M through the arc 90^0 to M$'$, and OQ$' = \cos(x+\frac{1}{2}\pi)1_r = -\sin x1_r$ becomes the measure of the operation; a second like multiplication advances 1_μ to M$''$, giving

$OQ''=\cos(x+\pi)1_r=-\cos x 1_r$ for measure; a third multiplication places 1_μ in M''', and gives $OQ'''=\cos(x+\frac{3}{2}\pi)1_r=+\sin x 1_r$ for measure; and the fourth multiplication restores 1_μ to M, where $OQ=\cos(x+2\pi)1_r=+\cos x 1_r$ is the measure as at the outset. Thus when the cosine is taken as the measure of the arc, a uniform direct motion in the circumference will generate the infinite series of periodical ratios $\cos x$, $-\sin x$, $-\cos x$, $+\sin x$, $+\cos x$, etc.; where again each term is the differential coefficient of the preceding, and the integral of the succeeding one.

It is obvious that, when the sine is taken as the measure of the operation, the same results would be had from the oscillation of the passive unit 1_μ in the diameter BB', namely, through OB, BO, OB', B'O, OB, etc.; and when the cosine is the measure adopted, the oscillation will be in the diameter AA', namely, through AO, OA', A'O, OA, AO, etc.

From its position [fig. 51] in A, the multiplicand 1_μ may reach the point M either through direct multiplication by the arc AM $=\theta.1_r=$ arc whose sine is $x.1_r$ (if $x.1_r=OP=\sin\theta.1_r$, whence $\cos\theta.1_r=\sqrt{(1-x^2)}1_r=OQ$); or through inverse multiplication by the arc AB'A'BM. Since inverse multiplication corresponds to division, while the first operation is equivalent to the product $x.1_r.1_\mu=\sin\theta.1_r.1_\mu=OP.1_\mu$, the second should be equivalent to the inverse product $\frac{1}{\sin\theta}.1_r.1_\mu$; to which corresponds the oscillation in the diameter through the steps OB', B'O, OB, BP, leaving $OP.1_\mu$ the same result as before. Effecting the entire product with both factors $\frac{1}{\sin\theta}.\sin\theta.1_r.1_\mu=1.1_r.1_\mu$, we see that 1_μ has traversed the diameter $AB'=2.1_r$ *twice*, and the ratio unity appears as the measure of the result; while at the same time, in the arc, the entire circumference, or absolute geometrical unit, has been described, and is the measure of the operation.

If in the equation $x.1_r=\sin\theta.1_r$ we introduce the unit of angular velocity by its measure the sine of the right angle, we pass to the differential, the mobile 1_μ advances from M to M', and the equation becomes $\sin(\theta+\frac{1}{2}\pi)1_r=\cos\theta.1_r=\sqrt{(1-x^2)}1_r=OP'$. But we could equally pass from M to M' through the inverse path MAB'A'M'; when, by the equivalence of the operations of division and inverse multiplication, the appropriate expression would be ---------- $\frac{1}{\cos\theta}.1_r=\frac{1}{\sqrt{(1-x^2)}}1_r$. This is still the differential of $\sin\theta.1_r=x.1_r$; so that if we now divide by the right angle, we return to the position M, and, taking finally the arc as measure, we have the integral of $\frac{1}{\sqrt{(1-x^2)}}1_r$ = arc sin $x.1_r$, the time being unity.

3° If $n=0$, then $x^0.1_l=1.1_l$, and the generated function is unity or the ratio 1; but the actual operation, if achieved by multiplication, consists in first effecting the direct product $x.1_\lambda.1_\mu$, and then multiplying this result by the inverse factor $\frac{1}{x}.1_\lambda$; by which means 1_μ is first transferred from O to P through a distance $x.1_l$, and then returned to O, thereby giving zero as the measure of the *magnitude* of the result, but at the same generating the *numerical ratio* 1. If we take the magnitude of the result as the measure of the operation, since that magnitude is zero, we can form no differential, and in fact the differential of unity is null; but if we take the generated ratio 1 as such measure, and introduce the unit of velocity 1_λ and divide by the time $x.1_t$, we get $\frac{1}{x}$ as the differential coefficient of $\frac{x}{x}.1_l$ (which last function we now suppose to be generated by differentiation in the time $x.1_t$, by the simultaneous direct and inverse motion of two mobiles 1_μ and $1'_\mu$, instead of the successive generation by multiplication in two intervals each $x1_t$). Inversely if we divide the differential $\frac{1}{x}.1_l$ by the unit of space 1_l, and multiply it by the time $x.1_t$, we get the integral 1.1_l. But here we have shown the very operations of differentiating log x and integrating for the same; a logarithm being in its nature an abstract number expressing the measure of a ratio, or more generally the number of times that 1_μ must be multiplied by a given factor, as $e.1_\lambda$, to produce the distance $x.1_l$ or ratio x. Having obtained the abstract number unity, or pure ratio 1, if we introduce the geometrical unit (which may be linear or circular), we might return and generate by multiplication any quantity whatever $x.1_l$, by expounding 1.1_λ^x into $x.1_\lambda$ [n° 17], provided the arithmetical and geometrical powers of unity coincided; but if instead of 1_λ we introduce the factor $e.1_\lambda$ (e being the base of napierian logarithms), we shall have $1.e^{\log x}.1_\lambda = x.1_\iota$, whatever be the value of x. Hence the base $e.1_\lambda$ has this advantage over the former base 1.1_λ, that it is capable to generate all possible ratios, while the ratio unity alone is all that can be obtained from the base unity.

The results of the operations expressed in the two lines

$x^1.1_\lambda.1_\mu \times x^{-1}.1_\lambda.1_\mu = x^{1-1}.1_\lambda.1_\mu = x^0.1_\lambda.1_\mu = 1.1_\lambda.1_\mu$, and

$e^{\log x}.1_\lambda.1_\mu \times e^{-\log x}.1_\lambda.1_\mu = e^0.1_\lambda.1_\mu = 1.1_\lambda.1_\mu$, are identical : the exponent 0, the logarithm of unity, indicates the equilibrium resulting from the combined direct and inverse multiplication of 1_μ by the factor $e.1_\lambda$, which is exactly equivalent to the performance of no operation at all upon the term 1.1_μ.

Therefore 1° the double operation expressed by $\frac{x}{x}.1_\lambda.1_\mu$ yields a pure unit ratio, the abstract number 1, while the magnitude of the single operation $x.1_\lambda.1_\mu$ will be greater as x is greater; 2° the meaning of the word *number* is capable of extension, so as to signify the number of operations (or magnitude of the operation) requisite to generate the quantity $x.1_\iota$, under which signification it answers to the term *logarithm*, the measure of a ratio, that is, of the operation which generates that ratio; and 3° by the adoption of this extension of meaning, a new species of quantity is originated, in which 0 is the measure of unity, whereas it was before the measure of zero.

47. The integral and differential of a function $fx.1_\iota$ are respectively the distance and velocity generated in the time $x1_\iota$. The function fx will necessarily have some dimension n, and be therefore of the form $fx1_\iota^n$, which leads to the differential by the development of the linear factor 1_ι^n into $n.1_\lambda$. When n is a positive whole number, the velocity will be positive; but when fractional or negative, the velocity will be negative. When $n = 0$, the function $fx1_\iota$ becomes unity, as resulting from the product of the factor $fx.1_\lambda$ by its reciprocal $(fx)^{-1}.1_\lambda$; and the velocity becomes null, as resulting from the equilibrium between a positive and negative force of the first order. If $fx.1_\iota = x.x^{-1}.1_\iota = 1.1_\iota$, it is the equation of the equilateral hyperbola referred to its asymptotes, in which x may have any positive or negative, whole or

fractional value whatever, and it is known that $\int x^{-1}.dx =$ the asymptotic area = the logarithm of the abscissa x; but if we substitute $\cos x$ for x, we have $\cos x.(\cos x)^{-1}.1_{l} = 1.1_{l}$, the factor $\cos x$ (as also $\sin x$) is confined within the limits 0 and 1, and $\frac{\cos x}{\cos x}.dx = \frac{d \sin x}{\sqrt{(1-\sin^2 x)}}$, whose integral is $(\text{arc}x)1_{r}$ = twice the area of the sector whose arc is x and sine is $\sin x$, and is therefore a circular logarithm of $\sin x$, the analogue of the hyperbolical logarithm of x in the former case.

NOTE ON THE RESULTANT OF TWO CONCURRING FORCES.

The *passive material unit*, or unit of mass, may be defined as a body incapable of self-motion, but susceptible of being moved by the application of the *unit of force* (translatory) *of the first order*, through the *unit of distance* in the *unit of time*, and in the direction of the action of the force.

1. Since the unit of translatory force carries the material unit through the unit of distance in the unit of time, it follows that n similar forces will carry the same mobile through n units of distance in the unit of time (and also that the unit of force will carry a mass equal to n material units, through the nth part of the unit of distance, in the unit of time).

2. The material unit cannot be moved in opposite directions at the same time : from which it follows that two equal and opposing forces will equilibrate, or destroy each other's effects; and when the forces are unequal, the material unit will move in the direction of the action of the greater force, through a distance in the unit of time equal to tbe difference of the measures of the two opposing forces.

The resultant (or combined effect) of two opposing or conspiring forces, therefore, is equal to the difference or sum of the forces (or of their separate effects).

3. Whatever be the direction of the action of a force, the measure of that action may always be estimated on two rectangular axes; and when the point of application and the plane of two concurring forces are made the origin and plane of the system of rectangular axes, each force will be estimated on both axes; the opposing and conspiring measures of the two forces on each axis will show what amount of effect is destroyed, and what is increased (no. 27); and since the material unit cannot move in two opposite directions at once, it will obey the resultant of the two concurring forces by describing the diagonal of the parallelogram constructed on the algebraical sum of the measures of the forces on the two rectangular axes.

CHAPTER III.

THE OPERATION OF ALGEBRAICAL DIVISION.

48. ADDITION and subtraction are mutually opposite operations ($+AC-BC$); and in the latter, we commonly take for result, not the measure of the operation performed ($-BC$), but the difference between it and the measure of the operation to which it is opposed ($+AC$), which gives a positive measure ($+AB$) [fig. 52] so long as the first operation is greater than the second; but in the contrary case, when the measure of the additive operation $+AC$ is less than that of the subtractive one $-BC$, the difference between the two operations ($+AC-BC$) is more than exhausted, and the full measure of the entire subtractive operation $-BC$ is reduced by the amount of the additive one $+AC$ to the $-AB$ [fig. 53], which is a negative measure, or the measure of that particular kind of negative operation termed subtraction. From this it appears that the operations of addition and subtraction may be illustrated by taking an origin, and introducing the linear unit 1_l as the measure of an operation performed in the unit of time 1_t by a force of the first order (constant velocity 1_λ): we should have $AC\times 1_l - AB\times 1_l = +Ab+1_l$ when $AC > AB$ [fig. 54], and $AC\times 1_l - AB\times 1_l = -Ab\times 1_l$ when $AC < AB$ [fig. 55]. Then when the subtrahend is 0 and the minuend is 1, the measure of the operation is $-1.1_l = -1.1_l.1_\mu$, which is equivalent to multiplying 1_μ by -1_λ, that is, to revolving the material unit 1_μ through two right angles.

49. Multiplication and division are mutually opposing (or mutually inverse) operations. Let 1_μ be the material unit (unit of burthen), and $Op = 1_l = 1_\lambda$ the unit of distance, equal to 1_t the unit of time. By successive multiplications of the material unit by the linear unit in so many units of time, I transfer the first from [fig. 56] O to p, p′, p″ and P, giving $OP\times 1_\lambda = x.1_\lambda.1_\mu$; and the measure of the whole operation is $x.1_l$. In opposing to

this the operation of division, I return the material unit 1_μ from P to O, say in the unit of time 1_t; and the measure of the operation is $\frac{x.1_t.1_\mu}{1_\lambda.1_\mu} = x$, an abstract number, a pure ratio, which expresses the number of times the operation $1_\lambda.1_\mu$ must be executed, in order to give for measure that of the dividend $x.1_t$. The result is positive when the dividend and divisor are each the measure of an operation executed in the same direction [fig. 57], as +AB and +Ab, or —AB′ and —Ab′; since the question is, How many times is $+Ab.1_t$ contained in $+AB.1_t$, or $-Ab'.1_t$ in $-AB'.1_t$, which can only yield a positive number for answer, because it requires just as many steps (or operations) each equal to Ab to measure AB in its direction, as to measure AB′ in its direction, so that the operation is truly expressed by

$$\frac{+AB.1_t}{+Ab.1_t} = \frac{-AB'.1_t}{-Ab'.1_t} = +\frac{AB}{Ab}.$$

But when the question is, How many times is $-Ab'.1_t$ contained in $+AB.1_t$, or $+Ab.1_t$ in $-AB'.1_t$, the first is equivalent to asking how many steps equal in magnitude and direction to $-Ab'.1_t$ must be taken to measure $+AB.1_t$, and the second merely changes $-Ab'.1_t$ into $+Ab.1_t$ and $+AB.1_t$ into $-AB'.1_t$; which requires that the divisors $-Ab'.1_t$ and $+Ab.1_t$ must respectively be brought into the directions +AB and —AB′, ere such operation of measurement can be performed; and this additional labor, which will be achieved by multiplying the lines $-Ab'.1_t$ and $+Ab.1_t$ by -1.1_λ, must be counted in the measure of the result, as thus :

$$-1.1_\lambda \times \frac{+AB.1_t}{-Ab'.1_t} = -1.1_\lambda \times \frac{-AB'.1_t}{+Ab.1_t} = -1.\frac{AB}{Ab}.1_\lambda.$$

50. Let [fig. 58] OP $= 1_t$, and PQ $= x1_t$; and divide OP by OQ, that is to say, divide 1_t by $(1+x)1_t$. This means, in the calculus of operations, that, the line OP $= 1_t$ being the measure of a direct operation, I am to operate inversely through the line OQ $= (1+x)1_t$ so as to bring about the result zero. By positive multiplication, the material unit has been transferred from O to P, giving $OP.1_\mu = 1_t.1_\mu$. Assuming the inverse factor $(1+x)1_\lambda$, I transfer 1_μ back from P to O by the first term 1.1_λ of the inverse factor; but the other term $x1$, prolongs the transfer to Q′, where

$OQ' = PQ = x1_\iota$, and I subtract the result, which gives .... $(1-(1+x))1_\lambda.1_\mu = (0-x)1_\iota.1_\mu = OQ'.1_\mu$, which is exactly the same thing as expressing the multiplication negatively. I next proceed to cancel the new term $-x1_\iota$ by a second inverted application of the factor $(1+x)1_\lambda$; but in order to bring 1_μ from Q' to O, I must multiply it positively by $x1_\lambda$, and this converts my factor into $x(1+x)1_\lambda$, which cancels the negative term $-x1_\iota$, and gives me $+x^2.1_\iota.1_\mu$ for the new position of 1_μ now on the right of the point O. To reduce 1_μ now to O, I must take the negative factor $-x^2(1+x)1_\lambda$, which will again place 1_μ on the left of O, but now at the distance expressed by $-x^3.1_\iota$; and a perpetual repetition of the process will successively place the material unit 1_μ on the right and on the left of the point, and at perpetually increasing distances when x is greater than 1. When [fig. 58] x is less than 1, the first negative position $x1_\iota = OQ''$ is less than $1_\iota = OP$; and x being a fraction, each successive power is a still smaller fraction of the distance 1_ι, and 1_μ will perpetually approach the point O. When $x = 1$, the successive positions will be OP, OQ‴, OP, OQ″, etc., that is, $+1_\iota$, -1_ι, $+1_\iota$, -1_ι, etc. to infinity in time.

The number of units of operation above performed is expressed by $1-x+x^2-x^3+$&c., this being the quantity and quality of the successive multiplications applied upon the divisor $(1+x)1_\iota$ in cancelling the successive dividends; for that even the very first operation was a multiplication of $(1+x)1_\iota$ by 1_λ, appears from the fact that if the dividend were $a.1_\iota$, the divisor must be made $a(1+x)1_\iota$.

51. If I am directed [fig. 58] to divide $1_\iota = OP$ by $(x+1)1_\iota$, I see that the requisite factor to bring 1_μ from P to O is $\frac{1}{x}.x1_\lambda$; so that I must multiply the given divisor $(x+1)1_\iota$ by $-1.\frac{1}{x}.1_\lambda$, which will bring 1_μ first to O and then to Q'', where we have $OQ'' = -1.\frac{1}{x}.1_\iota$; from whence we must return by means of the factor $+1.\frac{1}{x^2}(x+1)1_\lambda$, which will place 1_μ again on the right of O at the distance $+1.\frac{1}{x^2}.1_\iota$, and so on. Here when x is greater

than unity, we apprcximate to the point O; so that division by $x+1$ differs from that by $1+x$, for all values of x other than 1. Now this difference arises from the opposite directions in which the two systems of operation must necessarily be conducted, to wit, first, in the division by $x+1$, we proceed downwards from x operations to one operation; while, secondly, in the division by $1+x$, the proceeding is from one upwards to x operations; the first, when x is greater than unity, forming an infinite series of decreasing operations, and the second an increasing series, and *vice versa* when x is less than unity.

The first operation in division is really a negative multiplication, but it is a positive division; so that the first and all the successive terms of the quotient are truly written for positive division and negative multiplication.

52. To divide [fig. 58] $1_\iota = OP$ by $(1-x)1_\iota$, I multiply the divisor by -1.1_λ, which cancels 1_ι and produces $+1.x1_\iota$; that is, I transfer 1_μ from P to O, and then in the returning direction to Q^{iv}, because $OQ^{iv} = x1_\iota$. To cancel this remainder, I must multiply $(1-x)1_\iota$ by $-1.x1_\lambda$, which produces $(-1.x+1.x^2)1_\iota$, and carries 1_μ first to O, and then inversely to a distance on the right of O equal to $x^2.1_\iota$; and at each succeeding step of the process, we first return to the point O, and then depart successively further and further to the right, in all cases where x is greater than unity; but when $x < 1$, the successive steps will approximate to the point O; and thus we have in the former case a diverging, and in the latter a converging series. And if x were equal to 1, we should pace back and forth from P to O and O to P, to infinity in time.

Then in the division of unity by $1 + x$, accordingly as x is greater or less than, or equal to, unity, we operate an infinite series of oscillations of increasing, decreasing, or equal amplitude alternately on the right and left of the centre at zero; and in operating the division of unity by $1-x$, there are, under the same three relations of x to 1, a like increase, decrease, or equality of successive oscillations prolonged to infinity in time, but terminating from the right in the centre, which now forms the negative turning point of the mobile.

CHAPTER IV.

THE COMPOSITION AND DECOMPOSITION OF OPERATIONS.

53. An operation produces an effect, and requires for its determination the admeasurement of that effect in space and time. Two operations produce two effects, which require duplicate measures for their determination; that is to say, to render two operations determinate, they must each be subjected to two separate conditions of measurement, corresponding to the commencement and the termination of each operation in space and time.

Having [fig. 59] assumed an origin O and axis OX, the distance AB or AC may be measured in two different ways : 1° By measuring the distance OA (first operation), and then the distance AB or AC (second operation) : this method is an application of the ruler, or straight line. 2° By measuring first the line OA as before (first operation), and then the line OB or OC (second operation); and in case the second line as OB be equal to the first OA, the two separate operations may be reduced to one, namely, that of measuring the angle AOB : this is an application of the compasses, or of the circular arc. These two primitive instruments, the ruler and the compasses, enable us to measure the two first elements of space, to wit, *distance* and *direction;* and from the relation exhibited by the last of the above examples, in the reduction of the two measurements of a simple phenomenon to the performance of one single operation, we shall endeavor to deduce a method applicable to more complicated cases. The equality of the two distances OA, OB, determined by the operation of measuring the commencement and termination of the phenomenon in question, leads us to the notion of the principle of uniformity, or uniform law of action (measurement of equal distances); and by substituting the device of the compasses, the two separate but equal operations are reduced to the single one of describing the arc AB, in which case the arc becomes a measure of the operation, as also of the phenomenon itself. Inversely, then, this single circular operation being first assumed, it may afterwards be decomposed into two linear ones, and is therefore an equivalent of both the latter; which instance shows the possibility of proceeding similarly in other cases.

54. Now when a constant force (like that of gravitation) acts upon a material body during a unit of time, it performs an operation that may be regarded as *one* (analogous to describing the arc AB); which operation, as we shall see, afterwards branches into two others, and thereby affords an opportunity for referring one primitive operation to two distinct measures, the first being that of the distance described by the material body while under the immediate action of the force, *the simultaneous effect* (corresponding to the line OA); and the second measure being that of the distance described in the unit of time immediately following the suspension of the action of the force at the expiration of the first unit of time, which distance is due to the velocity generated in that first time, *the successive effect* (represented by line AC). Then [fig. 60] just as one same line OM may have at once two separate measures determinately related to each other as OP, ON, which require two separate operations for their measurement, and which two operations may be reduced to one as the measurement of the arc AM; so inversely may one single operation be decomposed into two operations (decomposition of operations). In the example of fig. 59, the single operation (arc AB) was decomposed into two equal operations (line OA = line OB); and the line AC, being referred to unequal radii OA, OC, could not then be treated : in the example of fig. 60, the single operation (arc AM) is decomposed into two unequal operations (lines OP, ON), but determinately related to each other. In all this, it is to be well understood that the measure of the operation is put for the operation itself.

Recurring to the case of the constant force : the condition of the uniform generation of velocity, or of the uniform increase of the motion of the body acted upon during the first unit of time, determines the relation of the distance described by the body during the second unit of time, and due alone to the velocity generated in the first unit of time, to the distance described in that first time under the action of the force, to be that of two to one. We have here then two distances determinately related to each other, and forming two measures (simultaneous and successive) of one primitive operation, the action of the generating force during the first unit of time. Now these two measures (which correspond to the lines AB & AC, or OP & ON, in number and office, but not in relative magnitude), being placed as chords to the same angle, will belong to two circles whose radii are to each other as 2 and 1; and, therefore, assuming for 1 any radius OA, we make [fig. 61] OA = 1 arbitrary unit of time 1_t,

$$OA' = 2\ OA, \text{ and chord } CC' = 1_t = 1_t;$$

whence chord $C''C''' = 2$ chord $CC' = 2.1_t$.

Here then are the two measures of our single primitive operation, the simultaneous CC′ and the successive C″C‴ measures. Now a line of the length $n1_t$, taken as the measure of one uniform operation in space (like that of uniform motion), is evidently equal to the sum of its n (equal or unequal) parts, even when each of these parts becomes itself the measure of a uniform operation proportional to the one measured by the whole line, for the operations are defined and based upon their measures alone; so that we say that the sum of n operations is equal to one operation of the quantity n. Therefore our second operation, performed in the second unit of time, and having the measure 2, may be replaced by, or decomposed into, two like operations, each of whose measures is half the measure of the undecomposed operation. Then on centres C, C′, and with radius OA, describe the arcs C″D, DC‴; and C″C‴ the measure of one operation of the magnitude 2, is divided into two (equal) measures, each of a like operation, of the magnitude 1 : and indeed the representation of the double operation is already provided for by the construction of the figure; for at the centre O, it will be an operation requiring double the exertion to describe the arc C″C‴, that it will require to describe the arc CC′ (according to the radii as well as the arcs).

Thus then the constant force generates velocity uniformly, and the velocity generates distance uniformly (after its own generation) : the distance generated in the first unit of time is 1_l; and in the second unit of time the velocity generated in the first unit of time will generate the distance 2.1_l, and a further accession of distance 1_l will be generated in this time by the action of the force itself, making the distance 4.1_l (square of the time) at the expiration of the second unit of time.

The proceeding here adopted amounts to the interpolation of one new operation (generation of velocity) between a primitive operation (uniform action of the force) and its complete or ultimate effect in space (the actual movement of the body under the operation of the force).

55. Let us next suppose that the relation of the second or successive measure to the first or simultaneous one may be that of 3 to 1; and as we have said that a constant force generates velocity uniformly, and the velocity (become constant after generation) generates distance uniformly, let us now assume a primitive force one degree higher, and conceive that this primitive force generates force of the degree previously considered uniformly, while this latter force (become constant after its generation) generates velocity uniformly, and the velocity (same condition) generates distance uniformly.

Construct [fig. 62] the circles OA to radius unity and OA″ to radius 3, and make the chord BB′ = OB = 1_l = 1_t. Call the primitive force *a force of the third order* ϕ'''; the generated force, *a force of the second order* ϕ''; and the velocity, *a force of the first order* ϕ', or 1_λ the unit of velocity, and equal to $1_l = 1_t$. Then ϕ''', ϕ'', ϕ', are units of force, such that each will generate the unit of distance in the unit of time.

The force ϕ''', like the force of the second order considered in the preceding example, has at once two different but determinately related measures, namely, the distance described by the mobile 1_μ in the time $1'_t$, under the action of the force ϕ''', which distance is measured by the chord BB′ = 1_l; and the distance described by the same mobile 1_μ in the time $1''_t$, under the action of the velocity generated by ϕ''' in $1'_t$. We for the present suppose the amount of this generated velocity to be 3.1_λ, to accommodate a preconceived order of succession beginning with the measure of a primitive velocity 1_λ, and followed by that of the velocity generated by a primitive force of the second order 2.1_λ; which indicates 3.1_λ for the amount of velocity which should be generated by a primitive force of the third order in the unit of time. The chord $DD''' = 3.1_l$ will therefore represent the distance described by the material unit 1_μ in the second unit of time $1''_t$, under the action of the generated velocity alone. As in the preceding case the velocity was generated uniformly, and was measured by two operations from the centres C, C′; so in this case, where it is force of the second order ϕ'' that is generated uniformly, this generated force will be measured by two operations from the centres B, B′, giving us the two chords CC′, C′C″, on the circle to radius $OA' = 2.1_l$; so that the measure of the force of the first order generated in the time $1'_t$ will be $2\phi'' = CC''$, exactly as in the former case of velocity ($2.1_\lambda = C''C'''$) uniformly generated in 1_t. In the case of the second order, the two chords C″D, DC‴ expressed the ratio of the distance generated by the velocity in $1''_t$, to that generated in $1'_t$; so here the chords CC′, C′C″ express the ratio of the velocity that the generated force of the second order will generate in the time $1''_t$, to that which it did generate in $1'_t$, which last we have *assumed* to be 3.1_λ. Then, at the expiration of the time $1'_t$, if the force ϕ''' be suspended, there will still remain, besides the velocity 3.1_λ, the force of the second order $2\phi''$, which, during the time $1''_t$, will generate the velocity $2.3.1_\lambda$; but we have seen that velocity, during the time of its own generation by a force of the second order, generates half the distance that it will generate in an equal time after its own generation; and therefore the amount $2.3.1_\lambda$ of velocity generated by the force $2\phi''$ in $1''_t$, will generate the distance 3.1_l in that time. Finally, if the force ϕ''' be supposed to continue its action also during $1''_t$, it will generate the distance 1_l in that time as before. We have, then, in all,

1_{ι} the distance generated in $1'_{t}$ by ϕ''';

3.1_{ι} the distance generated in $1''_{t}$ by $2\phi''$, which was generated in $1'_{t}$ by ϕ''';

3.1_{ι} the distance generated in $1''_{t}$ by 3.1_{λ}, which was generated in $1'_{t}$ by ϕ''', and

1_{ι} the distance generated in $1''_{t}$ by ϕ''' :

being $8.1_{\iota} = 2^{3}.1_{\iota}$, the cube of the time.

This amounts to the interpolation of two new operations between the immediate operation of a primitive power, and its ultimate effect in space. Viewed in an inverse order, the general process consists in reducing a number n of operations to $n-1$, these again to $n-2$, and so on until we arrive at 3, 2, and finally one operation commanding the whole subordinate series. A mere inspection of the figure will suggest the law by which we may prolong the process as far as we please, which we shall attempt to do, after generalizing the method made use of in n° 53 to reduce two operations to one.

56. Suppose [fig. 63] three lines AA′, BB′, CC′ are to be measured from the origin O : when these lines are disconnected, each will require two operations for its measurement, to wit :

1. From O to A, and from A to A′;
2. From A′ to B, and from B to B′; and
3. From B′ to C, and from C to C″.

But when these lines are so related that the termination of the first coincides with the origin of the second, and the termination of the second with the origin of the third, then, after the first twofold operation from O to A and from A to A′, each remaining line requires but one operation, namely, since A′ and B coincide, from B to B′ for the second, and from B to C′ for the third. In the former case the number of operations required was double the number of the lines, while in the latter they are reduced to one more than the number of the lines; but if measured by means of arcs, each system of lines will require only as many operations as there are lines.

Suppose now 7 equal distances are to be measured. Let them

be placed in symmetrical continuity, that is, in a straight line. Measured by arcs, they will require 7 centres; and these centres may be so placed on one straight line as to comprise between the extreme centres but six lines each equal to one of the first, so that the next measurement by arcs will require but 6 centres: these in their turn will comprise five lines between them, requiring 5 new centres of measurement, and so on until finally we are reduced to one line and one centre (origin of the resultant of all the system of operations).

57. Conversely to return from a resultant operation to any assigned inferior rank of component operations, we assume an origin A and angle of measurement BAB′ (it is more symmetrical to choose the angle of measurement equal to 60°, when the chords and radii may be made equal, and the triangle will be equilateral; but any isosceles triangle will serve).

Now to show the system in the operation of measurement:

1° The prime operator [fig. 64] A measures the chord BB′, and despatches two subordinate operators, one to each point B, B′, who measure the two lines CC′, C′C″.

2° Now were the lines CC′, C′C″ disconnected, it would require four operators to measure the three lines DD′, D′D″, D″D‴, and thus the prescribed law of measurement would be violated and the system of operations entirely defeated; but when the lines CC′, C′C″ are connected as they ought to be, B despatches one operator [fig. 65] to C and another to C′, and B′ despatches one operator to C″, and these three operators measure the three lines DD′, D′D″, D″D‴.

3° C despatches [fig. 65] one operator to D and another to D′, C′ despatches one to D″, and C″ one to D‴, making in all 4 operators to measure the 4 lines EE′, E′E″, E″E‴, E‴E^{iv}.

It thus appears, 1° That when a number n of operations is to be reduced to a lesser number, the lines which measure the operations must be placed in symmetrical continuity (as on one same straight line), so that each may be measured by one operation from a centre; 2° That the distances between these centres must also be placed in symmetrical continuity, so as to reduce the original number of measures to a new number less by one, whereby the number of operations of measurement to be next performed is reduced by one, and so on until we arrive at the final resultant operation of the whole system. And conversely to resolve a primitive or resultant operation into n components having equal measures, the distances which coordinate operators measure must be placed in symmetrical continuity, so that the number of coordinate operations in any particular rank shall exceed that of the preceding rank by one only, and thus finally reach the very number of components desired.

The law of these operations unfolds thus :

1° Each operator performs one operation of measurement; and,

2° Beginning with the prime operator, each successive operator in the first column despatches two subordinate operators to the next inferior station, while each operator in all the remaining columns despatches but one subordinate.

This law is but the mathematical expression of the physical development of *intension* into *extension*, the latter being converted into *number*.

If the intension of the force expended by each of the four operators, in measuring conjointly the final effect or phenomenon, be assumed unity, the line EE′ will be the unit measure of such expended force, or its intension converted into extension; and the whole line EE^{iv} will be the amount of extension resulting from the conversion of the intension of the combined force expended by the same four operators, which extension has been decomposed into this number 4 by the process of measurement.

The prime operator will require to expend a force equal in amount to the combined force expended by the four last operators, in describing by one operation in the unit of time the entire arc to radius AE and angle EAE^{iv}; so that by our process we have converted an original intension of the degree 4 and extension 1, into a final extension expressed by the number 4, the intension of each unit of the final extension being of the degree 1. The intension and extension of the interpolated forces (the forces expended by the intervening operators) are all exhibited by the figure.

CHAPTER V.

THE THEORY OF GENERATING POWERS.

58. In the second chapter of these researches, we sought the determination of various measures of *unity*, when that unity was given to us conditioned as being the final *effect* or phenomenon resulting from a system of known operations in space and time; these operations, all of one same degree, consisting in the conversion of constant velocity into distance. In the present chapter, we are to assume *unity* as a prime *cause*, of such degree as we please, and seek to determine its final *effect*, or the phenomena it will produce when subjected to an assigned law of uniform action in space and time.

When unity is given as a final effect, or as a cause whose degree is zero, its most general form is 1^n, where n may have any value, whole or fractional, positive or negative, real or imaginary, and we have endeavored to exhibit the different values of such different forms as before stated; but where the final effect given is not *unity*, but *multiplicity*, we will suppose it to be of the general form x^n or a^x (accordingly as the base is variable or constant, and the exponent is constant or variable); and thence we are to assume unity to be, not at the *foot*, but at the *summit* of the scale of cause and effect, and therewith to operate the generation of these two cardinal forms of algebraical ratio x^n and a^x, for positive and negative, whole and fractional values of the exponent of x, and for positive and negative, real and imaginary values of the exponent of a. The importance of this proceeding will be obvious when we observe that if the formation of these principal ratios be once shown to be comprised in the evolution of one single law of operation, the consideration of various other fractional, circular and elliptical ratios, and even that of fractional operations (fractional differentiation, for example), will doubtless be facilitated, and perhaps much light thrown upon many questions of philosophy and physics.

59. Algebra has been defined as that science in which the operations are prescribed, and we are to find their results; while in the science named the calculus of functions, the results are given, and we seek the operations which shall produce them. Why not generalize the relation which exists between the ideas expressed by these two definitions, and transfer them from the classificatory to the deductive form : view them not only as under the categories of quantity and quality, but also in that of relation, of cause and effect; not as being available only as constituent elements of the understanding, but as regulative principles of the reason ? In the algebraical question, the *cause* is given, namely, the form of the operation, and the *effect* is sought : in the calculus of functions, the *effect* is given, and we seek its *cause*, the form of the operation which shall produce it. Let these two ideas become regulative : try the category of relation, refer to the law of cause and effect; find the *cause* of this *cause*, the still simpler operation which shall produce the operation first sought in the calculus of functions; in a word, let us invent a calculus of successive functions, that may enable us to ascend from the complex to the simplest possible function, unity itself.

60. By differentiating successively the equation following,

$$fx = x^4+4x^3h+6x^2h^2+4xh^3+h^4, \quad \text{we obtain}$$

$$\frac{d\,fx}{dx} = 4(x^3+3x^2h+3xh^2+h^3),$$

$$\frac{d^2fx}{dx^2} = 4.3(x^2+2xh+h^2),$$

$$\frac{d^3fx}{dx^3} = 4.3.2(x+h), \text{ and}$$

$$\frac{d^4fx}{dx^4} = 4.3.2.1.$$

And by integrating successively the equation following,

$$\frac{d^4fx}{dx^4} = 1,$$ and determining the arbitrary constants symmetrically, we obtain

$$\frac{d^3fx}{dx^3} = x+h,$$

$$\frac{d^2fx}{dx^2} = \tfrac{1}{2}(x^2+2xh+h^2),$$

$$\frac{d\,fx}{dx} = \frac{1}{1.2.3}(x^3+3x^2h+3xh^2+h^3),$$ and

$$fx = \frac{1}{1.2.3.4}(x^4+4x^3h+6x^2h^2+4xh^3+h^4).$$

Thus the differential calculus does not evolve from the developed entire function $(x+k)^4$ the unity which is enveloped therein, but yields us the inverted factorial 4.3.2.1 : neither is the integral calculus competent to develop unity into a formula with entire coefficients, for it encumbers $(x+h)^4$ with the reciprocal of the factorial 1.2.3.4.

By differentiation, we ascend from an effect to its immediate cause; but each successive differential, in its turn becoming the effect, is treated precisely as was the first effect, that is, as the rational measure of a distance, of which a constant velocity is always the immediate cause. Thus by this method we can never get beyond the mechanical or first order of forces, and consequently can never rise into the region of pure dynamics, of generating forces or powers ascending in a graduated scale above the order unity : we remain in a mere treadmill, where each step does but reiterate the same level. So the integral calculus is incompetent to evolve the compound phenomenon $x^4+4x^3h+6x^2h^2+4xh^3+h^4$ from simple unity : it cannot achieve the conversion of intension into extension, but requires the dynamical unit 1^4 to be developed into the mechanical factorial 4.3.2.1 at the outset, so as to be enabled to proceed from velocity to distance, and thus merely to reverse the steps of the differential calculus as it ought to do. A new conception was therefore necessary, to show the origin and filiation and the mutual relations of the various forms of elementary mathematical development. Such conception I have labored strenuously to shadow forth in these pages; and if the delineation be not sufficiently clear and distinct, the reader may rest assured the obstacle lies in the want of proper facility in the artist, and not at all in any obscurity or sterility inherent in the conception itself.

61. In a general case of causation and production, I define a primitive power to be that noumenon or force which shall produce or generate a uniform effect in successive equal times. This effect may in its turn be a power or force, which shall, after its own generation, also generate an effect uniformly; but during its own generation, its effect would be variable and increasing. The same supposition may be repeated; and if each successive effect is conditioned to be one degree inferior to its immediate cause, we shall finally arrive at a power of the degree one, whose effect would necessarily be a power of the degree zero, and further production would cease with the cessation of causation.

Take for instance a primitive power of the fourth degree or order : I say that a power of the fourth order generates power of the third order uniformly, which generated power of the third order generates power of the second order, which power of the second order generates power of the first order (velocity), which power of the first order generates power of the order zero (distance), where the process of generation ceases : all commencing, proceeding, and terminating simultaneously with the time considered. And from this definition we are to show that the generated power of the third order will increase proportionally to the time; the power of the second order, proportionally to the square of the time; the power of the first order, the velocity, proportionally to the cube of the time; and finally that the distance generated will increase proportionally to the biquadrate or fourth power of the time.

62. Notations :

1° Let 1_μ represent the unit of body or material unit, which in all cases is the *patient* whereon the effort of the final *agent* (the power of the first order) is expended in generating the phenomenon, which phenomenon may be represented in a general manner by the transfer of such material unit (or an equivalent material point) through an assumed distance in space.

2° Let 1_t represent the unit of time, which may be appropriated to successive intervals by means of accents.

3° Let 1_l be the unit of distance, which is always the unit measure of the phenomenon, or of the effort expended by the power or force of the first order in transferring the material point through the unit of distance in the unit of time, which two last units (of space and of time) may or may not be made equal to each other.

4° Let ϕ^0, ϕ', ϕ'', ϕ''', ϕ^{iv}, etc. represent a series of powers in the ascending order, each one of which generates its immediately inferior, increasingly during its own generation, and uniformly afterwards.

63. If a material unit move uniformly, it will describe equal distances in equal times, and is therefore said to have a constant velocity; and if the distance described in a previously determined unit of time be taken for linear unit 1_l, the distance will be $x1_l$ described in the time $x1_t$, where the unit measure of time may also be taken equal to 1_l. I now transfer the term *velocity* from the *passive* to the *active* sense, and say that a constant velocity generates distance uniformly; and since the distance generated in the time 1_t is 1_l, the unit measure of velocity 1_λ will also be equal to 1_l. Since the distance generated by velocity is a truly passive existence, a physical zero, it answers to the definition of a force or power of the order zero, and a constant velocity is consequently a power of the first order ϕ'.

64. A constant force generates velocity uniformly, and will therefore generate x times the velocity in the time $x1_t$ that it generated in the time 1_t. As the velocity generated in any time $x1_t$ increased uniformly from zero, it will evidently generate twice the distance in an equal time $x1_t$ after its generation, that it did generate during the time of its own generation; and consequently at the expiration of the first time $\frac{1}{2}x1_t$, the amount of the generated velocity was such as would generate uniformly the same distance in the time $x1_t$ that was actually variably generated

in that time. Since a constant velocity answers to the definition of a power of the first order, it follows that the force which generates velocity uniformly will be of an order one degree higher, that is, a power of the second order ϕ''.

Let the force of the second order ϕ'' be applied to the material unit (act upon the unit of mass) 1_μ placed at the point O. In the first unit of time $1'_t$, ϕ'' will generate a velocity such as will generate uniformly, in the second unit of time $1''_t$, twice the distance generated by that velocity in the first unit of time $1'_t$ during its own generation : let this last mentioned distance be $OP = 1_l$, the linear unit (the linear and temporal units may be equal); and then the velocity generated will have for measure 2.1_l, the distance which it will afterwards generate uniformly during the unit of time, that distance being the unit measure of its effect or *production :* therefore 2.1_λ (equal to 2.1_l) may be written as the unit measure of this generated velocity or power of the first order, or of its *causation;* and since 2.1_λ is the unit measure of the immediate effect or production of ϕ'' in the time $1'_t$, and is measured by its own production in the time $1''_t$, it is truly the *successive measure* [n° 54] of the primitive power of the second order ϕ''. At the expiration of the first temporal unit $1'_t$, then, there will be generated immediately and mediately by the force ϕ'', the velocity 2.1_λ and the distance 1_l. During the second unit of time $1''_t$, the force ϕ'' will generate another increment of velocity 2.1_λ, which, during its own generation, will generate the distance 1_l; and the velocity 2.1_λ generated in the first temporal unit $1'_t$, will generate the distance 2.1_l, making the distance 3.1_l generated in the second unit of time $1''_t$; so that at the expiration of the second temporal unit $1''_t$, there is generated in all the velocity 4.1_λ and the distance 4.1_l. During the third temporal unit $1'''_t$, the precedingly generated velocity 4.1_λ will generate the distance 4.1_l, and the force ϕ'' will generate another increment of velocity 2.1_λ, which will generate the distance 1_l in the same time; so that at the expiration of the third unit of time $1'''_t$, there will be generated in all the velocity 6.1_λ and the distance 9.1_l. Then the velocity increases as the double of the time, and the distance as the square of the time.

Thus in the unit of time 1_t the force of the second order ϕ''

generates two units of velocity 2.1_λ uniformly, that is, a unit of of velocity 1_λ in the first semiunit of time $\frac{1}{2}'.1_t$, and another in the second semiunit of time $\frac{1}{2}''.1_t$; each of which units of velocity, *after* its generation, will generate the linear unit in the full unit of time, but only half that distance in an equal time *during* its own generation; so that $1'_\lambda$ generated $\frac{1}{4}.1_l$ during its own generation in $\frac{1}{2}'.1'_t$ and $\frac{1}{2}.1_l$ in $\frac{1}{2}''.1'_t$ after its generation, and $1''_\lambda$ generated $\frac{1}{4}.1_l$ during its generation in $\frac{1}{2}''.1'_t$, making in all the distance 1_l generated by the velocity 2.1_λ in the time 1_t *during* its own generation (its *simultaneous* measure), while the same velocity 2.1_λ will generate the distance 2.1_l (its *successive* measure) in the time $1''_t$ *after* its generation. Then when velocity is generated uniformly, it acquires the *intension* unity (increasing from 0 to 1) in a semiunit of time, but requires an entire unit of time for the conversion of this unit of intension into one of *extension* (generation of the unit of distance). Two *operations* of generation are therefore performed by the force of the second order in the unit of time, and their sum has two distinct measures: first, the distance 1_l, generated by the velocity 2.1_λ during its generation in $1'_t$ (the simultaneous effect); and, secondly, the distance 2.1_l generated by the same velocity in the time $1''_t$ after its generation (the successive effect). These measures are all expressed by their proportion to the assumed linear unit, and consist therefore of magnitude converted into number. Now we have seen (n° 46] that the term *number* may have its signification extended [n° 16] so as to include *number of operations;* and from this it shall follow, that as we have heretofore deduced number from magnitude, conversely we will hereafter deduce magnitude from number, in accordance with the precept at the close of n° 16; so that when we have logically determined the number of operations performed under an assigned law, we may determine the corresponding magnitude of the result.

In the case of power of the first order, which generates power of the order zero, a purely passive existence, a mere path in space, there is properly but one operation performed in the first unit of time $1'_t$, since the path or distance generated in that time (the simultaneous measure of the generated power of the first order) is always taken for the linear unit to which the measures of all the other operations are referred; but each power higher than that of the first order performs an entire operation in the semiunit of time. The power of the order zero is its own simultaneous measure : it generates nothing, and therefore has *no successive* measure; but every derivative or generated power other than zero has always a successive and a simultaneous measure, with a difference dependent upon the rate of increase of the power under generation, and to be determined according to the number (in quantity and quality) of the generating powers, whose unit of operation is performed (unit of intension produced) in the semiunit of time, and (extension) measured in the entire unit of time.

65. Assume now the primitive power of the third order ϕ''' : Subjected to the law of uniformity in action, the primitive power of the third order will generate in the time $1'_t$ an amount of power of the second order such as will generate in the time $1''_t$ twice the amount of power of the first order that it did generate in the time $1'_t$ during its own generation; that is, ϕ''' will generate $2\phi''$ uniformly in $1'_t$, which requires that $1\phi''$ be generated in $\frac{1}{2}'.1'_t$, and therefore ϕ''' performs one operation in the semiunit of time. Also the generated power of the second order, whose product (power of the first order) is also a generator, will perform one operation in each semiunit of time; but the generated power of the first order generates a non-productor (power zero), and therefore performs but one operation in the unit of time.

1° The primitive power ϕ''' performs one operation in $\frac{1}{2}'.1'_t$ and one in $\frac{1}{2}''.1'_t$, both equal, and amounting to $\phi''_1+\phi''_2 = 2\phi''$, which is the immediate successive measure of ϕ'''.

2° ϕ''_1 performs one operation in $\frac{1}{2}'.1'_t$ and one in $\frac{1}{2}''.1'_t$, and ϕ''_2 performs one in $\frac{1}{2}''.1'_t$, the first and third being each equal to half the second; but by n° 64 the measure of the sum of these operations is equal to their number, which is 3, and therefore we say that the generated or derivative power $2\phi''$ generates the power of the first order $3\phi'$ during the time $1'_t$ of its own generation, or that $3\phi' = 3.1_\lambda$ is the simultaneous measure of $2\phi''$; and we find that $\frac{3}{2}.1_\lambda$ was generated by ϕ''_1 in $\frac{1}{2}''.1'_t$, and $\frac{3}{4}.1_\lambda$ by ϕ''_1 and ϕ''_2 in $\frac{1}{2}'.1'_t$ and $\frac{1}{2}''.1'_t$ respectively.

3° As all the other generated or derivative powers, the power of the first order (the velocity 3.1_λ) is expressed in its own successive measure, since 3 is nothing but the ratio obtained by comparing the distance that the velocity will generate in the unit of time after its generation, to the distance which it did generate in the unit of time during its generation, which last is the linear unit $1_l = 1_t$ the unit of time.

In the unit of time $1'_t$, therefore, the primitive power of the third order ϕ''' generates the power of the second order $2\phi''$; which, during the same time $1'_t$, generates the power of the first order, or velocity 3.1_λ; which, during the same time $1'_t$, generates the power of the order zero, or distance 1_l.

In the second unit of time $1''_t$, the primitive power ϕ''' will generate the same as before; and,

1° The first derivative power $2\phi''$ will generate twice the velocity that it generated in $1'_t$, which will be $2.3.1_\lambda = 6.1_\lambda$:

2° This velocity 6.1_λ, being generated uniformly by $2\phi''$ in the time $1''_t$, will generate half the distance during this time of its own generation that it would generate in the succeeding time $1'''_t$, which will therefore be $\frac{6}{2}.1_l = 3.1_l$; and,

3° The velocity 3.1_λ (second derivative of ϕ'''), generated by $2\phi''$ in $1'_t$, will now generate the distance 3.1_l.

So that at the expiration of the second temporal unit, there will be generated in all the power of the second order $4\phi''$, the velocity 12.1_λ, and the distance 8.1_l; and we see that the power of the second order increases as the double of the time, the velocity increases as the triple square of the time, and the distance as the cube of the time.

66. Consider yet the primitive power of the fourth order :

1° The power of the fourth order ϕ^{iv} generates power of the third order uniformly in time : then, at the expiration of the first temporal unit $1'_t$, the amount of power of the third order generated is such as will generate, in the second temporal unit $1''_t$, twice the amount that it generated in the first unit $1'_t$; and therefore when expressed by the ratio formed by comparing the second effect to the first, the generated power of the third order will be $2\phi'''$.

2^0 Since the power $2\phi'''$ has been generated uniformly in the time $1'_t$, it follows that $1\phi'''$ was generated in the first semiunit of time $\frac{1}{2}'.1'_t$, and $1\phi'''$ in the second semiunit $\frac{1}{2}''.1'_t$; and therefore one complete operation, or unit of action, is performed by the primitive power ϕ^{iv} in a semiunit of time $\frac{1}{2}.1_t$, or two operations in the entire unit of time 1_t; so that the numerical coefficient of $2\phi'''$, the first derivative power of ϕ^{iv}, expresses the number of operations performed by its primitive in the unit of time, this *number* being the ratio obtained by comparing together the *magnitude* of the two effects generated by $2\phi'''$ in $1''_t$ and $1'_t$ as above.

3^0 During the generation of ϕ'''_1 in $\frac{1}{2}'.1'_t$, at the end of which time it has reached its individual growth or unit of magnitude, it also acts as a generator, and generates a certain amount of power of the second order; and during the time $\frac{1}{2}''.1'_t$ it acts as a *constant* generator (being now a full-grown individual unit of power), and generates twice that amount. And during the generation of ϕ'''_2 in $\frac{1}{2}''.1'_t$, this power also acts its part as a generator, and generates an amount of power of the second order equal to that generated by ϕ'''_1 in $\frac{1}{2}'.1'_t$. There are then in all three operations performed by the derivative power $2\phi'''$ in the unit of time $1'_t$, namely, one by ϕ'''_1 in $\frac{1}{2}'.1'_t$, and one by ϕ'''_2 and another by ϕ'''_1 in $\frac{1}{2}''.1'_t$. Now in order to *constitute* this *whole number three* of operations, the unit of operation should be made equal to the linear unit of the scale, so that the sum of the measures of the three (unequal) operations may be subsequently divided into three parts each equal to unity; and thus the *magnitude* of the successive effect (power of the second order) generated by the power $2\phi'''$ in $1'_t$ will be counted equal to the *number* of operations by which it was produced, and we say that $3\phi''$ is the amount of power of the second order generated by the power of the third order $2\phi'''$ during its own generation in the unit of time $1'_t$.

4^0 The power of the second order ϕ''_1, generated by ϕ'''_1 in the time $\frac{1}{2}'.1'_t$, performs one operation in that time, and another in the time $\frac{1}{2}''.1'_t$; and the $2\phi''_2$ generated by ϕ'''_1 and ϕ'''_2 in $\frac{1}{2}''.1'_t$, each perform one operation in the time $\frac{1}{2}''.1'_t$, making in all four operations performed by the derivative power $3\phi''$ in the unit of time $1'_t$; and as these operations consist in the generation of power of the first order, it follows from the preceding deductions that $4\phi'$ is the amount of power of the first order generated by the power of the second order $3\phi''$ during its own generation in the unit of time $1'_t$.

5° The power of the first order $4\phi'$, being of the lowest degree of intension, generates or produces an effect which will be the zero of power, and therefore an absolutely passive quantity, a definition which conforms exactly to that of empty extent, or to distance in space, taken as the measure of the immediate effect of the power of the first order. As is the case with all the other powers, the generated power of the first order $4\phi'$ is expressed by its successive measure, obtained by comparing its effect *after*, with that *during*, its generation; and as this effect (power zero) is a pure dynamical nullity having zero for its successive measure, but yet has a real *existence* as an element of space which is its own simultaneous measure, we take for the effect of $4\phi'$ in the unit of time $1'_t$ during its own generation (its simultaneous measure), the simultaneous measure of the power of the order zero which it has generated in that time; and whatever may be the magnitude of the effect or phenomenon thus produced, it will have a measure in space which can generally be expressed in a linear form, and, since the phenomenon and its measurement are each to be accomplished in the unit of time, that linear measure may conventionally be adopted as the unit of length 1_l, and conveniently made equal to the unit of time 1_t; and we say finally that $1\phi^0 = 1_l$ is the measure of the effect of the power $4\phi'$ in the time $1'_t$ (its simultaneous measure), and is at the same time the ultimate simultaneous measure of the primitive power of the fourth order ϕ^{iv}.

The following tablet exhibits the totality of this deduction :

No. of operations.	Powers generated.
$\frac{1}{2}'.1'_t + \frac{1}{2}''.1'_t$	$= 1'_t$, the time.
ϕ^{iv}	$= 1\phi^{iv}$, the primitive power :
$1\phi''' + 1\phi'''$	$= 2\phi'''$, the first derivative of ϕ^{iv};
$1\phi'' + 2\phi''$	$= 3\phi''$, the second derivative of ϕ^{iv};
$1\phi' + 3\phi'$	$= 4\phi'$, the third derivative of ϕ^{iv};
ϕ^0	$= 1\phi^0 = 1_l$, the simultaneous measure of $4\phi'$, and ultimate simultaneous effect of ϕ^{iv}.

The accents enumerate the intension (which corresponds to the rank or order), and the coefficients the extension of the several powers, which is always the same as the number of their operations in the unit of time*.

In the unit of time $1'_t$, therefore, the power of the fourth order ϕ^{iv} generates the unit of distance $1_\prime$, and the three generating powers $2\phi'''$, $3\phi''$, and $4\phi' = 4.1_\lambda$; which three derivatives, as well as their primitive ϕ^{iv}, will now be constant generators during the immediately succeeding unit of time $1''_t$, and the distance which each of them will generate in that time is yet to be determined.

In the series $2\phi'''$, $3\phi''$, $4\phi'$, generated simultaneously in the time $1'_t$, the coefficient of each power expresses the number of quantities of the simultaneously generated power of the next inferior order that it will generate in the succeeding unit of time

* It may be observed that the entire process of this deduction consists in the evolution of a purely rational formula, enunciated in no. 7 as the law of uniformity of action. The prime generator, being a *unit* of power, is so merely from the condition that it performs *one* operation, or produces *one* effect in the unit of time, wherefore the number 1 is its *simultaneous* measure; but as this primitive unit of power acts uniformly, and its immediate product (first derivative power) is also a generator, the amount of the latter at the expiration of the first unit of time is such as will generate twice the product (operate twice the effect) in the unit of time *after* its generation, that it did generate (operate) in the unit of time *during* its own generation; which result gives the number 2 as the *successive* measure [no. 54] of the primitive power, and fixes the semiunit as the time consumed in the performance of one operation of generation, so long as the product of that generation is itself a generator. On reaching the lowest step, the conversion of the noumenon of the lowest order into the phenomenon, or of the power of the order one into that of the order zero, when of course the last is not a generator, and therefore has no successive measure; we take this phenomenon itself (the ultimate simultaneous effect of the primitive power), as measured in space and time, for unit of operation, and a linear unit made proportional thereto will enchain the series of scalar operations under the law of uniformity of action in space and time, and compel each *successive* measure (generated power) to take its increase, from zero at the commencement, up to the magnitude indicated by its numerical coefficient (which is the same as its rank in the scale of *descent* from the primitive) at the termination, of the unit of time during its generation.

$1''_t$; for example, the quantity of power of the second order ϕ'' generated in $1'_t$ is 3, and 2 is the number of quantities (each $3\phi''$) that the generated power of the third order $2\phi''$ will generate in the time $1''_t$, that is, $2.3\phi''$; and similarly the generated power of the second power $3\phi''$ will generate 3 quantities (each $4\phi'$) of power of the first order in $1''_t$, that is, $3.4\phi'$. The coefficient of each generated power is then rightly the *successive unit measure* of its generator : it expresses at the same time the number of operations that were performed with an *increasing* energy in *its* generation, and the number that it will perform with a *constant* energy as a generator, in the unit of time; and it is always the same number as that which marks its own rank in descent from the primitive generator *inclusive*. Take for example $3\phi''$: the coefficient 3 is the successive unit measure of its generator $2\phi'''$, since the latter will generate $2.3\phi''$ in 1_t; the same coefficient 3 expresses at the same time the number of *increasing* operations concerned in its generation in $1'_t$, and the number of *constant* operations of generation it will perform in $1''_t$; and it is the third in rank of descent from the primitive power ϕ^{iv} inclusive.

Each coefficient in the series $2\phi'''$, $3\phi''$, $4\phi'$, is generated in a unit of time, at such rate that its intension increases from zero, up to the magnitude respectively indicated by the numbers 2, 3, 4, which express the amount of the succeeding constant generations; and therefore to return from the amount of any *constantly* generated power, to that which would be *increasingly* generated in an equal time, we must divide that amount by the coefficient of the generator; and as this coefficient marks the rank of the generator in descent from the primitive power *inclusive*, the precept takes this form : To obtain the *simultaneous* from the *successive* generated power, divide the coefficient of the latter by the number which marks the rank of its power in descent from the primitive power *exclusive*. For example, $3.4\phi'$ is the amount *constantly* generated by $3\phi''$ in $1''_t$, or is the *successive* power generated by $3\phi''$: then to return to the amount *increasingly* generated by $3\phi''$ in $1'_t$, we divide $3.4\phi'$ by the number 3 which marks its rank in descent from the primitive power ϕ^{iv} *exclusive*, and get $4\phi'$ the *simultaneous* power.

Thus the *successive unit measures* (coefficients of the successive) generating powers are always determined by the number which marks their rank in descent from the *independent* primitive power ϕ^{iv} *inclusive;* but the various *simultaneous* generators have their *unit measures* deduced always by means of the number which marks their rank in descent from their *particular* (*dependent* as $2\phi'''$ or $3\phi''$, or *independent* as ϕ^{iv}) primitive power *exclusive;* for we have seen that each generated power above the order zero, after its own generation, acts as a constant generator, and is therefore a *new* primitive, analogous to, but *dependent* for its existence and magnitude upon, the *independent* primitive power.

Ready for action at the beginning of the time $1''_t$, then, we have the hierarchy of powers $1\phi^{iv}$, $2\phi'''$, $3\phi''$ and $4\phi'$, each of which will perform the part of a primitive generator during that interval.

1° The power of the first order $4\phi' = 4.1_\lambda$, generated by $3\phi''$ in $1'_t$, will generate the distance 4.1_t in $1''_t$.

2° The power of the second order $3\phi''$, generated by $2\phi'''$ in $1'_t$, will generate the velocity $3.4.1_\lambda$ in $1''_t$ uniformly; and this velocity will generate half the distance during its own generation, that it will generate during an equal time afterwards, that is, $\frac{3.4}{1.2}.1_t = 6.1_t$.

3° The power of the third order $2\phi'''$, generated by ϕ^{iv} in $1'_t$, will generate the power of the second order $2.3\phi''$ in $1''_t$ uniformly; and this power of the second order will generate in $1''_t$ half the velocity $(2.3.4.1_\lambda)$ that it would generate in $1'''_t$, that is, $\frac{2.3.4}{1.2}.1_\lambda$. This last generator of the first order will generate the distance $\frac{2.3.4}{1.2}.1_t$ in the time $1'''_t$; but as it is the third in rank of descent under the *new* primitive generator $2\phi'''$, it will, by reason that it increases at a rate proportional to that of a growth from 0 to 3 in the unit of time, generate $\frac{1}{3}$ as much during the time of its own generation in $1''_t$, as it would afterwards generate in $1'''_t$, which gives $\frac{2.3.4}{1.2.3}.1_t = 4.1_t$ for the distance generated by $2\phi'''$ in $1''_t$.

4° The primitive power ϕ^{iv} will generate the same as before, to wit, in the time $1''_t$, the distance 1_l, the velocity 4.1_λ, the power of the second order $3\phi''$, and the power of the third order $2\phi'''$.

In all, we find generated by the power of the fourth order ϕ^{iv}, in two units of time $1'_t$ and $1''_t$, the power of the third order $4\phi'''$, the power of the second order $12\phi''$, the power of the first order (velocity) 32.1_λ, and the distance 16.1_l; and we see that the power of the third order increases as the double of the time, the power of the second order increases as the triple square of the time, the power of the first order increases as the quadruple cube of the time, and the distance as the biquadrate of the time*.

To show inductively that this law persists, we have constructed the following table for ten successive units of time, in which the columns under ϕ''' and ϕ'' are obtained, the first, by multiplying $A\phi'''$ by 3, 6 and 2 respectively for power of the second, first and zero*th* order; and the second, by multiplying $A\phi''$ by 4 and by 2 for power of the first and of the zeroth order, the other columns needing no explanation.

---

* Although only incidentally accessary to the significance of our language in relation to the *generation of distance*, it may be proper to give a short exposition of the physical constitution of matter, so far at least as concerns the production of motion. We define a material point (which may stand as the representative of the material unit 1μ, from the reaction of which we conceive motion to be originated by the application of a foreign force) to be merely the centre of a force that is infinite (indefinitely great) in space and time : infinite in quantity and quality, and in duration; emanating in all directions from that centre, and acting uniformly throughout all time. Under the head of quality, it is only necessary here to seek for a force emanating from such centre O [fig 77], and pulling in any direction as OP, which of course is counteracted by an equal force pulling in the opposite direction OP', so that the centre O is held in equilibrium, that is, does not move in any direction. Apply now a foreign force against the centre O, and acting in the direction P'OP : in a very short but sensible interval of time, it will destroy a portion of the force OP', and thereby leave during that time an equal amount of force in the opposite direction OP unequilibrated, which will consequently move the centre O in the direction OP.

An indefinite number of such centres [fig 78] placed in the direction of the applied force, and connected permanently by mutual attraction and repulsion, will transmit the impulsion or pressure from the first to the last, and the whole line will move with the velocity proper to a single centre as in the former case; but were the line of centres (connected as before) placed perpendicular (or even any how inclined) to the direction of the single force applied to the unique centre O [fig. 79] since each additional centre O' is now equilibrated by two equal opposing forces O'p and O'p' parallel to OP, just as is the unique centre O by OP and OP', it would require the application of as many new forces, each equal and parallel to that applied to O, as there are additional centres O', to beget a velocity of the line of centres in its present position, equal to that in its former one, and consequently the single force at O alone would give the system a velocity inversely proportional to the whole number of centres or material points.

Time.	Partial amounts generated by ϕ^{iv}.	ϕ'''.	ϕ''.	ϕ'.			..	Total amounts.
$1_t'$:	$2\phi'''$						..	$2\phi''' = 2.1$
	$3\phi''$						..	$3\phi'' = 3.1^2$
	$4\phi'$						..	$4\phi' = 4.1^3$
	$1\phi^0$						..	$1\phi^0 = 1^4$
$1_t''$:	$2\phi'''$						..	$4\phi''' = 2.2$
	$3\phi''$	$6\phi''$			=	$9\phi''$	..	$12\phi'' = 3.2^2$
	$4\phi'$	$12\phi'$	$12\phi'$		=	$28\phi'$	..	$32\phi' = 4.2^3$
	$1\phi^0$	$4\phi^0$	$6\phi^0$	$4\phi^0$	=	$15\phi^0$	..	$16\phi^0 = 2^4$
$1_t'''$:	$2\phi'''$						..	$6\phi''' = 2.3$
	$3\phi''$	$12\phi''$			=	$15\phi''$	..	$27\phi'' = 3.3^2$
	$4\phi'$	$24\phi'$	$48\phi'$		=	$76\phi'$	..	$108\phi' = 4.3^3$
	$1\phi^0$	$8\phi^0$	$24\phi^0$	$32\phi^0$	=	$65\phi^0$	..	$81\phi^0 = 3^4$
1_t^{iv} :	$2\phi'''$						..	$8\phi''' = 2.4$
	$3\phi''$	$18\phi''$			=	$21\phi''$	..	$48\phi'' = 3.4^2$
	$4\phi'$	$36\phi'$	$108\phi'$		=	$148\phi'$	..	$256\phi' = 4.4^3$
	$1\phi^0$	$12\phi^0$	$54\phi^0$	$108\phi^0$	=	$175\phi^0$	..	$256\phi^0 = 4^4$
1_t^{v} :	$2\phi'''$						..	$10\phi''' = 2.5$
	$3\phi''$	$24\phi''$			=	$27\phi''$	..	$75\phi'' = 3.5^2$
	$4\phi'$	$48\phi'$	$192\phi'$		=	$244\phi'$	..	$500\phi' = 4.5^3$
	$1\phi^0$	$16\phi^0$	$96\phi^0$	$256\phi^0$	=	$369\phi^0$	..	$625\phi^0 = 5^4$
1_t^{vi} :	$2\phi'''$						..	$12\phi''' = 2.6$
	$3\phi''$	$30\phi''$			=	$33\phi''$	..	$108\phi'' = 3.6^2$
	$4\phi'$	$60\phi'$	$300\phi'$		=	$364\phi'$	..	$864\phi' = 4.6^3$
	$1\phi^0$	$20\phi^0$	$150\phi^0$	$500\phi^0$	=	$671\phi^0$	..	$1296\phi^0 = 6^4$
1_t^{vii} :	$2\phi'''$						..	$14\phi''' = 2.7$
	$3\phi''$	$36\phi''$			=	$39\phi''$	..	$147\phi'' = 3.7^2$
	$4\phi'$	$72\phi'$	$432\phi'$		=	$508\phi'$	..	$1372\phi' = 4.7^3$
	$1\phi^0$	$24\phi^0$	$216\phi^0$	$864\phi^0$	=	$1105\phi^0$	..	$2401\phi^0 = 7^4$
1_t^{viii} :	$2\phi'''$						..	$16\phi''' = 2.8$
	$3\phi''$	$42\phi''$			=	$45\phi''$	..	$192\phi'' = 3.8^2$
	$4\phi'$	$84\phi'$	$588\phi'$		=	$676\phi'$	..	$2048\phi' = 4.8^3$
	$1\phi^0$	$28\phi^0$	$294\phi^0$	$1372\phi^0$	=	$1695\phi^0$	..	$4096\phi^0 = 8^4$
1_t^{ix} :	$2\phi'''$						..	$18\phi''' = 2.9$
	$3\phi''$	$48\phi''$			=	$51\phi''$	..	$243\phi'' = 3.8^2$
	$4\phi'$	$96\phi'$	$768\phi'$		=	$868\phi'$	..	$2916\phi' = 4.8^3$
	$1\phi^0$	$32\phi^0$	$384\phi^0$	$2048\phi^0$	=	$2465\phi^0$	..	$6561\phi^0 = 9^4$
1_t^{x} :	$2\phi'''$						..	$20\phi''' = 2.10$
	$3\phi''$	$54\phi''$			=	$57\phi''$	..	$300\phi'' = 3.10^2$
	$4\phi'$	$108\phi'$	$972\phi'$		=	$1084\phi'$	..	$4000\phi' = 4.10^3$
	$1\phi^0$	$36\phi^0$	$486\phi^0$	$2916\phi^0$	=	$3439\phi^0$	..	$10000\phi^0 = 10^4$

67. 1° The primitive power ϕ^{iv}, in the second unit of time $1_t''$, generates the power of the third order $2\phi'''$, which will generate the power of the second order $2.3\phi''$ in the time $1_t'''$, which will generate the power of the first order $2.3.4\phi'$ in the time 1_t^{iv}, which finally will generate the power zero $2.3.4\phi^0$ in the time 1_t^{v}; so that we may write these successive generations thus :

$1\phi^{iv}$, the independent primitive generator :
$1.2\phi'''$, generated in $1_t''$;
$1.2.3\phi''$, generated in $1_t'''$;
$1.2.3.4\phi'$, generated in 1_t^{iv}; and
$1.2.3.4.1\phi^0$, generated in 1_t^{v}.

Now ϕ^{iv} will generate precisely the same subordinate series or hierarchy of powers in $1_t''$, that it did in $1_t'$, namely, $2\phi'''$, $3\phi''$, $4\phi'$ and $1\phi^0$; so that to return from the above-written *successively* generated series, to the one *simultaneously* generated in the unit of time, we must introduce denominators as follows :

$$1\phi^{iv} = 1\phi^{iv};$$
$$\frac{1.2}{1}\phi''' = 2\phi''';$$
$$\frac{1.2.3}{1.2}\phi'' = 3\phi'';$$
$$\frac{1.2.3.4}{1.2.3}\phi' = 4\phi';$$
$$\frac{1.2.3.4.1}{1.2.3.4}\phi^0 = 1\phi^0.$$

2° The power of the third order $2\phi'''$, generated by ϕ^{iv} in $1_t'$, is now also a primitive generator, and will give us the following *successive* series (always including the primitive itself) :

$2\phi'''$, the first dependent primitive generator :
$2.3\phi''$, generated by $2\phi''$ in $1_t''$;
$2.3.4\phi'$, generated by $2.3\phi''$ in $1_t'''$; and
$2.3.4.1\phi^0$, generated by $2.3.4\phi'$ in 1_t^{iv}.

And to return from this to the *simultaneous* series due to the dependent primitive generator $2\phi'''$ in $1_t''$, we apply the precept [p. 91] by introducing denominators as follows :

$$2\phi''' = 2\phi''',$$

$$\frac{2.3}{1}\phi'' = 6\phi'',$$

$$\frac{2.3.4}{1.2}\phi' = 12\phi',$$

$$\frac{2.3.4.1}{1.2.3}\phi^0 = 4\phi^0.$$

3° The power of the second order $3\phi''$, generated by $2\phi'''$ in $1'_t$, is in its turn a primitive generator, and gives the successive series :

$3\phi''$, the second dependent primitive generator :
$3.4\phi'$, generated by $3\phi''$ in $1''_t$; and
$3.4.1\phi^0$, generated by $3.4\phi'$ in $1'''_t$.

Which, by the precept, is converted into the simultaneous series due to the primitive generator $3\phi''$ in $1''_t$, thus :

$$3\phi'' = 3\phi'',$$

$$\frac{3.4}{1}\phi' = 12\phi',$$

$$\frac{3.4.1}{1.2}\phi^0 = 6\phi^0.$$

4° The power of the first order $4\phi'$, generated by $3\phi''$ in $1'_t$, become a primitive generator, gives the two successive terms :

$4\phi'$, the third dependent primitive generator : and
$4.1\phi^0$, generated by $4\phi'$ in $1''_t$.

Which are written simultaneous for $1''_t$ thus :

$$4\phi' = 4\phi',$$

$$\frac{4.1}{1}\phi^0 = 4\phi^0.$$

For convenience of reference, we throw the whole process of the fourth order, for the two first units of time $1'_t$ and $1''_t$ as above given, into the following tablet, and follow up the same by tablets similarly constructed for the third and second orders.

1. TABLET OF THE FOURTH ORDER.

$$\underbrace{1'_t.}\qquad \overbrace{\qquad\qquad\qquad\qquad 1''_t. \qquad\qquad\qquad\qquad}$$

$$1\phi^{iv};\quad \frac{1.2}{1}\phi''',\ \frac{1.2.3}{1.2}\phi'',\ \frac{1.2.3.4}{1.2.3}\phi',\ \frac{1.2.3.4}{1.2.3.4}\phi^0 = 1\phi^0.$$

$$2\phi''';\quad \frac{2.3}{1}\phi'',\ \frac{2.3.4}{1.2}\phi',\ \frac{2.3.4}{1.2.3}\phi^0 = 4\phi^0.$$

$$3\phi'';\quad \frac{3.4}{1}\phi',\ \frac{3.4}{1.2}\phi^0 = 6\phi^0.$$

$$4\phi';\quad 4\phi^0.$$

$$1\phi^0.$$

That is, $(1+4+6+4+1=16=2^4)\phi^0$, the complete production, or final result of the terminated causation of the power of the fourth order during the time 2.1_t, is equal (proportional) to the biquadrate of the time.

2. TABLET OF THE THIRD ORDER.

$$\underbrace{\tfrac{1}{2}'.1'_t+\tfrac{1}{2}''.1'_t= 1'_t.}\qquad \overbrace{\qquad\qquad\qquad 1''_t. \qquad\qquad\qquad}$$

$$1\phi''' \quad = 1\phi''';\quad \frac{1.2}{1}\phi'',\ \frac{1.2.3}{1.2}\phi',\ \frac{1.2.3}{1.2.3}\phi^0 = 1\phi^0.$$

$$1\phi''+1\phi'' = 2\phi'';\quad \frac{2.3}{1}\phi',\ \frac{2.3}{1.2}\phi^0 = 3\phi^0.$$

$$1\phi'+1\phi' = 3\phi';\quad 3\phi^0.$$

$$1\phi^0 \quad = 1\phi^0.$$

Or $(1+3+3+1=8=2^3)\phi^0$ is equal to the cube of the time.

3. TABLET OF THE SECOND ORDER.

$$\underbrace{\tfrac{1}{2}'.1'_t+\tfrac{1}{2}''.1'_t= 1'_t.}\qquad \overbrace{\qquad\quad 1''_t. \qquad\quad}$$

$$1\phi'' \quad = 1\phi'';\quad \frac{1.2}{1}\phi',\ \frac{1.2}{1.2}\phi^0 = 1\phi^0.$$

$$1\phi' + 1\phi' = 2\phi';\quad 2\phi^0.$$

$$1\phi^0 \quad = 1\phi^0.$$

That is, $(1+2+1=4=2^2)\phi^0$, equal to the square of the time.

68. The simultaneous part of the process may be succinctly resumed as follows :

$$
\begin{array}{l}
\phi^{iv}: \\
\frac{1}{2}'.1'_t,\ \frac{1}{2}''.1'_t = 1'_t. \\
1\phi''',\ 1\phi''' = 2\phi'''; \\
1\phi'',\ 2\phi'' = 3\phi''; \\
1\phi',\ 3\phi' = 4\phi'; \\
\phi^0 = 1\phi^0.
\end{array}
$$

A generating power is assumed of a certain order, whose attribute (in common with that of all the subordinate powers until the order zero) it is to generate a new power of the next inferior order in each half unit of time; while each power thus subordinately generated, in its turn, also generates a new power of the order next inferior to its own in each half unit of time, and so on until the order zero : the series of subordinate powers thus generated in the unit of time forms a true *hierarchy*, and may be termed THE SIMULTANEOUS SERIES OF POWERS, namely, $1\phi^{iv}$, $2\phi'''$, $3\phi''$, $4\phi'$ and $1\phi^0$, in contradistinction from THE SUCCESSIVE SERIES $1\phi^{iv}$, $1.2\phi'''$, $1.2.3\phi''$, $1.2.3.4\phi'$ and $1.2.3.4.1\phi^0$.

There are two distinct elements involved in the process, to wit, the operations (of generation), and their measure in space; and these of course are arbitrary, or may be assumed at pleasure. We have chosen the relation between the operations to be that of equality at the outset, and uniformity of action throughout; and the relation of the operations to their measure in space is left to be discovered or assumed at the point of contact between ϕ' and ϕ^0. The law of the operations is defined arbitrarily; but it is the relation between the ultimate or lowest operation and its measure in space that fixes the extent or *height* of the scale, that is, the order of the independent primitive power. Thus if the relation between ϕ' and ϕ^0 is discovered (as in phenomenal or *objective* problems) or assumed (as in rational or *purely subjective* theorems) to be such that the material unit 1_μ shall pass through four distances in the unit of time, each equal to $\phi^0 = 1_l$, this requires that four distinct operations shall be reduced to one [n° 57], so that one single power may be enabled to command the same; which fixes the fourth order ϕ^{iv} to be that of the independent primitive power to be assumed.

69. We have calculated the amount of production yielded by the power of the fourth order ϕ^{iv}, first, in a single unit of time 1_t [p. 87 – 90]; and, secondly, in the two first units of time 2.1_t

[p. 92, 93], which last result is the development of the formula $(1+1)^4$. This calculation has enabled us to proceed by successive units of time, as in the table on page 94, from 2^4 up to 10^4, and may be prolonged to any extent, so as to give the amount of production or ultimate effect of ϕ^{iv} for the time $x1_t$, which we now see in advance will be x^4 when expressed by its ratio only; but the process of successive generation, and subsequent conversion of the series of powers thus generated (the successive series) into the corresponding simultaneous series [n° 67], will achieve the generation of x^4 in one interval of time equal to $x1_t$.

In the series $1\phi^{iv}$, $1.2\phi'''$, $1.2.3\phi''$, $1.2.3.4\phi'$, $1.2.3.4.1\phi^0$, the successive generations are all uniform; that is, the generated quantities all increase uniformly, just as in the case of uniform motion, where the distance described increases uniformly with the time. In any case of uniform causation, therefore, the amount of immediate production increases uniformly with the time; so that what was ϕ^n at the expiration of the time 1_t, becomes $x\phi^n$ at the expiration of the time $x1_t$. Then if the primitive generator ϕ^{iv} generates $1.2\phi'''$ uniformly in the unit of time 1_t, it will generate $1.2x\phi'''$ uniformly in the time $x1_t$; and if $1.2x\phi'''$ be now in its turn a uniform generator, and generate $1.2.3x\phi''$ in the unit of time 1_t, it will generate $1.2.3x^2\phi''$ in a second interval of time $x'1_t$: if, again, $1.2.3x^2\phi''$ be now a uniform generator, and generate $1.2.3.4x^2\phi'$ in the unit of time, it will generate $1.2.3.4x^3\phi'$ in the third interval of time $x'''1_t$; and finally $1.2.3.4x^3\phi'$, become a uniform generator, will generate $1.2.3.4.1x^3\phi^0$ in the unit of time, and $1.2.3.4.1x^4\phi^0$ in the fourth interval $x^{iv}1_t$. So that while our former series expressed the successive generations accomplished in four successive units of time, we may now write a similar series for four successive equal intervals of x units of time, as follows :

0.1_t.	$x'1_t$.	$x''1_t$.	$x'''1_t$.	$x^{iv}1_t$.
$1\phi^{iv}$,	$1.2x\phi'''$,	$1.2.3x^2\phi''$,	$1.2.3.4x^2\phi'$,	$1.2.3.4.1x^4\phi^0$.

By applying denominators to this successive series, as we have heretofore done to the successive series $1\phi^{iv}$, $1.2\phi'''$, etc., we shall convert it into its corresponding simultaneous series, namely,

$$1\phi^{iv},\ \frac{1.2}{1}x\phi''',\ \frac{1.2.3}{1.2}x^2\phi'',\ \frac{1.2.3.4}{1.2.3}x^3\phi',\ \frac{1.2.3.4.1}{1.2.3.4}x^4\phi^0.$$

which is equal to $1\phi^{iv}$, $2x\phi'''$, $3x^2\phi''$, $4x^3\phi'$, $1x^4\phi^0$; in which form it expresses the extension of the series $1\phi^{iv}$, $2\phi'''$, $3\phi''$, $4\phi'$, $1\phi^0$, from one unit of time to an interval of x successive units of time.

Otherwise we might have conducted the explanation thus :

$2x\phi'''$, generated by ϕ^{iv} in $x'1_t$, will generate $2.3x^2\phi''$ in $x''1_t$, and consequently would generate $\frac{1}{2}.2.3x^2\phi''=3x^2\phi''$ in $x'1_t$;

$3x^2\phi''$ will generate $3.4x^3\phi'$ in $x''1_t$, and therefore would generate $\frac{1}{3}.3.4x^3\phi'=4x^3\phi'$ in $x'1_t$;

$4x^3\phi'$ will generate $4.1x^4\phi^0$ in $x''1_t$, and therefore would generate $\frac{1}{4}.4.1x^4\phi^0=x^4\phi^0$ in $x'1_t$.

At the commencement of the generative process, it requires a unit of time to determine the several units of operation, which increase from 0 to 2, to 3, to 4, ..., etc. according to the position or degree of subordination of the generated power below the independent primitive; but from and after the expiration of the first unit of time, all the units of operation are constant, and we can only determine the amount that would be *increasingly* generated by any subordinate generator, by dividing the *constantly* generated amount by 2, 3, 4, etc. according to the rank as above expressed : just as in the case of the action of the force of gravity, we divide the distance 2.1_l that will be generated by the velocity 2.1_λ generated in the unit of time, by 2, to obtain the distance 1_l that would be *increasingly* generated in that same time; for half the velocity generated by gravity during the unit of time, would generate *uniformly* the same distance that was *increasingly* generated by the velocity while it increased from 0 to 2, or was acquiring its unit of magnitude as a generator.

70. Having the simultaneous series ϕ^{iv}, $2x\phi'''$, $3x^2\phi''$, $4x^3\phi'$, $x^4\phi^0$, for a first interval of time $x1_t$, we may, as heretofore with two successive unit intervals $1_t'$ and $1_t''$ has been done, extend the process of generation to a second interval $h1_t$ of time.

1° The independent primitive generator $1\phi^{iv}$ will generate $1.2h\phi'''$ in $h'1_t$, which will generate $1.2.3h^2\phi''$ in $h''1_t$, which will generate $1.2.3.4h^3\phi'$ in $h'''1_t$, which will generate $1.2.3.4.1h^4\phi^0$ in $h^{iv}1_t$; that is, the successive series $1.2h\phi'''$, $1.2.3h^2\phi''$, $1.2.3.4h^3\phi'$, $1.2.3.4.1h^4\phi^0$ in four successive intervals of time each $h1_t$.

2° The first dependent primitive generator $2x\phi'''$ will generate $2.3xh\phi''$ in $h'1_t$, which will generate $2.3.4xh^2\phi'$ in $h''1_t$, which will generate $2.3.4.1xh^3\phi^0$ in $h'''1_t$; that is, the successive series $2.3xh\phi''$, $2.3.4xh^2\phi'$, $2.3.4.1xh^3\phi^0$ in three successive intervals each $h1_t$.

3° The second dependent primitive generator $3x^2\phi''$ will generate $3.4x^2h\phi'$ in $h'1_t$, which will generate $3.4.1x^2h^2\phi^0$ in $h''1_t$; that is, the successive series $3.4x^2h\phi'$, $3.4.1x^2h^2\phi^0$ in two successive intervals of time each $h1_t$.

4° The third dependent primitive generator $4x^3\phi'$ will generate $4.1x^3h\phi^0$ in the time $h1_t$.

In this stage of the deduction, the tablet of operations stands thus:

SIMULTANEOUS.	SUCCESSIVE.			
$x1_t$	$h'1_t$.	$h''1_t$.	$h'''1_t$.	$h^{iv}1_t$.
$1\phi^{iv}$;	$1.2h\phi'''$,	$1.2.3h^2\phi''$,	$1.2.3.4h^3\phi'$,	$1.2.3.4.1h^4\phi^0$.
$2x\phi'''$;	$2.3xh\phi''$,	$2.3.4xh^2\phi'$,	$2.3.4.1xh^3\phi^0$.	
$3x^2\phi''$;	$3.4x^2h\phi'$,	$3.4.1x^2h^2\phi^0$.		
$4x^3\phi'$;	$4.1x^3h\phi^0$.			
$1x^4\phi^0$.				

Now by the introduction of denominators, these several successive series are converted into their corresponding simultaneous ones, and we have the totality of the production of the power of the fourth order ϕ^{iv} for the time $(x+h)1_t$ as follows :

$x1_t$.	$h1_t$.			
$1\phi^{iv}$;	$\frac{1.2}{1}h\phi'''$,	$\frac{1.2.3}{1.2}h^2\phi''$,	$\frac{1.2.3.4}{1.2.3}h^3\phi'$,	$\frac{1.2.3.4}{1.2.3.4}h^4\phi^0=h^4\phi^0$.
$2x\phi'''$;	$\frac{2.3}{1}xh\phi''$,	$\frac{2.3.4}{1.2}xh^2\phi'$,	$\frac{2.3.4}{1.2.3}xh^3\phi^0=4xh^3\phi^0$.	
$3x^2\phi''$;	$\frac{3.4}{1}x^2h\phi''$,	$\frac{3.4}{1.2}x^2h^2\phi^0=6x^2h^2\phi^0$.		
$4x^3\phi'$;	$4x^3h\phi^0$.			
$1x^4\phi^0$.				A′

That is, $(x^4+4x^3h+6x^2h^2+4xh^3+h^4)\phi^0 = (x+h)^4\phi^0$, which is equal to the biquadrate of the time $(x+h)1_t$; and we have not only the ultimate effect, or phenomenon, but also all the intermediate effects, the full hierarchy of generated noumena, to wit :

$(4x^3+12x^2h+12xh^2+4h^3)\phi' = 4(x+h)^3\phi'$, proportional to the cube of the time;
$(3x^2+6xh+3h^2)\phi'' = 3(x+h)^2\phi''$, proportional to the square of the time; and
$(2x+2h)\phi''' = 2(x+h)\phi'''$, proportional to the time.

For the purpose of numerical verification, let $x=5$, $h=4$: then

$$(625+2000+2400+1280+256)\phi^0 = 9^4\phi^0 = 6561\phi^0,$$
$$(500+1200+960+256)\phi' = 4.9^3\phi' = 2916\phi',$$
$$(75+120+)\phi'' = 3.9^2\phi'' = 243\phi'', \text{ and}$$
$$(10+8)\phi''' = 2.9\phi''' = 18\phi''';$$ which may be compared with the table on page 94.

71. Suppose now that we introduce this condition, to wit, that after the expiration of the first interval of time $x1_t$, each then succeeding and subordinate generative action shall be of the opposite quality to that of its immediately preceding and governing one, that is, if ϕ''' generate $-2\phi''$ in $1'_t$, this latter shall generate $(-2)(-3)\phi'=+6\phi'$ in $1''_t$, and therefore $+3\phi'$ in $1'_t$. Then for the first interval $x1_t$, we have as before the simultaneous series $1\phi^{iv}$, $2x\phi'''$, $3x^2\phi''$, $4x^3\phi'$, $1x^4\phi^0$; but for the second interval $h1_t$, the subordinate generations are to be consecutively inverted throughout the scale; so that the requisite modification of the process (conducted by the successive method) will consist in making each generator invert its successor, whence $2x\phi'''$ must generate $2(-3)xh\phi''$ in the time $h'1_t$, which must generate $2(-3)(-4)xh^2\phi'$ in the time $h''1_t$, which must finally generate $2(-3)(-4)(-1)xh^3\phi^0$ in the time $h'''1_t$; and similarly with respect to the two remaining subordinate generators $3x^2\phi''$ and $4x^3\phi'$, as also the independent primitive ϕ^{iv} itself. In this way the several successive series will arise thus :

From $1\phi^{iv}$: $1(-2)h\phi'''$ in $h'1_t$,
$1(-2)(-3)h^2\phi''$ in $h''1_t$,
$1(-2)(-3)(-4)h^3\phi'$ in $h'''1_t$, and
$1(-2)(-3)(-4)(-1)h^4\phi^0$ in $h^{iv}1_t$;
from $2x\phi'''$: $2(-3)xh\phi''$ in $h'1_t$,
$2(-3)(-4)xh^2\phi'$ in $h''1_t$, and
$2(-3)(-4)(-1)xh^3\phi^0$ in $h'''1_t$;
from $3x^2\phi''$: $3(-4)x^2h\phi'$ in $h'1_t$, and
$3(-4)(-1)x^2h^2\phi^0$ in $h''1_t$; and
from $4x^3\phi'$: $4(-1)x^3h\phi^0$ in $h'1_t$.

Accordingly as the number of negative factors in each factorial is odd or even, the factorial itself will be negative or positive, and will consequently retain but one single sign as a prefix; and by introducing denominators as heretofore, the several successive series are rendered simultaneous, and the complete deduction furnishes the following tablet :

$x1_t$. $h1_t$.

$$1\phi^{iv};\quad -\frac{1.2}{1}h\phi''',\ +\frac{1.2.3}{1.2}h^2\phi'',\ -\frac{1.2.3.4}{1.2.3}h^3\phi',\ +\frac{1.2.3.4}{1.2.3.4}h^4\phi^0.$$

$$2x\phi''';\quad -\frac{2.3}{1}xh\phi'',\ +\frac{2.3.4}{1.2}xh^2\phi',\ -\frac{2.3.4}{1.2.3}xh^3\phi^0.$$

$$3x^2\phi'';\quad -\frac{3.4}{1}x^2h\phi',\ +\frac{3.4}{1.2}x^2h^2\phi^0.$$

$$4x^3\phi';\quad -4x^3h\phi^0.$$

$$1x^4\phi^0. \qquad\qquad A''$$

And the results are $(x^4-4x^3h+6x^2h^2-4xh^3+h^4)\phi^0=(x-h)^4\phi^0$;
$(4x^3-12x^2h+12xh^2-4h^3)\phi'=4(x-h)^3\phi'$;
$(3x^2-6xh+3h^2)\phi''=3(x-h)^2\phi''$;
$(2x-2h)\phi'''=2(x-h)\phi'''$.

Here if in the coefficient of ϕ^0 we make $x=h=1$, we get

$$(1-4+6-4+1)\phi^0 = (1-1)^4\phi^0 = 0\phi^0.$$

If we write the last diagonal line of each of the tablets A′ and A″ with the numerators reversed, we have

$$x^4 \pm 4x^3h + \frac{4.3}{1.2}x^2h^2 \pm \frac{4.3.2}{1.2.3}xh^3 + \frac{4.3.2.1}{1.2.3.4}h^4,$$

which is the common form of development of the fourth power of the sum and difference of x and h, obtained by applying the binomial theorem.

For the primitive power of the third order ϕ''', the successive deduction will stand as follows :

$x1_t.$	$h'1_t.$	$h''1_t.$	$h'''1_t.$
$1\phi'''$;	$1(-2)h\phi''$,	$1(-2)(-3)h^2\phi'$,	$1(-2)(-3)(-1)h^3\phi^0$.
$2x\phi''$;	$2(-3)xh\phi'$,	$2(-3)(-1)xh^2\phi^0$.	
$3x^2\phi'$;	$3(-1)x^2h\phi^0$.		
$1x^3\phi^0$.			

Which reverts to the simultaneous form thus :

$x1_t.$	$h1_t.$		
$1\phi'''$;	$-\frac{1.2}{1}h\phi''$,	$+\frac{1.2.3}{1.2}h^2\phi'$,	$-\frac{1.2.3.1}{1.2.3}h^3\phi^0$.
$2x\phi''$;	$-\frac{2.3}{1}xh\phi'$,	$+\frac{2.3.1}{1.2}xh^2\phi^0$.	
$3x^2\phi'$;	$-3x^2h\phi^0$.		
$1x^3\phi^0$.			

That is, $(x^3-3x^2h+3xh^2-h^3)\phi^0 = (x-h)^3\phi^0$,
$(3x^2-6xh+3h^2)\phi' = 3(x-h)^2\phi'$, and
$(2x-2h)\phi'' = 2(x-h)\phi''$.

For the primitive power of the second order ϕ'', we give the simultaneous form at once :

$x1_t.$	$h1_t.$	
$1\phi''$;	$\frac{1(-2)}{1}h\phi'$,	$\frac{1(-2)(-1)}{1.2}h^2\phi^0$.
$2x\phi'$;	$2(-1)xh\phi^0$.	
$1x^2\phi^0$.		

That is, $(x^2-2xh+h^2)\phi^0 = (x-h)^2\phi^0$, and
$(2x-2h)\phi' = 2(x-h)\phi'$.

From the simultaneous series $1\phi^{iv}$, $2x\phi'''$, $3x^2\phi''$, $4x^3\phi'$ and $x^4\phi^0$, we have now deduced two successive forms, namely, $1\phi^{iv}$, $1.2h\phi'''$, $1.2.3h^2\phi''$, $1.2.3.4h^3\phi'$, $1.2.3.4.1h^4\phi^0$, for the time $4h1_t$; and $1\phi^{iv}$, $1(-2)h\phi'''$, $1(-2)(-3)h^2\phi''$, $1(-2)(-3)(-4)h^3\phi'$, $1(-2)(-3)(-4)(-1)h^4\phi^0$, for the time $4(-h)1_t$. Now the coefficients of the several terms of the latter series are

$$\begin{aligned}
1 &= 1,\\
1(-2) &= 1.2(-1) = -1.2,\\
1(-2)(-3) &= 1.2(-1)3(-1) = 1.2.3(-1)^2\\
&\qquad\qquad\qquad = +1.2.3,\\
1(-2)(-3)(-4) &= 1.2(-1)3(-1)4(-1)\\
&= 1.2.3.4(-1)^3 = -1.2.3.4, \text{ and}\\
1(-2)(-3)(-4)(-1) &= 1.2(-1)3(-1)4(-)1(-1)\\
&= 1.2.3.4.1(-1)^4 = +1.2.3.4.1;
\end{aligned}$$

so that to pass from the first series to the second, we must multiply each factor except the first in each factorial by -1, or, which is the same thing, multiply each factorial by such power of -1 as is expressed by the number of its factors minus one. We will then have the second series written thus :

$$1\phi^{iv},\ 1.2(-1)h\phi''',\ 1.2.3(-1)^2h^2\phi'',\ 1.2.3.4(-1)^3h^3\phi', \text{ and }\ 1.2.3.4.1(-1)^4h^4\phi^0; \quad \text{or,}$$

$$1\phi^{iv},\ -1.2h\phi''',\ +1.2.3h^2\phi'',\ -1.2.3.4h^3\phi',\ +1.2.3.4.1h^4\phi^0.$$

This simplifies the notation, but conceals the genesis of the coefficients, which is achieved under the condition that, for the function $(x-h)^n$, each generator, after the first interval of time $x1_t$, must invert its successor; or, if we call each generator an *antecedent*, and its successive and subordinate effect its *consequent*, then, each antecedent shall invert the direction of its consequent, by revolving it through an angle of 180°. So that in order that the ultimate effect produced by ϕ^{iv} in $1_t''$ shall destroy that produced in $1_t'$, we find that, throughout the scale of operations, each antecedent must invert its consequent.

72. The theory here attempted is with us merely the expression of a rational and purely subjective formula, to which, perhaps, in the general case, there corresponds no objective counterpart; although for the case of the second order we have the remarkably

appropriate and fundamental example of the constant force of gravity, which has enabled us to mount from the first to the second step in the scale, and thus inductively to attain finally to the full and complete notion of a perfect hierarchy of powers. The same formula, however, departs somewhat from its purely *spiritual* acceptation, and puts on more of a *physical* character, when expressed as consisting in the conversion of *intension* into *extension*. Without here inquiring into the nature or manner of such physical conversion, of which the fluxion of heat would furnish an apposite example, we may briefly show its numerical analogy with the generation of hierarchical powers.

Given the intension 4, which has the extension 1 : required to reduce this intension gradually to zero, by converting it into extension.

The intension being truly a *unit*, will be properly expressed as 1^4, where the exponent marks the degree of the intension, and may be interpreted as signifying the number of descending steps to be taken in the process of effecting the conversion. Numerically the solution of the problem is achieved by dividing the column headed *intension*, and multiplying the one headed *extension*, successively by 1; interpreting the powers of unity according to n° 18, until reaching the foot of the scale where the intension unity exhausts itself in zero, as follows :

INTENSION.		EXTENSION.
$1^4 = 4$	:	$1^1 = 1,$
$1^3 = 3$	:	$1^2 = 2,$
$1^2 = 2$	:	$1^3 = 3,$
$1^1 = 1$	:	$1^4 = 4,$
$1^0 = 0$	:	$1^0 = 1.$

The last column comprises the coefficients of the simultaneous series of hierarchical powers for the fourth order; and they may be obtained by successive subtraction and subsequent addition from the second column under *intension*, just as the first column under *extension* is obtained from the first under *intension* by successive division and subsequent multiplication.

Hence is shown the development of the dynamical unit 1^4 into the *integral* formula $x^4+4x^3h+6x^2h^2+4xh^3+h^4$, which was a desideratum with the integral calculus [n° 60]; and now to show its complement for the differential calculus, we need do no more than retrace our steps, that is, reconvert our given *extension* into *intension*, by inverting the preceding columns; or, in the scheme of generation, since each generating or antecedent power exhausts itself in its consequent power or effect, conversely we may say that each consequent completely absorbs or destroys its antecedent for the time of its operation; so that when there are given the phenomenon $\phi^0=1$ and its immediate antecedent the noumenon of the first order $4\phi'$, we know, from all the preceding synthesis, that just as the full unit measure 4.1_λ of $4\phi'$ was exhausted in generating its consequent $1\phi^0$, so has $4\phi'$ exhausted (or destroyed) its antecedent generator $3\phi''$, which in its turn has destroyed its antecedent $2\phi'''$, which finally has destroyed the unit antecedent (the independent primitive generator) ϕ^{iv}, in each instance by absorbing the full effort of the generative action during the unit of time. Since the reasoning will be entirely the same, when, instead of $\phi^0=1$ we have $\phi^0=x^4 1$, we now see how to ascend from the multiple phenomenon x^4 to its simple primitive noumenon 1^4, which was the desideratum of the differential calculus [n° 60]; and, further, as the foregoing synthesis has also shown how to determine the ultimate effect of each noumenon in the series $1x^4\phi^0$, $4x^3\phi'$, $3x^2\phi''$, $2x\phi'''$, $1\phi^{iv}$, for the time $\pm h1_t$, we have but to invert the descending order of the lines composing the several tablets for the power of the fourth order on pages 97, 101 and 103, to exhibit the respective developments of $(1+1)^4$ and $(x\pm h)^4$ by this inverse method, which corresponds to that of the binomial theorem of Newton, but arranges the factors in the numerators in the ascending order as they should be.

73. We will now construct a diagram [fig. 80] to show the actual motion of the material unit 1_μ, subjected to the application of the force of the fourth order during two intervals of time each 1_t; that is, the distance generated by the power ϕ^{iv} in the time 2.1_t.

1° The straight lines X′X and Y′Y being perpendicular to each other, and the point O fixed upon as origin, let $OP=PP'=1_l$, and make $P'Q=1.1_l$, $QQ'=4.1_l$, $Q'Q''=6.1_l$, $Q''Q'''=4.1_l$, and $Q'''M'=1.1_l$;

Draw PM and QM respectively equal and parallel to P′Q and and P′P, and divide MQ into four equal parts Mp, pp′ p′p″, p″Q.

2° Draw MQ′, and, from p, draw a parallel to Y′Y, intersecting MQ′ in N;

Draw NQ″, and, from p′, draw a parallel to Y′Y, intersecting NQ″ in N′;

Draw N′Q‴, and, from p″, draw a parallel to Y′Y, intersecting N′Q‴ in N″; and finally draw N″M′.

Place now the material unit 1_μ at the origin O, and let it be simultaneously acted upon by a constant velocity 1_λ in the direction X′X, and by the force of the fourth order ϕ^{iv} in the direction Y′Y. Under this compound action, the mobile 1_μ will describe the arc OM of the curve expressed by the equation $y = x^4$, in the first unit of time $1'_t$; at which point M we have

$$y = \mathrm{PM} = \mathrm{OP} = x = 1.1_l,$$

that is, the distance 1_l generated in the time 1_t. But besides this distance 1_l or $1\phi^0$, there are also generated in the time $1'_t$ the several forces $4\phi'$, $3\phi''$, $2\phi'''$, which, together with the primitive force ϕ^{iv} itself, will all act upon the mobile 1_μ in the direction Y′Y, in conjunction with the velocity 1_λ in the direction X′X, during the second unit of time $1''_t$. Now were all the forces above those of the first order annihilated at the commencement of the time $1''_t$, the material unit 1_μ would move uniformly, by virtue of the forces $4\phi'=4.1_\lambda$ and 1_λ, through the distance MQ in the time $1''_t$, MQ being the diagonal of the parallelogram constructed on $\mathrm{MQ}=1_\lambda$ and $\mathrm{QQ}'=4.1_\lambda$. Here

$$\frac{\mathrm{Q'Q}}{\mathrm{QM}} = \frac{4.1_l}{1.1_l} = 4 = \frac{\sin \mathrm{Q'MQ}}{\cos \mathrm{Q'MQ}} = \tan \mathrm{Q'MQ},$$

and therefore $y' = \tan \mathrm{Q'MQ}.h1_l = 4h1_l$ is the equation of the straight line MQ′, which is in general the geometrical tangent of the curve at any point M; and, also, tan Q′MQ (which in this example is equal to 4) is always equal to the coefficient of the first power of h in the development of $(x+h)^4$, and is the trigonometrical tangent of the angle that the curve makes with the axes at the point M. This tangent line MQ′ is then the direction in which the mobile 1_μ actually *trends* at the instant it leaves the point M; but as the forces $3\phi''$, $2\phi'''$ and ϕ^{iv} are not annihilated at the commencement of the time $1''_t$, but act upon 1_μ conjointly with $4\phi'$ and 1_λ, their united action deflects that mobile from the tangent MQ′, by virtue of the velocities which they respectively generate during $1''_t$. To estimate this deflection, we must endeavor to separate the simultaneous actions of the different forces into successive periods, as indicated by the lines Mp, pp′, etc.

At the beginning of the second unit of time $1''_t$, the velocity 4.1_λ is already generated, and commences its action *immediately* upon the mobile 1_μ; while the several forces $3\phi''$, $2\phi'''$ and ϕ^{iv} can only touch the mobile *mediately*, through the velocity they are to generate from the beginning of and during this second unit of time $1''_t$. Now from $3\phi''$ to ϕ^0 there are two genetic operations, namely, $12\phi'$ and $6\phi^0$ (see tablet on page 97); from $2\phi'''$ to ϕ^0, three genetic operations, $6\phi''$, $12\phi'$ and $4\phi^0$; and from ϕ^{iv} to ϕ^0 there are four genetic operations, $2\phi'''$, $3\phi''$, $4\phi'$ and $1\phi^0$. Let these three systems of genetic operations commence with the time $1''_t$, and let each single operation (amounting to the full effect of that which, under the former and *true* supposition, is accomplished in the entire unit of time $1''_t$) be performed in the time $\frac{1}{4}.1_t$, which is measured by Mp, etc. Under these suppositions,

1° The force $3\phi''$ will generate the velocity 12.1_λ in the time $\frac{1}{4}'.1''_t$, one-half of which velocity (that is, its *simultaneous* measure, p. 92) will generate the distance 6.1_l in the unit of time. Arrived at N at the end of the time $\frac{1}{4}'.1''_t$, by virtue of the velocity 4.1_λ, the mobile 1_μ will receive an accession of velocity equal to 6.1_λ, which, with its former amount, would carry it to Q″ at the end of the time $1''_t$.

2° The force $2\phi'''$ will generate the force $6\phi''$ in $\frac{1}{4}'.1''_t$, which will generate the velocity 12.1_λ in $\frac{1}{4}''.1''_t$, one-third of which velocity (its simultaneous measure) will generate the distance 4.1_l in the unit of time. Arrived at N′ at the end of the time $\frac{1}{4}''.1''_t$, by virtue of the velocities $(4+6)1_\lambda$, the mobile 1_μ will receive an accession of velocity equal to 4.1_λ, which, with its former amount, would now carry it to Q‴ at the end of the time $1''_t$.

3° Finally, always under the same suppositions, the force ϕ^{iv} will generate the force $2\phi'''$ in $\frac{1}{4}'.1''_t$, which will generate the force $3\phi''$ in $\frac{1}{4}''.1_t''$, which will generate the velocity 4.1_λ in $\frac{1}{4}'''.1_t''$, one-fourth of which velocity (its simultaneous measure) will generate the distance 1_l in the unit of time. Arrived at N″ at the end of the time $\frac{1}{4}'''.1_t''$, by virtue of the velocities $(4+6+4)1_\lambda$, the mobile 1_μ will finally receive an accession of velocity equal to 1_λ, which, together with its former amount, will carry it to M′ at the end of the time $1_t''$.

By these operations, the mobile 1_μ will describe the sides MN, NN′, N′N″, N″M′, of a polygon, each in the time $\frac{1}{4}.1_t''$; but this scheme of operations, and its results, though made for the unit of time, would be equally true for any time whatever $h1_t$. We may, in general, then, make OP $= x1_l$ and PP′ $= h1_l$, when we shall have $(x+h)^4 1_l = (x^4+4x^3h+6x^2h^2+4xh^3+h^4)1_l$ in place of P′M′; and by taking h sufficiently small (for instance, if ..... $h = \frac{1}{1000000}.1_l =$ MQ), the points M, p, p′, p″, Q, will approach excessively near to each other, and reduce the sides of the polygon to infinitesimal dimensions, so as finally to merge in the curve which is the true resultant of the system of simultaneous operations here represented successively. But however closely the points M, N, N′, N″, M′, may be approximated, they must never coincide, since they must ultimately mark the positions of the mobile 1_μ at successive points of time; and since the only limitation to this reduction of the distance between M and N is that these two points shall not actually coincide, but shall remain successive positions of the mobile however small the change of position may be, in its last possible minuteness MN must be a straight line (a single step as it were of the mobile 1_μ), and so also NN, N′N″, etc.; and we may say that 1_μ truly moves in the tangent from M to its immediately successive position in N, and in the arc of the circle of curvature from M to its second successive position in N′, since a straight line and a circle can always be described respectively through two and three points.

From this example we may infer the reason for the practice of rejecting the infinitesimals of the second and higher orders, and retaining those of the first order only, from the equation of a curve in which $x+dx$ and $y+dy$ are respectively substituted for x and y, when the rectilinear tangent is the *quæsitum* of the problem. The tangent line is coincident with the direction in which the mobile would proceed with its acquired velocity at the point M, during the next succeeding instant of time, which velocity is the coefficient of the first power of dx in the developed equation of the curve; while the deflection from the tangent is produced by the velocity *to be* generated by the accelerating forces *during* this succeeding instant, and which therefore does not exist at the *beginning* of this instant, and so can not affect the mobile in its very first step from M. The first item of the newly generated velocity is the coefficient of the second power of dx in the development; and that it is not rejected, in the research for the tangent, merely because it may be neglected on account of its smallness, is evident from the fact that it is retained in the research for the circle of curvature. The true reason for its rejection in the former case, is because it has no place in the phenomenon sought, which is that of rectilinear tangence at the point M; and in the latter case, where circular contact is the sought phenomenon, the first step of the deflection produced by the accelerating forces after the mobile has left M, is requisite to complete the number three of points necessary to determine a circle, that is, both the first and second powers of dx must be retained, the third being yet rejected, etc. If the third power of dx were also retained, we should have contact of third order; with the fourth power, contact of the fourth order, and so on.

74. For the sake of convenience in the number of terms to operate with, we have taken a power of the fourth order to exemplify the theory of generation; but the following three rules will serve to find all the terms of the whole process for two equal unit intervals of time, for a power of any order whatever :

1° During the first unit of time, $n\phi^{(m)}$ begets $(n+1)\phi^{(m-1)}$, until the accent reduces to 1, when the last power appears as $1\phi^{0}$.

2° In successive generation, $n\phi^{(m)}$ begets $n(n+1)\phi^{(m-1)}$, until the accent reduces to one, when the last power ϕ^{0} introduces into the factorial no new factor but unity.

3° To return from successive to simultaneous generation, any power is referred to the preceding unit of time by dividing its coefficient by the number which marks its own rank in descent from its primitive generator exclusive.

CHAPTER VI.

THE THEORY OF DESTROYING POWERS.

75. No principle in philosophy is better established than this, namely, that a single (non-creative) unopposed power or force, proceeding continuously in space and time, and having nothing whereon to act, can produce no effect, will engender no phenomenon. Without limitation, no reality : without opposition, no composition : where there is no evil to be encountered, no good can be educed : an eternal fixity of the thermometer would leave impossible all the effects which now result from change of temperature; nay, would ignore the very existence of any such phenomenon as temperature at all.

The evolution of phenomena by the positive power ϕ^{iv}, therefore, requires an encountering or opposing power, such as the reaction offered by the material unit 1_μ in the examples of the preceding chapter; which reaction, we have seen, exhausts or destroys the entire effort of the power ϕ^{iv}, successively during each unit of time, by converting the same into the phenomenon. In this instance, the material unit acts the part of a power of the first order ϕ', capable always of yielding a magnitude of extension proportional to the intension of the agent brought to bear upon it, and thus finally reducing that intension to zero, where the process terminates. But although the power ϕ^0 is a physical or noumenal zero, it is not an absolute zero, but a true phenomenal *existence* [n° 5], in general represented by its measure in space as $x^n.1_l$ or 1_l. Suppose, now, that, having reduced the noumenon $\phi^{(n)}$ to zero, and finding the phenomenon ϕ^0 remaining, we also demand to reduce the phenomenon to zero, or, in other words, to eliminate its measure 1_l, and obtain the pure ratio unity? We call in aid a negative power of the first order $\phi^{-\prime}$, which destroys the phenomenon ϕ^0 in the time $1'_t$, and sets free the pure ratio 1; but this negative power persists in its calling, and generates the negative phenomenon $-\phi^0 = -1_t$ in $1''_t$; so that we must now call on the negative power of the second order $\phi^{-''}$, which in its turn generates $1(-2)\phi'$ in $1''_t$, which in its turn generates $1(-2)(-1)\phi^0$ in $1'''_t$, and consequently $\frac{1}{2}.1(-2)(-1)\phi^0 = +1\phi^0$ in $1''_t$; thereby destroying the negative phenomenon $-\phi^0$ by eliminating its measure 1_t, and leaving free the ratio -1. In its place, the power $\phi^{-''}$ has generated the positive phenomenon $+\phi^0$ in $1''_t$, which must be destroyed by calling in the negative power of the third order $\phi^{-'''}$, which generates $1(-2)\phi''$ in $1''_t$, which will generate $1(-2)(-3)\phi'$ in $1'''_t$, which will generate $1(-2)(-3)(-1)\phi^0$ in 1^{iv}_t; and consequently there is generated $\frac{1}{3}(-2)(-3)(-1)\phi^0$ in $1'''_t$, and $\frac{1}{2}.\frac{1}{3}(-2)(-3)(-1)\phi^0 = -1\phi^0$ in $1''_t$; thereby destroying the positive phenomenon $+1\phi^0$ by eliminating its measure, and freeing the ratio $+1$. The negative phenomenon $-1\phi^0$, generated by $\phi^{-'''}$ in $1''_t$, must be destroyed by bringing in the negative power of the fourth order $1\phi^{-iv}$, which generates $1(-2)\phi'''$ in $1''_t$, which again will generate $1(-2)(-3)\phi''$ in $1'''_t$, which will generate $1(-2)(-3)(-4)\phi'$ in 1^{iv}_t, which will generate $1(-2)(-3)(-4)(-1)\phi^0$ in 1^{v}_t; and consequently there is generated

$$\tfrac{1}{4}.1(-2)(-3)(-4)(-1)\phi^0 \text{ in } 1^{iv}_t,$$
$$\tfrac{1}{3}.\tfrac{1}{4}.1(-2)(-3)(-4)(-1)\phi^0 \text{ in } 1'''_t, \text{ and}$$
$$\tfrac{1}{2}.\tfrac{1}{3}.\tfrac{1}{4}.1(-2)(-3)(-4)(-1)\phi^0 = +1\phi^0 \text{ in } 1''_t;$$

which destroys the negative phenomenon $-\phi^0$ by eliminating its measure 1_t, and frees the ratio -1. The process continues *ad infinitum*, as pointed out by the two following tablets, the first being the successive deduction rendered simultaneous in the second :

$1'_t$.	$1''_t$.	$1'''_t$.	1^{iv}_t.
$1\phi^0$.			
$1\phi^{-'}$;	$-1\phi^0$.		
$1\phi^{-''}$;	$1(-2)\phi'$,	$1(-2)(-1)\phi^0$.	
$1\phi^{-'''}$;	$1(-2)\phi''$,	$1(-2)(-3)\phi'$,	$1(-2)(-3)(-1)\phi^0$.
&c.	&c.		

$$\begin{array}{ll} \underbrace{1'_t.} & \overbrace{\qquad\qquad\qquad 1''_t. \qquad\qquad\qquad} \\ 1\phi^0. & \\ 1\phi^{-\prime}; & 1(-1)\phi^0 = -1\phi^0. \\ 1\phi^{-\prime\prime}; & \frac{1(-2)}{1}\phi', \quad \frac{1(-2)(-1)}{1\,.\,2}\phi^0 = +1\phi^0. \\ 1\phi^{-\prime\prime\prime}; & \frac{1(-2)}{1}\phi'', \quad \frac{1(-2)(-3)}{1\,.\,2}\phi', \quad \frac{1(-2)(-3)(-1)}{1\,.\,2\,.\,3}\phi^0 = -1\phi^0. \\ \&c. & \&c. \end{array}$$

If we gather the coefficients of ϕ^0 from this last tablet, we have $(1-1+1-1+1-\&c.)\phi^0$, which, since the process continues *ad infinitum*, is the development of $(1+1)^{-1}\phi^0$.

By expunging the factors common to the numerator and denominator of the coefficient of each power in the last tablet, and attending to the signs, we have it more conveniently expressed as follows :

$$\begin{array}{lllll} \underbrace{1'_t.} & \overbrace{\qquad\qquad 1''_t. \qquad\qquad} & & & \\ +1\phi^0; & & & & \\ +1\phi', & -1\phi^0; & & & \\ +1\phi'', & -2\phi', & +1\phi^0; & & \\ +1\phi''', & -2\phi'', & +3\phi', & -1\phi^0; & \\ +1\phi^{iv}, & -2\phi''', & +3\phi'', & -4\phi', & +1\phi^0, \quad \&c. \end{array}$$

Now we know from n°s 69 and 70, that in each line of this tablet, the second unit of time $1''_t$ may be extended to $x1_t$, and therefore we may at once write the tablet following :

$$\begin{array}{lllll} \underbrace{1'_t.} & \overbrace{\qquad\qquad x1_t. \qquad\qquad} & & & \\ +1\phi^0. & & & & \\ +1\phi'; & -1x\phi^0. & & & \\ +1\phi''; & -2x\phi', & +1x^2\phi^0. & & \\ +1\phi'''; & -2x\phi'', & +3x^2\phi', & -1x^3\phi^0. & \\ +1\phi^{iv}; & -2x\phi''', & +3x^2\phi'', & -4x^3\phi', & +1x^4\phi^0. \quad \&c. \end{array}$$

Here the coefficient of ϕ^0 gives us $(1-x+x^2-x^3+x^3-\&c.)\phi^0$ $=(1+x)^{-1}\phi^0$ in the time $(1+x)1_t$; and this infinite series has arisen from the attempt to eliminate the measure in space of a phenomenal unit, whereby to obtain the pure rational unit 1. The entire series, indeed, is now a proper ratio, a mere numerical coefficient of ϕ^0; but suppose now that we demand the measure of this ratio? We must regard it as the coefficient of a power of the first order, and find the distance that such power generates during its own generation, its simultaneous measure, as thus :

$$(1-x+x^2-x^3+x^4-\&c.)\phi' = (1_\lambda - x1_\lambda + x^2 1_\lambda - x^3 1_\lambda + x^4 1_\lambda - \&c.,$$

where the first term is a constant velocity; the second term is a velocity generated by a force of the second order; the third, a velocity generated by a force of the third order; the fourth, a velocity generated by a force of the fourth order, etc., each in the time $x1_t$. Therefore during the time of its own generation in $x1_t$, the series of velocities will generate this series of distances :

$$(x-\tfrac{1}{2}x^2+\tfrac{1}{3}x^3-\tfrac{1}{4}x^4+\tfrac{1}{5}x^5-\&c.)1_l = \log(1+x)1_l,$$

that is, *the measure of the ratio* expressed by the proposed series $(1-x+x^2-x^3+x^4-\&c.)$; and if $x = 1$, this measure becomes $(1-\frac{1}{2}+\frac{1}{3}-\frac{1}{4}+\frac{1}{5}-\&c.)1_l$ = the napierian logarithm of 2.

At the commencement of this example, the phenomenon, represented by its measure 1_l, was destroyed by opposing to it a power 1_λ exactly equal to that which generated it; so that *the measure* 1_l was reduced to zero (or eliminated), and the ratio 1 abstracted : this gives zero as the measure of the ratio of equality, or 0 is the logarithm of unity. The supernumerary term 0.1_l was not necessary to be retained in the deduction of the preceding tablets; but when the measure of the ratio of the coefficient of ϕ^0 is sought, the neglected term has its signification, and ought to be restored, whereby we find $(0+x-\frac{1}{2}x^2+\frac{1}{3}x^3-\frac{1}{4}x^4+\&c.)1_l$ $= (\log 1)1_l+(x-\frac{1}{2}x^2+\frac{1}{3}x^3-\frac{1}{4}x^4+\&c.)1_l$ to be the complete expression for $\log(1+x)1_l$. When $a1_\lambda$ instead of 1_λ is opposed to 1.1_l, the ratio 1 is reduced to its ath part $\frac{1}{a}$, and the measure of the ratio expressed by the coefficient of ϕ^0 will be

$$(\log a+\frac{x}{a}-\tfrac{1}{2}\frac{x^2}{a^2}+\tfrac{1}{3}\frac{x^3}{a^3}-\tfrac{1}{4}\frac{x^4}{a^4}+\&c.)1_l = \log(a+x)1_l,$$

as may better appear hereafter.

When, in the preceding chapter, a phenomenon of any assigned degree x^n was required to be *generated*, it was done by assuming, or calling into operation, a power of the proper order $\phi^{(n)}$ competent to produce that particular effect. Here, where a phenomenon, or a succession of phenomena are required to be *destroyed*, as in the example just treated, it is done by always assuming a negative power (a power acting inversely) corresponding to the degree of the particular phenomenon to be destroyed. This method, which is derived from an examination of the operation of division [n° 50], is the first that offers itself in the investigation of the subject of negative generation, and might be further pursued; but by contrasting with the idea of positive generation under a different point of view, a route, more readily accessible, and leading to more extensive results, has been discovered.

76. In positive generation, we calculated the complete series of effects produced in two successive semiunits of time, while the prime generator $\phi^{(n)}$ performed two equal operations. In negative generation, the primitive generator $\phi^{(-n)}$ should also be calculated by its equal operations in two successive semiunits of time; but here the first operation must furnish a positive result, something which may be submitted to destruction or diminution by the second operation. Then in the two first semiunits of time, *let all the simultaneous generations be of the same quality, and all the successive generations be of the opposite quality.*

Generation being the first act, and destruction the second, let the first operations, equal in quantity and opposite in quality, be

$$\phi^{-\prime} \ : \ \overset{\frac{1}{2}'.1'_t,}{1} - \overset{\frac{1}{2}''.1'_t.}{1} = 0\phi = \phi^0 = 1;$$ the noumena exhausted, the phenomenon destroyed (its measure 1_t eliminated), and the ratio unity abstracted and preserved of record.

While the prime destroyer $\phi^{(-n)}$ generates the power zero absolute 0ϕ, and abstracts the ratio 1, in the time $1'_t$, it also generates a power of the first negative order, which we in this example suppose to be of the extension -1, and therefore write it $-\phi'$; and continuing the operations, we obtain the following tablet :

$\frac{1}{2}'.1'_t$, $\frac{1}{2}''.1'_t$.

$1 - 1 = 0\phi = 1\phi^0.$
$1 - 2 = -1\phi';$
$1 - 3 = -2\phi'';$
$1 - 4 = -3\phi''';$
$1 - 5 = -4\phi^{iv};$
&c. *ad infinitum.*

Each simultaneous operation is of the same quality, and each successive operation of the opposite quality. For instance, the 1 on the left in the second line generates $+1$ in $\frac{1}{2}'.1'_t$, and -1 in $\frac{1}{2}''.1'_t$; and the -2 on the right generates -2 in $\frac{1}{2}''.1'_t$, making together -3; and the difference $1-3 = -2\phi''$.

We have here a simultaneous series of negative powers, $1\phi^0$, $-\phi'$, $-2\phi''$, $-3\phi'''$, $-4\phi^{iv}$, etc., generated in the first unit of time $1'_t$ by the independent prime destroyer $\phi^{-\prime}$; each of which powers will act the part of a primitive generator during the second unit of time $1''_t$, as in the case of negative generation considered in n° 75, but with this difference : During the time $1''_t$, in the example referred to, as well as in that of n° 71, negative generation was performed by positive powers acting negatively, whereby each intension was gradually reduced to zero, by being converted into a series of increasing negative extensions; while in the present example, on the contrary, each generation is to be performed by a negative power acting positively, so as to reduce negative intension ascendingly to zero, by converting the same into a series of decreasing negative extensions. In both cases the consequent is always rendered opposite in quality to its antecedent, by being inverted in its direction, that is, revolved through an angle of 180°. Therefore, recollecting that positive increase is negative decrease (that the series 1, 2, 3, etc. and -3, -2, -1, etc. are both increasing series), we may, without further explanation, proceed to the following tablet :

$1'_t$.	$1''_t$.		
$+1\phi^0$.			
$-1\phi'$;	$-1\phi^0$.		
$-2\phi''$;	$\frac{(-2)(-1)}{1}\phi'$,	$\frac{(-2)(-1)1}{1\,.\,2}\phi^0 = +1\phi^0$.	
$-3\phi'''$;	$\frac{(-3)(-2)}{1}\phi''$,	$\frac{(-3)(-2)(-1)}{1\,.\,2}\phi'$,	$\frac{(-3)(-2)(-1)1}{1\,.\,2\,.\,3}\phi^0 = -1\phi^0$.
&c.	&c.		

That is, $(1-1+1-1+1-\&c.)\phi^0 = (1+1)^{-1}\phi^0$.

For a second example, we propose to destroy the phenomenon whose measure is of the degree $1^{-2}.1_{\iota}=1.1_{\iota}$; which requires that we assume the prime destroyer $\phi^{-'''}$, which eliminates the measure 1_{ι}, liberates the ratio $1^{-2}=1$, generates the negative power of the first order $-2\phi'$, and sets in operation the entire series of simultaneous and successive generators as follows :

$$\overbrace{\tfrac{1}{2}'.1'_{\iota},\ \tfrac{1}{2}''.1'_{\iota}.}^{1'_{\iota}.}\qquad \overbrace{\qquad\qquad\qquad\qquad}^{1''_{\iota}.}$$

$$1-1=0\phi=1\phi^{0}.$$

$$1-3=-2\phi';\quad (-2)1\phi^{0}=-2\phi^{0}.$$

$$1-4=-3\phi'';\quad \frac{(-3)(-2)}{1}\phi',\quad \frac{(-3)(-2)1}{1\,.\,2}\phi^{0}=+3\phi^{0}.$$

$$1-5=-4\phi''';\quad \frac{(-4)(-3)}{1}\phi'',\quad \frac{(-4)(-3)(-2)}{1\,.\,2}\phi',\quad \frac{(-4)(-3)(-2)1}{1\,.\,2\,.\,3}\phi^{0}=-4\phi^{0}.$$

$$1-6=-5\phi^{\text{iv}};\quad \frac{(-5)(-4)}{1}\phi''',\quad \frac{(-5)(-4)(-3)}{1\,.\,2}\phi'',\quad \frac{(-5)(-4)(-3)(-2)}{1\,.\,2\,.\,3}\phi',$$

$$\frac{(-5)(-4)(-3)(-2)1}{1\,.\,2\,.\,3\,.\,4}\phi^{0}=+5\phi^{0}.$$

&c. &c.

Or $(1-2+3-4+5-\&c.)\phi^{0}=(1+1)^{-2}\phi^{0}$.

We give some more examples of the degree 1^{n}, for different values of n, as follow :

EXAMPLE 3. For the phenomenon $1^{\frac{1}{2}}.1_{\iota} = 1.1_{\iota}$, take the power of the negative order $-\frac{1}{2}$.

$$\overbrace{\tfrac{1}{2}'.1_{\iota}',\ \tfrac{1}{2}''.1_{\iota}'.}^{1_{\iota}'.} \qquad \overbrace{\qquad\qquad\qquad\qquad\qquad\qquad\qquad\qquad}^{1_{\iota}''.}$$

$$1 - 1 = 0\phi = 1\varphi^{0}.$$

$$1 - \tfrac{1}{2} = +\tfrac{1}{2}\phi';\quad (+\tfrac{1}{2})1\phi^{0} = +\tfrac{1}{2}\phi^{0}.$$

$$1 - \tfrac{3}{2} = -\tfrac{1}{2}\phi'';\quad \frac{(-\frac{1}{2})(+\frac{1}{2})}{1}\phi',\quad \frac{(-\frac{1}{2})(+\frac{1}{2})1}{1\ .\ 2}\phi^{0} = -\tfrac{1}{1}\cdot\tfrac{1}{2}(\tfrac{1}{2})^{2}\phi^{0}.$$

$$1 - \tfrac{5}{2} = -\tfrac{3}{2}\phi''';\quad \frac{(-\frac{3}{2})(-\frac{1}{2})}{1}\phi'',\quad \frac{(-\frac{3}{2})(-\frac{1}{2})(+\frac{1}{2})}{1\ .\ 2}\phi',\quad \frac{(-\frac{3}{2})(-\frac{1}{2})(+\frac{1}{2})1}{1\ .\ 2\ .\ 3}\phi^{0} = +\tfrac{1}{1}\cdot\tfrac{1}{2}\cdot\tfrac{3}{3}(\tfrac{1}{2})^{3}\phi^{0}.$$

$$1 - \tfrac{7}{2} = -\tfrac{5}{2}\phi^{\text{iv}};\quad \frac{(-\frac{5}{2})(-\frac{3}{2})}{1}\phi''',\ \frac{(-\frac{5}{2})(-\frac{3}{2})(-\frac{1}{2})}{1\ .\ 2}\phi'',\ \frac{(-\frac{5}{2})(-\frac{3}{2})(-\frac{1}{2})(+\frac{1}{2})}{1\ .\ 2\ .\ 3}\phi',\ \frac{(-\frac{5}{2})(-\frac{3}{2})(-\frac{1}{2})(+\frac{1}{2})1}{1\ .\ 2\ .\ 3\ .\ 4}\phi^{0}$$

$$= -\tfrac{1}{1}\cdot\tfrac{1}{2}\cdot\tfrac{3}{3}\cdot\tfrac{5}{4}(\tfrac{1}{2})^{4}\phi^{0}.$$

&c. &c.

That is, $\{1+\frac{1}{2}-\frac{1}{1}\cdot\frac{1}{2}(\frac{1}{2})^{2}+\frac{1}{1}\cdot\frac{1}{2}\cdot\frac{3}{3}(\frac{1}{2})^{3}-\frac{1}{1}\cdot\frac{1}{2}\cdot\frac{3}{3}\cdot\frac{5}{4}(\frac{1}{2})^{4}+\text{\&c.}\}\phi^{0} = (1+1)^{\frac{1}{2}}\phi^{0} = \sqrt{2}.\phi^{0}.$

EXAMPLE 4. For the phenomenon $1^{-\frac{1}{2}}.1_{\iota} = 1.1_{\iota}$, assume the power of the negative order $-\frac{3}{2}$.

$$\overbrace{\tfrac{1}{2}'.1_{\iota}', \ \tfrac{1}{2}''.1_{\iota}'.}^{1_{\iota}'.} \qquad \overbrace{\qquad\qquad\qquad\qquad\qquad\qquad}^{1_{\iota}''.}$$

$$1 - 1 = 0\phi = 1\phi^0.$$

$$1 - \tfrac{3}{2} = -\tfrac{1}{2}\phi'; \quad (-\tfrac{1}{2})1\phi^0 = -\tfrac{1}{2}\phi^0.$$

$$1 - \tfrac{5}{2} = -\tfrac{3}{2}\phi''; \quad \frac{(-\frac{3}{2})(-\frac{1}{2})}{1}\phi', \quad \frac{(-\frac{3}{2})(-\frac{1}{2})1}{1\,.\,2}\phi^0 = +\tfrac{1}{1}\cdot\tfrac{3}{2}(\tfrac{1}{2})^2\phi^0.$$

$$1 - \tfrac{7}{2} = -\tfrac{5}{2}\phi'''; \quad \frac{(-\frac{5}{2})(-\frac{3}{2})}{1}\phi'', \quad \frac{(-\frac{5}{2})(-\frac{3}{2})(-\frac{1}{2})}{1\,.\,2}\phi', \quad \frac{(-\frac{5}{2})(-\frac{3}{2})(-\frac{1}{2})1}{1\,.\,2\,.\,3}\phi^0 = -\tfrac{1}{1}\cdot\tfrac{3}{2}\cdot\tfrac{5}{3}(\tfrac{1}{2})^3\phi^0.$$

$$1 - \tfrac{9}{2} = -\tfrac{7}{2}\phi^{\text{iv}}; \quad \frac{(-\frac{7}{2})(-\frac{5}{2})}{1}\phi''', \quad \frac{(-\frac{7}{2})(-\frac{5}{2})(-\frac{3}{2})}{1\,.\,2}\phi'', \quad \frac{(-\frac{7}{2})(-\frac{5}{2})(-\frac{3}{2})(-\frac{1}{2})}{1\,.\,2\,.\,3}\phi', \quad \frac{(-\frac{7}{2})(-\frac{5}{2})(-\frac{3}{2})(-\frac{1}{2})1}{1\,.\,2\,.\,3\,.\,4}\phi^0$$

$$= +\tfrac{1}{1}\cdot\tfrac{3}{2}\cdot\tfrac{5}{3}\cdot\tfrac{7}{4}(\tfrac{1}{2})^4\phi^0.$$

&c. &c.

That is, $\{1-\frac{1}{2}+\frac{1}{1}\cdot\frac{3}{2}(\frac{1}{2})^2-\frac{1}{1}\cdot\frac{3}{2}\cdot\frac{5}{3}(\frac{1}{2})^3+\frac{1}{1}\cdot\frac{3}{2}\cdot\frac{5}{3}\cdot\frac{7}{4}(\frac{1}{2})^4-\&c.\}\phi^0 = (1+1)^{-\frac{1}{2}}\phi^0 = \sqrt{\frac{1}{2}}.\phi^0.$

EXAMPLE 3. For the phenomenon whose measure is $1^{\frac{1}{3}}.1_{\iota} = 1.1_{\iota}$, take the negative power $-\frac{2}{3}\phi'$.

$$\overbrace{\tfrac{1}{2}'.1'_{\iota},\ \tfrac{1}{2}''.1'_{\iota}.}^{1'_{\iota}.}\qquad\qquad \overbrace{\qquad\qquad\qquad\qquad\qquad\qquad}^{1''_{\iota}.}$$

$$1 - 1 = 0\phi = 1\phi^0.$$

$$1 - \tfrac{2}{3} = +\tfrac{1}{3}\phi';\quad (+\tfrac{1}{3})1\phi^0 = +\tfrac{1}{3}\phi^0.$$

$$1 - \tfrac{5}{3} = -\tfrac{2}{3}\phi'';\quad \frac{(-\frac{2}{3})(+\frac{1}{3})}{1}\phi',\quad \frac{(-\frac{2}{3})(+\frac{1}{3})1}{1\ .\ 2}\phi^0 = -\tfrac{1}{1}.\tfrac{2}{2}(\tfrac{1}{3})^2\phi^0.$$

$$1 - \tfrac{8}{3} = -\tfrac{5}{3}\phi''';\quad \frac{(-\frac{5}{3})(-\frac{2}{3})}{1}\phi'',\quad \frac{(-\frac{5}{3})(-\frac{2}{3})(+\frac{1}{3})}{1\ .\ 2}\phi',\quad \frac{(-\frac{5}{3})(-\frac{2}{3})(+\frac{1}{3})1}{1\ .\ 2\ .\ 3}\phi^0 = +\tfrac{1}{1}.\tfrac{2}{2}.\tfrac{5}{3}(\tfrac{1}{3})^3\phi^0.$$

$$1 - \tfrac{11}{3} = -\tfrac{8}{3}\phi^{iv};\quad \frac{(-\frac{8}{3})(-\frac{5}{3})}{1}\phi''',\quad \frac{(-\frac{8}{3})(-\frac{5}{3})(-\frac{2}{3})}{1\ .\ 2}\phi'',\quad \frac{(-\frac{8}{3})(-\frac{5}{3})(-\frac{2}{3})(+\frac{1}{3})}{1\ .\ 2\ .\ 3}\phi',\quad \frac{(-\frac{8}{3})(-\frac{5}{3})(-\frac{2}{3})(+\frac{1}{3})1}{1\ .\ 2\ .\ 3\ .\ 4}\phi^0$$

$$= -\tfrac{1}{1}.\tfrac{2}{2}.\tfrac{5}{3}.\tfrac{8}{4}(\tfrac{1}{3})^4\phi^0.$$

&c. &c.

That is, $\{1+\frac{1}{3}-\frac{1}{1}.\frac{2}{2}(\frac{1}{3})^2+\frac{1}{1}.\frac{2}{2}.\frac{5}{3}(\frac{1}{3})^3-\frac{1}{1}.\frac{2}{2}.\frac{5}{3}.\frac{8}{4}(\frac{1}{8})^4+\&c.\}\phi^0 = (1+1)^{\frac{1}{3}}\phi^0 = \sqrt[3]{2}.\phi^0.$

EXAMPLE 4. For the phenomenon $1^{-\frac{1}{3}}.1_{\iota} = 1.1_{\iota}$, assume the negative power of the first order $-\frac{4}{3}\phi'$.

$$\overbrace{\tfrac{1}{2}'.1'_{\iota},\ \tfrac{1}{2}''.1'_{\iota}.}^{1'_{\iota}.} \qquad \overbrace{\qquad\qquad\qquad\qquad\qquad\qquad\qquad\qquad}^{1''_{\iota}.}$$

$$1 - 1 = 0\phi = 1\phi^0.$$

$$1 - \tfrac{4}{3} = -\tfrac{1}{3}\phi'; \quad (-\tfrac{1}{3})1\phi^0 = -\tfrac{1}{3}\phi^0.$$

$$1 - \tfrac{7}{3} = -\tfrac{4}{3}\phi''; \quad \frac{(-\frac{4}{3})(-\frac{1}{3})}{1}\phi', \quad \frac{(-\frac{4}{3})(-\frac{1}{3})1}{1\ .\ 2}\phi^0 = +\tfrac{1}{1}.\tfrac{4}{2}(\tfrac{1}{3})^2\phi^0.$$

$$1 - \tfrac{10}{3} = -\tfrac{7}{3}\phi'''; \quad \frac{(-\frac{7}{3})(-\frac{4}{3})}{1}\phi'', \quad \frac{(-\frac{7}{3})(-\frac{4}{3})(-\frac{1}{3})}{1\ .\ 2}\phi', \quad \frac{(-\frac{7}{3})(-\frac{4}{3})(-\frac{1}{3})1}{1\ .\ 2\ .\ 3}\phi^0 = -\tfrac{1}{1}.\tfrac{4}{2}.\tfrac{7}{3}(\tfrac{1}{3})^3\phi^0.$$

$$1 - \tfrac{13}{3} = -\tfrac{10}{3}\phi^{\text{iv}}; \quad \frac{(-\frac{10}{3})(-\frac{7}{3})}{1}\phi''', \quad \frac{(-\frac{10}{3})(-\frac{7}{3})(-\frac{4}{3})}{1\ .\ 2}\phi'', \quad \frac{(-\frac{10}{3})(-\frac{7}{3})(-\frac{4}{3})(-\frac{1}{3})}{1\ .\ 2\ .\ 3}\phi', \quad \frac{(-\frac{10}{3})(-\frac{7}{3})(-\frac{4}{3})(-\frac{1}{3})1}{1\ .\ 2\ .\ 3\ .\ 4}\phi^0$$

$$= +\tfrac{1}{1}.\tfrac{4}{2}.\tfrac{7}{3}.\tfrac{10}{4}\tfrac{1}{3}()^4\phi^0.$$

&c. &c.

That is, $\{1-\frac{1}{3}+\frac{1}{1}.\frac{4}{2}(\frac{1}{3})^2-\frac{1}{1}.\frac{4}{2}.\frac{7}{3}(\frac{1}{3})^3+\frac{1}{1}.\frac{4}{2}.\frac{7}{3}.\frac{10}{4}(\frac{1}{3})^4-\text{\&c.}\}\phi^0 = (1+1)^{-\frac{1}{3}}\phi^0 = \sqrt[3]{\tfrac{1}{2}}.\phi^0.$

77. The five last preceding examples are given here merely to show the applicability of the method, which is susceptible of further generalization; but it is necessary first to estimate the effect of negative generation, when extended from the unit of time 1_t, to the interval of time $x1_t$.

In the generative series $1\phi^{iv}$, $2x\phi'''$, $3x^2\phi''$, $4x^3\phi'$, $1x^4\phi^0$, of n° 69, the dimensions of x increase with the decrease of the order of the generating powers, the lowest dimension beginning with the highest order of power. In a destructive series, this law will apply in the inverse direction, so that the highest dimension of x shall begin with the lowest order of negative generating power; an increase of negative intensity in a power, and an increase of negative dimension in x, being both counted as a positive decrease. For if a magnitude be unity 1.1_t, its dimension is 1, and division by 1_t reduces it to 1, the dimension 0; a second division by 1_t reduces the latter to $1^{-1}.1_t$, which has the dimension -1; a third division by 1_t reduces the latter to $1^{-2}.1_t$, which has the dimension -2, and so on indefinitely : and if the divisions of 1 be commenced with the divisor $x1_t$ instead of 1_t, we shall get the series of quotients $x^{-1}.1_t$, $x^{-2}.1_t$, $x^{-3}.1_t$, etc., each term of which is one dimension lower than the preceding. Also if the division of 1 by 1_t require the time 1_t for its performance, there will be required the time $x1_t$ to divide 1 by $x1_t$; so that the successive divisions of 1 by $x1_t$ would occupy a series of intervals of time $x'1_t$, $x''1_t$, $x'''1_t$, etc. equal to the number of successive divisions to be performed. Now the series of terms 1.1_t, $\frac{1}{x}.1_t$, $\frac{1}{x^2}.1_t$, $\frac{1}{x^3}.1_t$, etc., instead of being deduced from each other by successive division, may be regarded as severally generated by the corresponding powers in the series $1\phi^0$, $-1\phi'$, $-1\phi''$, $-1\phi'''$, etc. of n° 75 (the negative sign of the indices or accents being transferred to the coefficients), each simultaneously in one interval of time $x1_t$. From the same n° 69 we also learn that when the phenomenon $x^n\phi^0$ is generated in the time $x1_t$, it is accompanied by the simultaneous series of noumena $nx^{n-1}.\phi'$, $(n-1)x^{n-2}.\phi''$, $(n-2)x^{n-3}.\phi'''$, etc.; and therefore when the phenomenon $x^{-n}\phi^0$ is generated, we should have also the simultaneous series of noumena $-nx^{-n-1}.\phi'$, $(-n-1)x^{-n-2}.\phi''$, $(-n-2)x^{-n-3}.\phi'''$, etc. Then when $x^{-1}.\phi^0$ is the generated phenomenon, we must have also the simultaneous series $-1x^{-2}\phi'$, $-2x^{-3}\phi''$, $-3x^{-4}\phi'''$, $-4x^{-5}\phi^{iv}$, etc,; and thus we see the simultaneous series of negative powers $1\phi^0$, $-1\phi'$, $-2\phi''$, $-3\phi'''$, $-4\phi^{iv}$, etc. extended from the time 1_t to the time $x1_t$, as here written :

$$\frac{1}{x}\phi^0, \quad -\frac{1}{x^2}\phi', \quad -\frac{2}{x^3}\phi'', \quad -\frac{3}{x^4}\phi''', \quad -\frac{4}{x^5}\phi^{iv}, \ \&c.$$

With the phenomenon $x^{-2}\phi^0$, we should have also the simultaneous series $-2x^{-3}\phi'$, $-3x^{-4}\phi''$, $-4x^{-5}\phi'''$, etc.; and so on for any value of n in the phenomenon $x^{-n}\phi^0$.

The only positive power in the series $+1x^{-1}\phi^0$, $-1x^{-2}\phi'$, $-2x^{-3}\phi''$, $-3x^{-4}\phi'''$, etc. is of the order zero, and no new genetic operation is made by the primitive power after the first unit $1'_t$ or interval $x1_t$ of time, as is the case in positive generation; but all further operation is in the hands of the negative powers generated in the first unit of time, and which form an unlimited series increasing in negative intension. During the second unit of time, then, each negative power reacts, and resumes the generation of its proper simultaneous series of hierarchical powers terminating in the order zero; the reaction consisting in the reduction of the negative intension conferred on each power by the prime destroyer in the time $1'_t$, by the continual inversion of consequent by their antecedent powers, until the successive steps of the ascending noumena reach the pristine level where each lowest (in order but highest in rank) noumenon merges into its phenomenon, and thus gradually restores the measure of the entire negative genesis. When these several simultaneous series are written as in the tablets of nº 76, each one in the descending direction is of an order one step higher (in rank one step lower) than the preceding, and consequently must occupy one term more in reaching the level of ϕ^0, and so we have finally an infinite series of terms consisting of multiples of ϕ^0, obeying some law predetermined by the original assumption made for the index of the prime destroyer $\phi^{(-n)}$.

As therefore the law of successive generation is the same in negative as in positive genesis, with only the additional attention to the principle of continual inversion, the time $1''_t$ may be extended to $h1_t$, and the tablet of operations for the index $n = -1$ presented as follows :

NEGATIVE DEVELOPMENT OF A BINOMIAL SUM.

$$\overbrace{\qquad x1_t. \qquad}\qquad\qquad\qquad\qquad \overbrace{\qquad\qquad\qquad\qquad h1_t. \qquad\qquad\qquad\qquad}$$

$$+\frac{1}{x^1}\phi^0.$$

$$-\frac{1}{x^2}\phi'; \quad \frac{(-1)1h}{1}\frac{}{x^2}\phi^0=-1\frac{h}{x^2}\phi^0.$$

$$-\frac{2}{x^3}\phi''; \quad \frac{(-2)(-1)h}{1}\frac{}{x^3}\phi', \quad \frac{(-2)(-1)1h^2}{1\ .\ 2}\frac{}{x^3}\phi^0=+1\frac{h^2}{x^3}\phi^0.$$

$$-\frac{3}{x^4}\phi'''; \quad \frac{(-3)(-2)h}{1}\frac{}{x^4}\phi'', \quad \frac{(-3)(-2)(-1)h^2}{1\ .\ 2}\frac{}{x^4}\phi', \quad \frac{(-3)(-2)(-1)1h^3}{1\ .\ 2\ .\ 3}\frac{}{x^4}\phi^0=-1\frac{h^3}{x^4}\phi^0.$$

$$-\frac{4}{x^5}\phi^{\text{iv}}; \quad \frac{(-4)(-3)h}{1}\frac{}{x^5}\phi''', \quad \frac{(-4)(-3)(-2)h^2}{1\ .\ 2}\frac{}{x^5}\phi'', \quad \frac{(-4)(-3)(-2)(-1)h^3}{1\ .\ 2\ .\ 3}\frac{}{x^5}\phi', \quad \frac{(-4)(-3)(-2)(-1)1h^4}{1\ .\ 2\ .\ 3\ .\ 4}\frac{}{x^5}\phi^0=+\frac{h^4}{x^5}\phi^0.$$

&c. &c.

Which is $\left(\frac{1}{x}-\frac{h}{x^2}+\frac{h^2}{x^3}-\frac{h^3}{x^4}+\frac{h^4}{x^5}-\text{\&c.}\right)\phi^0 = (x+h)^{-1}\phi^0.$

78. The principle of the inversion of consequents by their antecedents, first introduced in n° 71, may now be alluded to for the purpose of facilitating its further application.

1° Let each negative genetic operation be regarded as consisting of an act of positive generation combined with revolution through the angle of 180°. In the example referred to, the genesis having been positive during the first interval $1'_t$ or $x1_t$ of time, each new (as well as the independent) primitive generator imprints a unit of semirevolution upon its immediate consequent, which is transmitted consecutively to all the consequents in the series, during the second interval $1''_t$ or $h1_t$ of time. In positive genesis, the inversion could only commence with the second interval of time.

In negative genesis, on the other hand, the inversion commences with the first interval $1'_t$ or $x1_t$ of time; the prime destroyer accompanying its first and only genetic operation with one of revolution through the angle 180°, which runs simultaneously throughout the descending hierarchy, placing all the series of powers in negative position. The reaction commences with the second interval $1''_t$ or $h1_t$ of time, by each new primitive generator transmitting the unit of semirevolution imprinted upon it by the independent primitive, combined with its own genetic operation, to its immediate consequent; whence the revolving operation is prolonged in each series until the lowest negative power in it is destroyed, when the inversion ceases, and the genesis proceeds in the positive form.

2° As a new condition, suppose now that the prime destroyer accompany its first and only genetic operation with an operation of revolution through the angle 360°, which shall govern the whole series of powers generated in the time $1'_t$ or $x1_t$, and place the entire hierarchy in the positive region. During the time $1''_t$ or $h1_t$, then, each new primitive generator will transmit the unit of revolution imprinted upon it by the independent primitive, combined with its own genetic operation, to its immediate consequent; which transmission and consequent revolution will take place consecutively throughout each series, so that all the powers will be affected with the positive sign, and the genesis be conducted entirely in the positive form. Therefore we shall comply with this new condition by multiplying each negative factor in each factorial in the last tablet by -1, to render all the factorials positive. Having done this, we find the following new tablet :

$$\begin{array}{llllll}
\overbrace{x1_t.} & \multicolumn{5}{c}{\overbrace{\qquad\qquad\qquad h1_t. \qquad\qquad\qquad}} \\
+\frac{1}{x}\phi^0. & & & & & \\
+\frac{1}{x^2}\phi'; & \frac{1.1h}{1\,x^2}\phi^0=+\frac{h}{x^2}\phi^0. & & & & \\
+\frac{2}{x^3}\phi''; & \frac{2.1h}{1\,x^3}\phi', & \frac{2.1.1h^2}{1.2\,x^3}\phi^0=+\frac{h^2}{x^3}\phi^0. & & & \\
+\frac{3}{x^4}\phi'''; & \frac{3.2h}{1\,x^4}\phi'', & \frac{3.2.1h^2}{1.2\,x^4}\phi', & \frac{3.2.1.1h^3}{1.2.3\,x^4}\phi^0=+\frac{h^3}{x^4}\phi^0. & & \\
+\frac{4}{x^5}\phi^{iv}; & \frac{4.3h}{1\,x^5}\phi''', & \frac{4.3.2h^2}{1.2\,x^5}\phi'', & \frac{4.3.2.1h^3}{1.2.3\,x^5}\phi', & \frac{4.3.2.1.1h^4}{1.2.3.4\,x^5}\phi^0=+\frac{h^4}{x^5}\phi^0. & \\
\&c. & \&c. & & & &
\end{array}$$

Which is $\left(\frac{1}{x}+\frac{h}{x^2}+\frac{h^2}{x^3}+\frac{h^3}{x^4}+\frac{h^4}{x^5}+\&c.\right)\phi^0 = (x-h)^{-1}\phi^0.$

79. We are now to proceed with the method opened at the commencement of n° 76. This method, which is based on the division of the first unit of time into halves, and combining the two separate operations performed by the prime generator in those intervals, may be so generalized as to give the development of each of the four functions $(x\mp h)^{\mp n}$. At the same time its discussion will serve to throw additional light upon the subject of the conversion of intension into extension, and to explain the phrase *destruction of phenomena.*

In the first semiunit of time $\frac{1}{2}'.1'_t$, then, the immediate operation of the prime destroyer must always be positive : a quantity must be generated, be brought into existence, ere it can be increased or diminished, retained or divided, preserved or destroyed. It is necessary, further, to assume that all the series of subordinate genetic operations performed during the first semiunit of time shall also be positive; but they may be either positive or negative during the second semiunit of time, according to conditions to be fulfilled. We have thus the simultaneous series $1.1_{\iota}=1^{n}.1_{\iota}$, $1\phi'$, $1\phi''$, $1\phi'''$, $1\phi^{iv}$, etc. of powers generated in the time $\frac{1}{2}'.1'_{\iota}$, and forming an ascending hierarchy, ready to combine operations in the time $\frac{1}{2}''.1'_{\iota}$ with the new hierarchy to be generated by the prime destroyer in that time.

In the second semiunit of time $\frac{1}{2}''.1'_{\iota}$, the immediate operation of the prime destroyer must of course be negative, and equal (in linear magnitude) to that performed in the first interval $\frac{1}{2}'.1'_{\iota}$, so as to destroy the same; for this destruction is essential to the success of the method. But the subordinate series of genetic operations put in action by the prime destroyer during this second interval $\frac{1}{2}''.1'_{\iota}$ may be either positive or negative (but all the terms must be of the same quality), and of such primitive intension as shall be imposed, according to conditions to be fulfilled. We shall thus have a simultaneous series $1^{n}.1_{\lambda}=1_{\iota}$, $\pm n\phi'$, $\pm n\phi''$, $\pm n\phi'''$, $\pm n\phi^{iv}$, etc. of powers generated in the time $\frac{1}{2}''.1'_{\iota}$, and forming also an ascending hierarchy, which will combine operations with the simultaneous series of the first interval $\frac{1}{2}'.1'_{\iota}$, and thus beget a new ascending hierarchy, which will be the resultant simultaneous series for the first entire unit of time $1'_{\iota}$.

[We have said that the two immediate operations of the prime destroyer in the intervals $\frac{1}{2}'.1'_{\iota}$ and $\frac{1}{2}''.1'_{\iota}$ must be equal; that is to say, equal in linear magnitude, so as to destroy, reduce to zero, or eliminate the measure 1_{ι} of the given phenomenon (represented here as generated in $\frac{1}{2}'.1'_{\iota}$), and liberate its ratio to the measure of the phenomenon opposed to it (generated in $\frac{1}{2}''.1'_{\iota}$) by the destroyer. The simple demand of the question on page 118 would be : Required to divide 1_{ι} by $1^{2}.1_{\iota}$ that is, 1.1_{ι} by $1^{3}.1_{\iota}$? Now the line 1_{ι} has really no meaning, in the calculus of operations, except as the measure of a phenomenon; and this measure we are asked to eliminate or destroy, by opposing to it an equal measure ($1^{3}.1_{\iota}=1.1_{\iota}$ in linear magnitude). The elimination being performed, we have the ratio $1^{-2} = 1.1_{\iota}\div 1^{3}.1_{\iota}$ abstracted; and we know by the deduction exhibited in n° 77, which is a mere application of the principles of the general theory of generating powers, that the power which generates the phenomenon $1^{-n}.1_{\iota}$, at the same time generates the power of the first order $-n\phi'$.

So that when asked to divide 1_t by $1^2.1_t$, we make the coefficients of the linear unit equal by virtue of the arithmetical property $1=1^n$, and now the proper operation can be performed; but since the ratio is found to be 1^{-2}, and this is the result to be retained, the notation of the process is simplified by taking $1^{-2}.1_t=1_t$ at once for the measure of the given phenomenon, which is to be eliminated by the destroyer, which, in so doing, generates the phenomenon 1.1_t in $\frac{1}{2}'.1'_t$ and the phenomenon of equal measure $1^{-3}.1_t$ in $\frac{1}{2}''.1'_t$, which give the measure 0.1_t and the ratio 1^{-2}, while the accompanying powers of the first order $1\phi'$ and $-3\phi'$ combine into the resultant $-2\phi'$ as seen in the example quoted.]

Let the two series of powers separately generated in the first and second semiunits of time be respectively denominated the *first* and *second* simultaneous series; then,

$$
\begin{aligned}
\tfrac{1}{2}'.1'_t+\tfrac{1}{2}''.1'_t &= 1'_t.\\
1^{-1}.1_t-1^{n-1}.1_t &= 0.1_t \ \&\ 1^n\phi^0.\\
1\phi' +(n-1)\phi' &= +n\phi',\\
1\phi'' +(n-2)\phi'' &= (+n-1)\phi'',\\
1\phi''' +(n-3)\phi''' &= (+n-2)\phi''',\\
1\phi^{iv} +(n-4)\phi^{iv} &= (+n-3)\phi^{iv},\\
\&c. \qquad & \qquad \&c.
\end{aligned}
$$

I. The second simultaneous series being positive, let the *successive* operations of the first simultaneous series be negative: the resultant simultaneous series will give the development of the function $(x+h)^n$.

$$
\begin{aligned}
\tfrac{1}{2}'.1'_t+\tfrac{1}{2}''.1'_t &= 1'_t.\\
1^{-1}.1_t-1^{n-1}.1_t &= 0.1_t \& 1^{-n}\phi^0.\\
1\phi' +(n-1)\phi' &= +n\phi',\\
1\phi'' +n\phi'' &= (+n+1)\phi'',\\
1\phi''' +(n+1)\phi''' &= (+n+2)\phi''',\\
1\phi^{iv} +(n+2)\phi^{iv} &= (+n+3)\phi^{iv},\\
\&c. \qquad & \qquad \&c.
\end{aligned}
$$

II. The second simultaneous series being still positive, let the successive operations of the first simultaneous series be positive: the resultant simultaneous series will give the development of the function $(x-h)^{-n}$.

$$
\begin{aligned}
\tfrac{1}{2}'.1'_t+\tfrac{1}{2}''.1'_t &= 1'_t.\\
1^{-1}.1_t-1^{-n-1}.1_t &= 0.1_t \& 1^n\phi^0.\\
1\phi' -(n+1)\phi' &= -n\phi',\\
1\phi'' -n\phi'' &= (-n+1)\phi'',\\
1\phi''' -(n-1)\phi''' &= (-n+2)\phi''',\\
1\phi^{iv} -(n-2)\phi^{iv} &= (-n+3)\phi^{iv},\\
\&c. \qquad & \qquad \&c.
\end{aligned}
$$

III. The second simultaneous series being negative, let the successive operations of the first simultaneous series be positive: the resultant simultaneous series will give the development of the function $(x-h)^n$.

$\frac{1}{2}'.1'_t+\frac{1}{2}''.1'_t = 1'_t.$
$1^{-1}.1_t-1^{-n-1}.1_t = 0.1_t \& 1^{-n}\phi^0.$
$1\phi' -(n+1)\phi' = -n\phi',$
$1\phi'' -(n+2)\phi'' = (-n-1)\phi'',$
$1\phi''' -(n+3)\phi''' = (-n-2)\phi''',$
$1\phi^{iv} -(n+4)\phi^{iv} = (-n-3)\phi^{iv},$
&c. &c.

IV. The second simultaneous series being yet negative, let the successive operations of the first simultaneous series be negative: the resultant simultaneous series will give the development of the function $(x+h)^{-n}$.

We give an example of each of the above four combinations, for $n = 4$.

The question now takes this more general form : Required to reduce to zero the measure of a unit phenomenon, by opposing to it the phenomenon whose measure is $1\pm^4.1_t$? The phenomena are to be brought in opposition by means of the powers which generate them, and these may be combined according to either one of the four different laws above propounded.

EXAMPLE I. *The second simultaneous series acts positively, and the first negatively, during the time* $\frac{1}{2}''.1'_t$.

Formation of the resultant series in the unit of time.

$(\frac{1}{2}'+\frac{1}{2}'')1'_t = 1'_t.$
$(1^{-1}-1^3)1_t = 0.1_t \& 1^4\phi^0.$
$(1+3)\phi' = 4\phi',$
$(1+2)\phi'' = 3\phi'',$
$(1+1)\phi''' = 2\phi''',$
$(1+0)\phi^{iv} = 1\phi^{iv},$
$(1-1)\phi^{v} = 0\phi^{v},$
et cetera desunt.

We replace the terms $1_t = 1^4 1_t$ by $1.1_t = 1^5.1_t$, when they give

$$1^{-1}.1_t-1^3.1_t = 0,$$

and $1^3.1_t \div 1^{-1}.1_t = 1^4$, and ensure the resultant $4\phi'$ from the combination $(1+3)\phi'$ of the first mediate consequents of the genesis.

Tablet of operations for $(x+h)$ units of time.

$1'_t.$ $\qquad 1''_t.$

$1x^4\phi^0.$

$4x^3\phi';\quad 4.1x^3h\phi^0 = 4x^3h\phi^0.$

$3x^2\phi'';\quad \frac{3.4}{1}x^2h\phi',\quad \frac{3.4.1}{1.2}x^2h^2\phi^0 = 6x^2h^2\phi^0.$

$2x\phi''';\quad \frac{2.3}{1}xh\phi'',\quad \frac{2.3.4}{1.2}xh^2\phi',\quad \frac{2.3.4.1}{1.2.3}xh^3\phi^0 = 4xh^3\phi^0.$

$1\phi^{iv};\quad \frac{1.2}{1}h\phi''',\quad \frac{1.2.3}{1.2}h^2\phi'',\quad \frac{1.2.3.4}{1.2.3}h^3\phi',\quad \frac{1.2.3.4.1}{1.2.3.4}h^4\phi^0 = 1h^4\phi^0.$

That is, $(x^4+4x^3h+6x^2h^2+4xh^3+h^4)\phi^0 = (x+h)^4\phi^0.$

EXAMPLE II. *The second simultaneous series acts positively, and the first also positively, during the time* $\frac{1}{2}''.1'_t$.

Formation of the resultant series in the unit of time.

$(\frac{1}{2}'+\frac{1}{2}'')1'_t = 1'_t.$
$(1^{-1}-1^3)1_t = 0.1_t \& 1^{-4}\phi^0.$
$(1+3\phi\phi' = 4\phi',$
$(1+4)\phi'' = 5\phi'',$
$(1+5)\phi''' = 6\phi''',$
$(1+6)\phi^{iv} = 7\phi^{iv},$
et cetera.

We replace the terms $1_t = 1^4.1_t$ by $1.1_t = 1^5.1_t$, when they give $1^{-1}.1_t - 1^3.1_t = 0$, and $1^3.1_t \div 1^{-1}.1_t = 1^4$, or as well $1^{-1}.1_t \div 1^3.1_t = 1^{-4}$, and ensure the resultant $4\phi'$ from the combination $(1+3)\phi'$ of the first mediate consequents.

Tablet of operations for $(x-h)$ units of time.

$x1_t$ ... $h1_t$.

$$+\frac{1}{x^4}\phi^0.$$

$$+\frac{1}{x^5}\phi'; \quad \frac{4.1h}{1\ x^5}\phi^0 = +4\frac{h}{x^5}\phi^0.$$

$$+\frac{5}{x^6}\phi''; \quad \frac{5.4h}{1\ x^6}\phi', \quad \frac{5.4.1h^2}{1.2\ x^6}\phi^0 = +10\frac{h^2}{x^6}\phi^0.$$

$$+\frac{6}{x^7}\phi'''; \quad \frac{6.5h}{1\ x^7}\phi'', \quad \frac{6.5.4h^2}{1.2\ x^7}\phi', \quad \frac{6.5.4.1h^3}{1.2.3\ x^7}\phi^0 = +20\frac{h^3}{x^7}\phi^0. \quad \&c.$$

That is, $(x^{-4}+4x^{-5}h+10x^{-6}h^2+20x^{-7}h^3+\&c.)\phi^0=(x-h)^{-4}\phi^0.$

EXAMPLE III. *The second simultaneous series acts negatively, and the second positively, during the time* $\frac{1}{2}''.1_t$.

Formation of the resultant series in the unit of time.

$(\frac{1}{2}'+\frac{1}{2}'')1'_t = 1'_t.$
$(1^{-1}-1^{-5})1_t = 0.1_t \& 1^4\phi^0.$
$(1-5)\phi' = -4\phi',$
$(1-4)\phi'' = -3\phi'',$
$(1-3)\phi''' = -2\phi''',$
$(1-2)\phi^{iv} = -1\phi^{iv},$
$(1-1)\phi^{v} = 0\phi^{v},$
et cetera desunt.

We replace the terms $1_t = 1^4.1_t$ by $1.1_t = 1^5.1_t$, when they give $1.1_t - 1^5.1_t = 0$, and $1^5.1_t \div 1.1_t = 1^4$, or as well $1^{-1}.1_t \div 1^{-5}.1_t = 1^4$, and ensure the resultant $-4\phi'$ from the combination $(1-5)\phi'$ of the first mediate consequents.

Tablet of operations for $(x-h)$ units of time.

$$\overbrace{x1_t.}\qquad\qquad\qquad\qquad h1_t.$$

$$+1x^4\phi^0.$$

$$-4x^3\phi';\quad \frac{(-4)1}{1}x^3h\phi^0 = -4x^3h\phi^0.$$

$$-3x^2\phi'';\quad \frac{(-3)(-4)}{1}x^2h\phi',\quad \frac{(-3)(-4)1}{1\,.\,2}x^2h^2\phi^0 = +6x^2h^2\phi^0.$$

$$-2x\phi''';\quad \frac{(-2)(-3)}{1}xh\phi'',\quad \frac{(-2)(-3)(-4)}{1\,.\,2}xh^2\phi',\quad \frac{(-2)(-3)(-4)1}{1\,.\,2\,.\,3}xh^3\phi^0 = -4xh^3\phi^0.$$

$$-1\phi^{iv};\quad \frac{(-1)(-2)}{1}h\phi''',\quad \frac{(-1)(-2)(-3)}{1\,.\,2}h^2\phi'',\quad \frac{(-1)(-2)(-3)(-4)}{1\,.\,2\,.\,3}h^3\phi',\quad \frac{(-1)(-2)(-3)(-4)1}{1\,.\,2\,.\,3\,.\,4}h^4\phi^0 = +1\phi^0.$$

That is, $(x^4-4x^3h+6x^2h^2-4xh^3+h^4)\phi^0 = (x-h)^4\phi^0.$

[I give here three outline forms of the second combination :

1. Outline of operations when $x=h=1$, and $n=1$.

$$1-1=1\phi^0.$$
$$1+0=1\phi'; \quad 1\phi^0.$$
$$1+1=2\phi''; \quad \frac{2.1}{1}\phi', \quad \frac{2.1.1}{1.2}\phi^0=1\phi^0.$$
$$1+2=3\phi'''; \quad \frac{3.2}{1}\phi'', \quad \frac{3.2.1}{1.2}\phi', \quad \frac{3.2.1.1}{1.2.3}\phi^0=1\phi^0, \text{ \&c.}$$

Or $(1+1+1+1+\&c.)\phi^0=(1-1)^{-1}\phi^0$, the series of units.

2. The same, for $n = 2$.

$$1-1=1\phi^0.$$
$$1+1=2\phi'; \quad 2\phi^0.$$
$$1+2=3\phi''; \quad \frac{3.2}{1}\phi', \quad \frac{3.2.1}{1.2}\phi^0=3\phi^0.$$
$$1+3=4\phi'''; \quad \frac{4.3}{1}\phi'', \quad \frac{4.3.2}{1.2}\phi', \quad \frac{4.3.2.1}{1.2.3}\phi^0=4\phi^0, \text{ \&c.}$$

Or $(1+2+3+4+\&c.)\phi^0=(1-1)^{-2}\phi^0$, the natural numbers.

3. The same, for $n = 3$.

$$1-1=1\phi^0.$$
$$1+2=3\phi'; \quad 3\phi^0.$$
$$1+3=4\phi''; \quad \frac{4.3}{1}\phi', \quad \frac{4.3.1}{1.2}\phi^0=6\phi^0.$$
$$1+4=5\phi'''; \quad \frac{5.4}{1}\phi'', \quad \frac{5.4.3}{1.2}\phi', \quad \frac{5.4.3.1}{1.2.3}\phi^0=10\phi^0, \text{\&c.}$$

Or $(1+3+6+10+\&c.)\phi^0=(1-1)^{-3}\phi^0$, the triangular numbers.]

EXAMPLE IV. *The second simultaneous series acts negatively, and the first also negatively, during the time* $\frac{1}{2}''.1'_t$.

Formation of the resultant series in the unit of time.

$$(\tfrac{1}{2}'+\tfrac{1}{2}'')1'_t = 1'_t.$$
$$(1^{-1}-1^{-5})1_t = 0.1_t \& 1^{-4}\phi^0.$$
$$(1-5)\phi' = -4\phi',$$
$$(1-6)\phi'' = -5\phi'',$$
$$(1-7)\phi''' = -6\phi''',$$
$$(1-8)\phi^{iv} = -7\phi^{iv},$$

et cetera.

We replace the terms $1_t = 1^4.1_t$ by $1.1_t = 1^5.1_t$, when they give

$$1.1_t - 1^5.1_t = 0,$$

and $1^5.1_t \div 1.1_t = 1^4$, or as well $1^{-5}.1_t \div 1^{-1}.1_t = 1^{-4}$, and ensure the resultant $-4\phi'$ from the combination $(1-5)\phi'$ of the first mediate consequents.

Tablet of operations for $(x+h)$ units of time.

$$\underbrace{x1_t.}\qquad\qquad\qquad\qquad \underbrace{h1_t.}$$

$$+\frac{1}{x^4}\phi^0.$$

$$-\frac{4}{x^5}\phi'; \quad \frac{(-4)1h}{1x^6}\phi^0=-4\frac{h}{x^5}\phi^0.$$

$$-\frac{5}{x^6}\phi''; \quad \frac{(-5)(-4)h}{1x^6}\phi', \quad \frac{(-5)(-4)1h^2}{1\,.\,2x^6}\phi^0=+10\frac{h^2}{x^6}\phi^0.$$

$$-\frac{6}{x^7}\phi'''; \quad \frac{(-6)(-5)h}{1x^7}\phi'', \quad \frac{(-6)(-5)(-4)h^2}{1\,.\,2x^7}\phi', \quad \frac{(-6)(-5)(-4)1h^3}{1\,.\,2\,.\,3x^7}\phi^0=-20\frac{h^3}{x^7}\phi^0.$$

$$-\frac{7}{x^8}\phi^{\mathrm{iv}}; \quad \frac{(-7)(-6)h}{1x^8}\phi''', \quad \frac{(-7)(-6)(-5)h^2}{1\,.\,2x^8}\phi'', \quad \frac{(-7)(-6)(-5)(-4)h^3}{1\,.\,2\,.\,3x^8}\phi', \quad \frac{(-7)(-6)(-5)(-4)1h^4}{1\,.\,2\,.\,3\,.\,4x^8}\phi^0=+35\frac{h^4}{x^8}\phi^0.$$

&c. &c.

That is, $(x^{-4}-4x^{-5}h+10x^{-6}h^2-20x^{-7}h^3+35x^{-8}h^4-\&c.)\phi^0 = (x+h)^{-4}\phi^0.$

80. The proof of the correctness of the result of the operation of division is contained in the fact that the product of the divisor and quotient must be equal to the dividend. Now no multiplication can be performed unless one at least of the factors contain the linear unit, or unit measure of operation : then if the quotient be an abstract ratio, the divisor must contain the linear measure, and therefore must always represent the result or measure of an operation, or the measure of a phenomenon. If then a unit be proposed for division, it must in the first place be linear, or represent a magnitude that can be divided; and it must also possess a ratio as coefficient, to signify that it is the measure of a phenomenon. Thus having to divide 1_l by $1^n.1_l$, we supply a coefficient to the linear dividend by multiplying both it and the divisor by some power of 1, when the operation commences by assuming for the quotient such number or ratio as, when the divisor is multiplied by it, will produce a phenomenon whose measure will be exactly equal to the dividend; so that, for instance, if the phenomenon measured by the dividend consist in the transport of the material unit 1_μ through the distance 1_l in the time 1_t, in a direction which, being primitive, may be termed positive, then the product of the quotient and divisor must effect the return of the mobile 1_μ in the negative or opposite direction, to its point of departure, also in a unit of time; that is, must annul or destroy the phenomenon of which the dividend is the measure, by reducing that measure to zero. Thus the linear unit is eliminated from the dividend and divisor, and the ratio is abstracted and placed of record in the quotient.

81. The few examples given in n° 79 are sufficient to show the generality and simplicity of the method of negative generation, which serves for the development of the function $(x\pm h)^n$ for all values whatever of n, positive or negative, whole or fractional.

Referring to those examples (in which $n = 4$, and is positive or negative), 1° the first form of combination gives the development of $(x+h)^4$, by a process equivalent to that of dividing $(x+h)^5$ by $x+h$. Suppose we are required to divide the quantity $1^4.1_l$ by 1_l; which requisition we generalize into that of employing the second quantity as the measure of an opposing operation which shall reduce the first quantity to zero (because the divisor must be made to destroy the dividend)? We affect the magnitude 1_ι with a *rational* coefficient, by multiplying both quantities by the ratio unity, and have

$1^5.1_\iota - 1.1_\iota = 0.$ Then if we divide 1^5 successively by unity, and
$1^4 = 4,$ interpret the results according to n° 19, we get
$1^3 = 3,$ the coefficients of a simultaneous series of po-
$1^2 = 2,$ wers of the fourth order, but arranged in the
$1^1 = 1,$ inverse order from that of the corresponding
$1^0 = 0.$ series of n° 68, in which the terms were such as may be obtained from the gradual reduction of the primitive intension 4 [n° 62], while here they arise from a similar reduction of the dimension of the primitive unit 1^4 coefficient of the measure of the phenomenon generated by that same intension 4.

2° The second form of combination gives the development of $(x-h)^{-4}$, or the division of unity by $(x-h)^4$. To divide 1_ι by $1^4.1_\iota$, we multiply by 1 as before, and now are to have

$1.1_\iota - 1^5.1_\iota = 0$, and also $1.1_\iota \div 1^5.1_\iota = 1^{-4}$. Then dividing succes-
$1^{-4} = -4,$ sively by unity, we get the coefficients of a
$1^{-5} = -5,$ negative simultaneous series. The dimension
$1^{-6} = -6,$ -4 of the primitive unit 1^{-4} follows the same
&c. = &c. law of reduction as the dimension of the primitive unit in the preceding case, and therefore the series of powers will be arranged in the same inverse order; but if they are conditioned to act *inversely* after their generation [n° 71], their sign will change from negative to positive as they stand in the second example.

In the first example, the primitive intension, which was developed into the phenomenon $1^4.1_\iota$, was of the degree 4, and was always gradually reduced to zero under each dependent simultaneous series of powers. In the present example, the primitive intension of 1_ι was made equal to unity (for $1.1_\iota = 1_\lambda$, a power of the first order); and, therefore, the intension being here similarly reduced by successive division, must yet be always gradually reduced to zero under each dependent simultaneous series.

3° The third form of combination gives the development of $(x-h)^4$, by a process equivalent to the division of $(x-h)^5$ by $x-h$. We divide $1^4.1_\iota$ by 1_ι just as in the first example, and get the same series 4, 3, 2, 1, of coefficients of a simultaneous series of powers of the fourth order, arranged in the same inverse order; but if these powers are conditioned to operate negatively after their generation [n° 71], they will change sign from positive to negative as they stand in the third example.

4° The fourth form of combination gives the development of $(x+h)^{-4}$, or the division of unity by $(x+h)^4$. We divide 1_t by $1^4.1_t$ as in the second example, and get the same coefficients -4, -5, -6, etc. of a simultaneous series of negative powers; and if these powers are conditioned to act *directly* after their generation, their sign will remain negative as they stand in the fourth example.

82. The rules for the employment of the combination series may be indicated as follows :

1° When a function x^n is to be developed by negative generation, then, accordingly as n is positive or negative, $+n$ or $-n$ will be the coefficient of the first term of the resultant simultaneous series; which resultant series is to be formed in each case by the genetic operations of the second simultaneous series, all of the same quality as its own first term, during the time $\frac{1}{2}''.1'_t$, combined in both cases with the negative genetic operations of the first simultaneous series during that time, with the addition of the always positive genetic operations of this series during the time $\frac{1}{2}'.1'_t$; provided, in both cases, the development is to be prolonged for a positive time $h1_t$.

2° But if the development is to be prolonged for a negative time $-h1_t$, the coefficient n must have its sign changed in each case; and the genetic operations of the second simultaneous series during the time $\frac{1}{2}''.1'_t$, always of the same sign with that of the governing coefficient n of the resultant series, must in both cases be combined with the positive genetic operations of the first simultaneous series during that time, added to the positive genetic operations of this series during the time $\frac{1}{2}'.1'_t$ as before.

3° For positive fractional values of n, the sign of the genetic operations of the second simultaneous series changes from positive to negative, by passing over the zero which would be encountered if the denominator of n were unity; so that this transition occurs in the first term of the series when the numerator of the fraction n is unity, and beyond that term when the numerator exceeds unity.

4° The exponents of x decrease from n by unity, and those of h increase from 0 by unity.

5° The factorials in the numerators of the coefficients of the powers generated by the resultant series tend by unit steps towards n, and terminate in that number with the several powers of the first order, with always the introduction of the factor unity in the power zero [n° 74].

6° The factors in the denominators of the coefficients, similarly as in positive generation, increase from 1 by unity, being always one less in number than the factors of the corresponding numerator.

83. The two methods of positive and negative generation may be instructively compared by means of their different relations to unity.

When the symbol 1 of simple unity is placed before us, instead of regarding it as the representative of a mere magnitude or inert existence from which nothing further can be educed, we may view it as the coefficient of a single living and producing energy, which, in harmony with the numerical property $1=1^n$, and under the law of uniformity of action, shall, in the unit of time, beget the phenomenon whose degree of multiplicity is n. This view resolves itself into the method of direct or positive generation, as shown in the preceding chapter, which convenes only to the case of positive values for n, and leaves unexplored the genesis of negative exponents.

But when unity is given us under the form 1^n, we regard it as the coefficient of a multiple phenomenon, and, the theory of positive generation being now understood, we know the power of the first order by which it was immediately produced; whence, by a process analogous to that in n° 56, and which is conducted by a different method in n° 78, we ascend gradually to the simple origin of the multiple phenomenon; so that now the mere appearance of the phenomenon ($1^4.1_l$ for instance) reveals, by the exponent which expresses its degree of multiplicity, the existence of the entire hierarchy of powers ($4\phi'$, $3\phi''$, $2\phi'''$, $1\phi^{iv}$) which concurred in its genesis. The multiplicity of the phenomenon, which is in general of the degree n, reduces gradually through $n-1$, $n-2$, ..., to $n-(n-1)=1$ the undecomposable unit; and the corresponding series of analized powers of unity, for $n=4$, would be $1^4=1^1\times1^3$, $1^3=1^1\times1^2$, $1^2=1^1\times1^1$, $1^1=1$ or simple unity.

But if unity be given in the form 1^{-n} : even if $n=1$, the unit is not simple; for it is equal to $1^0\times1^{-1}$, or to $1^1\times1^{-2}$, where the second factor $1^{-2}=1^1\times1^{-3}$, which again gives $1^{-3}=1^1\times1^{-4}$, and so on to infinity, and never arriving at simple unity. Then by analogy with the preceding case, we may say that the appearance of the phenomenon $1^{-4}.1_l$ reveals, by the endless multiplicity involved in its exponent, the existence of the infinite hierarchy of negative powers $-1\phi'$, $-2\phi''$, $-3\phi'''$, $-4\phi^{iv}$, etc. which concurred in its genesis.

84. We must now inquire into the movements of the material unit 1_μ, so far as may serve to elucidate the construction of the two different kinds of factorials, positive and negative, which compose the numerators of the coefficients of the several powers generated in the second unit of time $1''_t$: premising that since the noumena are not developable in space and time (See KANT *passim*), all their measures are fictitious (unpossessed of linear extent), and correspond to the physical condition of intension unconverted into extension; so that none but the powers zero ϕ^0 can appear by measure upon the diagram.

First referring to the effect produced on 1_μ by the positive force of the fourth order in the unit of time, as shown in n° 73, we find the distance 1_l, and the several forces $2\phi'''$, $3\phi'$ and $4\phi'$, generated in the time $1'_t$; and that with the commencement of the time $1''_t$, the mobile 1_μ receives successively the accessions of velocity 4.1_λ, 6.1_λ, 4.1_λ, 1.1_λ all positive, and which, when the accessions succeed each other instantaneously, carry it through the distance 15.1_l in the time $1''_t$; but if these several accessions are received after successive units of time, the mobile 1_μ will describe the distances 4.1_l in $1''_t$, 6.1_l in $1'''_t$, 4.1_l in 1^{iv}_t, and 1_l in 1^{v}_t, by the action of each successive velocity alone. Here the order in time in which the several forces succeed each other in their action on 1_μ, is $4\phi'$, $3\phi''$, $2\phi'''$, $1\phi^{iv}$, and is actually the same as that in which they are obtained by negative genesis in the first example of n° 79.

1° We may, then, under the fiction of successivity in action, envisage the several factorials of the first form of development as follows :

$4\phi'$ carries 1_μ the distance 4.1_l in $1_t''$;

$3\phi''$ generates $3.4\phi'$ in $1_t''$, and $\frac{1}{2}.3.4\phi'=6\phi'$ will carry 1_μ the distance 6.1_l in $1_t'''$;

$2\phi'''$ generates $2.3\phi''$ in $1_t''$, which generates $2.3.4\phi'$ in $1_t'''$, and $\frac{1}{2}.\frac{1}{3}.2.3.4\phi'=4\phi'$ will carry 1_μ the distance 4.1_l in 1_t^{iv};

$1\phi^{iv}$ generates $1.2\phi''$ in $1_t''$, which generates $1.2.3\phi''$ in $1_t'''$, which generates $1.2.3.4\phi'$ in 1_t^{iv}, and $\frac{1}{2}.\frac{1}{3}.\frac{1}{4}.1.2.3.4\phi'=1\phi'$ will carry 1_μ the distance 1_l in the time 1_t^{v}.

Here the fictitious measures of the factorials are all positive, the development being that of $(x+h)^4$.

2° If the operations during the second interval $1_t''$ of time are negative, we are referred to the form of development given in the third example of n° 79, namely, $(x-h)^4$, and shall have what follows :

$-4\phi'$ carries 1_μ the negative distance -4.1_l in $1_t''$;

$-3\phi''$ generates $(-3)(-4)\phi'$ in $1_t''$, and $\frac{1}{2}(-3)(-4)\phi'=+6\phi'$ will carry 1_μ the positive distance $+6.1_l$ in $1_t'''$;

$-2\phi'''$ generates $(-2)(-3)\phi''$ in $1_t''$, which generates .... $(-2)(-3)(-4)\phi'$ in $1_t'''$, and $\frac{1}{2}.\frac{1}{3}(-2)(-3)(-4)\phi'=-4\phi'$ will carry 1_μ the negative distance -4.1_l in 1_t^{iv};

$-1\phi^{iv}$ generates $(-1)(-2)\phi'''$ in $1_t''$, which generates .... $(-1)(-2)(-3)\phi''$ in $1_t'''$, which generates $(-1)(-2)(-3)(-4)\phi'$ in 1_t^{iv}, and $\frac{1}{2}.\frac{1}{3}.\frac{1}{4}(-1)(-2)(-3)(-4)\phi'=+1\phi'$ will carry 1_μ the positive distance $+1_l$ in 1_t^{v}.

Here the fictitious measures of the factorials alternate from negative to positive, as each antecedent power inverts its consequent [n° 71]. Taking the sum of the distances, we find

$$(-4+6-4+1)1_l.1_\mu = -1.1_l.1_\mu;$$

so that the mobile 1_μ, having described the positive distance $+1.1_l$ in $1_t'$, will now have returned to its point of departure.

By referring to fig. 80, the various positions of 1_μ may be pointed out; and by superposing the third, fourth and fifth units of time upon the second $1_t''$, we shall return from the fictitious to the true state of the genesis during that time.

The fictitious measures of the factorials in the developments of $(x-h)^{-4}$ and $(x+h)^{-4}$ are respectively quite similar to those of $(x+h)^4$ and $(x-h)^4$, and are easily determined by referring to the above examples of the latter.

85. Without intending unduly to multiply forms of combination under the theory embraced in this chapter, I have yet one to offer, which originates directly from the principle of the conversion of intension into extension, falls immediately under the law which governs the operations in the examples of n° 79, and produces results agreeing precisely with those furnished by the method of positive generation, of which it is a form, but so extended as to include all the cases resolved in the preceding paragraphs by the negative method. It is of unlimited extent for the two functions $(x+h)^{\mp n}$, and immediately convertible for $(x-h)^{\mp n}$ by changing the signs of the factors in the numerators, and may be readily written for fractional values of n. It is given in outline in Table B opposite. The successive powers of unity, interpreted by n° 18,

INTENSION : ..... 1^{-4}, 1^{-3}, 1^{-2}, 1^{-1}, 1^0, 1^1, 1^2, 1^3, 1^4, ...;

EXTENSION: ..... -4, -3, -2, -1, 0, 1, 2, 3, 4, ...;

represent the gradual conversion of a series (of infinite extent in both directions, so that the origin and degree of the primary intension are both arbitrary) of intensions into extensions, and form the third column of the table; the genesis of which column, as a resultant simultaneous series, is also given in the second column, by the combination of the positive genetic operations of the first simultaneous series during both semiunits of time, with the direct (negative or positive) genetic operations of the second simultaneous series during the second semiunit of time, the sign of this series changing at the point of zero. The powers of x govern horizontally, and those of h perpendicularly. To fill the outline for any particular exponent, 5 for instance : In the third column, on the line beginning with x^5, stands the number 6; proceed diagonally upwards and towards the right, and divide all the terms on that diagonal line by 6, and the quotients will be the coefficients of the development of $(x+h)^5$; while the numerical triangle above the diagonal line, whose base is indicated by the division line at zero, comprises the coefficients of all the powers concerned in the genesis, arranged in the direct form corresponding to that in n° 70, with the prime generator at x^0.

For $\log(x+h)$, begin where $x^{-1}\times x^1$ and h^0 meet, and divide all the terms of the diagonal by $\log 1=0$, and you get

$$\log x+1x^{-1}h-\tfrac{1}{2}x^{-2}h^2+\tfrac{1}{3}x^{-3}h^2-\tfrac{1}{4}x^{-4}h^4+\&c.$$

For $(x+h)^{-1}$, begin where x^{-1} and h^0 meet, and divide the diagonal by 0, and you get

$$x^{-1}-x^{-2}h+x^{-3}h^2-x^{-4}h^3+x^{-5}h^4-\&c.$$

For $(x+h)^{-2}$, begin where x^{-2} and h^0 meet, and divide the diagonal by -1, and you get

$$x^{-2}-2x^{-3}h+3x^{-4}h^2-4x^{-5}h^3+5x^{-6}h^4-\&c.$$

And similarly for any negative exponent whatever.

The column under h^0, which is the base or root of the table, may all be evolved from the simple formula $1-n$, by successive additions of unity.

To form a table for a fractional exponent, choose for n any odd number, divide it by the denominator of the fraction, and proceed as before. For example, if the exponent be $-\frac{1}{2}$, I take $n=9$, and obtain

$$1-\tfrac{9}{2}=-\tfrac{7}{2},$$
$$1-\tfrac{7}{2}=-\tfrac{5}{2},$$
$$1-\tfrac{5}{2}=-\tfrac{3}{2},$$
$$1-\tfrac{3}{2}=-\tfrac{1}{2},$$
$$1-\tfrac{1}{2}=+\tfrac{1}{2},$$

etc., from which to write out the table.

CHAPTER VII.

THE THEORY OF REPEATING POWERS.

86. In commencing the investigation of the theory of generating powers, we assumed the causes and laws which should realize the production of phenomena, and thereby discovered the first form of positive development. The phenomenon being now given, we reversed the process, and, in prosecuting the theory of destroying powers, we assumed an opposing cause, which should annihilate the phenomenon, and enable us to retrace the steps of its production; whereby we found the several forms of negative development. Thus, in the first case, a purely synthetical process of reasoning, a strict deduction from assumed premises, has unfolded the genesis of a mathematical formula of high import, hitherto known only by induction; and, in the second case, the analytical counterpart of the first process has explained the transition from positive to negative in the exponent of the formula, and introduced various different forms of genesis, which yield as many different species of development, as it were by reproduction. By the conditions assigned in both cases, the genetic process encountered no fixed obstacle, but operated freely in its proper linear direction positive or negative, whereby the results in the first case should increase with the increase of the first interval of time $x1_{t}$, and decrease with the increase of that interval in the second case; and the developments obtained have all been of that class in which the base of the function is variable and the exponent constant, as x^{n} and x^{-n}. But we are now to assign a condition which shall circumscribe the freedom of the genetic process, by compelling it to assume a circular direction, to be confined to the circumference, in such manner that the results of the genesis in the first interval of time can not exceed the radius of the circle;

so that the base of the function generated must needs be constant, but the exponent may be variable, as e^x and a^x.

In positive genesis, under the prime generator, the measure of the phenomenon increases from zero to unity in the first unit of time, and the ratio of the phenomenon increases with the increase of the time $x1_t$; while in negative genesis, under the prime destroyer, the measure of the phenomenon decreases from unity to zero in the first unit of time, and the ratio of the phenomenon decreases with the increase of the time $x1_t$. But we have now to undertake a third or neutral kind of genesis, in which the measure of the phenomenon is neither generated or destroyed, but preexists and is conserved; and this reminds us of the theory of repeating powers, under which the same ratio is repeated in the successive genetic operations, as $e^x\phi'''$ generates $e^x\phi''$, which generates $e^x\phi'$, which generates $e^x\phi^0$.

87. Suppose then that a primitive power $\phi^{(n)}$ is so resisted or hindered in its operation, that the coefficient of the power which it generates in the unit of time shall only equal and not exceed its own coefficient : its immediate consequent will be $1\phi^{(n-1)}$; and the law being assumed to govern throughout the genesis, $1\phi^{(n-1)}$ will generate $1\phi^{(n-2)}$, which will generate $1\phi^{(n-3)}$, and so on until we reach the power zero ϕ^0. Let $n = 4$: we have a hierarchy or series of simultaneous powers $1\phi^{iv}$, $1\phi'''$, $1\phi''$, $1\phi'$, $1\phi^0$, corresponding to that of n° 68, but with unit coefficients throughout; and since instead of being equal to 4, n is really indeterminate, we may reverse the order of the hierarchy, so as to correspond with the order common to the various forms arising by negative generation, whence we have the simultaneous series $1\phi^0$, $1\phi'$, $1\phi''$, $1\phi'''$, $1\phi^{iv}$, etc. for the time $1'_t$. Each of these powers being in its turn a primitive generator, and subjected to the same condition of hindrance in its operation, will, in successive units of time, beget new powers with unit coefficients as follows :

$1\phi'$ generates $1\phi^0$ in $1''_t$;

$1\phi''$ generates $1.1\phi'$ in $1''_t$, which will generate $1.1.1\phi^0 = 1^2.1\phi^0$ in $1'''_t$;

$1\phi'''$ generates $1.1\phi''$ in $1''_t$, which will generate $1.1.1\phi'$ in $1'''_t$, which will generate $1.1.1.1\phi^0 = 1^3.1\phi^0$ in 1^{iv}_t;

$1\phi^{iv}$ generates $1.1\phi'''$ in $1''_t$, which will generate $1.1.1\phi''$ in $1'''_t$, which will generate $1.1.1.1\phi'$ in 1^{iv}_t, which will generate $1.1.1.1.1\phi^0 = 1^4.1\phi^0$ in 1^v_t, etc.

Now these successive powers of unity are directly interpretable with reference to the circle as in n° 18, the power of 1 in each coefficient of ϕ^0 being formed by the immediate antecedent $1^n\phi'$ transferring the material unit 1_μ through the circumference in the unit of time as often as there are units in its exponent, that is, three times for 1^3, etc.; while the fictitious measures [n° 84] of the several generating powers superior to the first order will obviously admit a similar interpretation. We therefore write the coefficient unity under the absolute form $+1$ [n° 30]; and rendering the successive deduction simultaneous, we get the following tablet :

$$\overbrace{1-1 = 1\phi^0.}^{1'_t.} \qquad \overbrace{\qquad\qquad\qquad\qquad\qquad\qquad\qquad\qquad}^{1''_t.}$$

$$1 = +1\phi'; \quad 1\phi^0.$$

$$1 = +1\phi''; \quad \frac{(+1)(+1)}{1}\phi', \quad \frac{(+1)(+1)1}{1\ .\ 2}\phi^0 = \frac{1^2}{1.2}\phi^0.$$

$$1 = +1\phi'''; \quad \frac{(+1)(+1)}{1}\phi'', \quad \frac{(+1)(+1)(+1)}{1\ .\ 2}\phi',$$

$$\frac{(+1)(+1)(+1)1}{1\ .\ 2\ .\ 3}\phi^0 = \frac{1^3}{1.2.3}\phi^0.$$

&c. &c.

That is, $\left(1+1+\frac{1^2}{1.2}+\frac{1^3}{1.2.3}+\frac{1^4}{1.2.3.4}+\&c.\right)\phi^0 = e^{+1}\phi^0.$

88. We have made the condition of hindrance to fulfil itself by compelling the genetic operations to be performed in an angular instead of linear direction, whereby each unit of operation consists of one revolution confined to the radius of the circle unity, the first and all the succeeding revolutions commencing with the origin of the angle at the extremity of the radius on the axis of x positive; but the origin remaining the same, the condition may require the first operation of the genesis to have the measure 180°, giving the power of the first order $-\phi'$; and all the re-

maining operations always proceeding by complete units, we shall get the simultaneous series $1\phi^0$, $-1\phi'$, $-1\phi''$, $-1\phi'''$, $1\phi^{iv}$, etc., and consequently have the following tablet :

$$\begin{array}{ll}
\overbrace{1-1 = 1\phi^0.}^{1'_{\prime}.} & \overbrace{\qquad\qquad\qquad\qquad\qquad\qquad\qquad\qquad}^{1''_{\prime}.} \\
-1 = -1\phi'; & -1\phi^0. \\
-1 = -1\phi''; & \frac{(-1)(-1)}{1}\phi', \quad \frac{(-1)(-1)1}{1\,.\,2}\phi^0 = +\frac{1}{1.2}\phi^0. \\
-1 = -1\phi'''; & \frac{(-1)(-1)}{1}\phi'', \quad \frac{(-1)(-1)(-1)}{1\,.\,2}\phi', \\
 & \qquad \frac{(-1)(-1)(-)1}{1\,.\,2\,.\,3}\phi^0 = -\frac{1}{1.2.3}\phi^0. \\
\&c. & \&c.
\end{array}$$

That is, $\left(1-1+\frac{1}{1.2}-\frac{1}{1.2.3}+\frac{1}{1.2.3.4}-\&c.\right)\phi^0 = e^{-1}\phi^0.$

If, in each of the preceding results, we introduce the successive increasing powers of x, beginning with zero, we will have the respective developments of e^{-x} and e^{-x}.

89. With the same origin, take respectively 90° and 270° for the measure of the first genetic operation : we shall then have the powers of the first order $+\sqrt{-1}\phi'$ and $-\sqrt{-1}\phi'$; and all the remaining operations proceeding by complete units, we get the corresponding simultaneous series

$$1\phi^0, \ +\sqrt{-1}\phi', \ +\sqrt{-1}\phi'', \ +\sqrt{-1}\phi''', \ +\sqrt{-}\phi^{iv}, \text{ etc.}$$

and

$$1\phi^0, \ -\sqrt{-1}\phi', \ -\sqrt{-1}\phi'', \ -\sqrt{-1}\phi''', \ -\sqrt{-}\phi^{iv}, \text{ etc.,}$$

which furnish the two following tablets, the results of which, by the introduction of the successive powers of x, will be converted into the respective developments of $e^{+\sqrt{-1}x}$ and $e^{-\sqrt{-1}x}$.

Development of the positive imaginary exponential $e^{+\sqrt{-1}.x}$.

$$\overbrace{1-1 = 1\phi^0.}^{1'_t.} \qquad \overbrace{\qquad\qquad\qquad\qquad\qquad\qquad}^{1''_t.}$$

$$+\sqrt{-1} = +\sqrt{-1}\phi'; \quad \frac{(+\sqrt{-1})1}{1}\phi^0 = +\sqrt{-1}\phi^0.$$

$$+\sqrt{-1} = +\sqrt{-1}\phi''; \quad \frac{(+\sqrt{-1})(+\sqrt{-1})}{1}\phi', \quad \frac{(+\sqrt{-1})(+\sqrt{-1})1}{1\ .\ 2}\phi^0 = -\frac{1}{1.2}\phi^0.$$

$$+\sqrt{-1} = +\sqrt{-1}\phi'''; \quad \frac{(+\sqrt{-1})^2}{1}\phi'', \quad \frac{(+\sqrt{-1})^3}{1\ .\ 2}\phi', \quad \frac{(+\sqrt{-1})^3 1}{1.2.3}\phi^0 = \frac{-\sqrt{-1}}{1.2.3}\phi^0.$$

$$+\sqrt{-1} = +\sqrt{-1}\phi^{iv}; \quad \frac{(+\sqrt{-1})^2}{1}\phi''', \quad \frac{(+\sqrt{-1})^3}{1\ .\ 2}\phi'', \quad \frac{(+\sqrt{-1})^4}{1.2.3}\phi', \quad \frac{(+\sqrt{-1})^4.1}{1.2.3.4}\phi^0 = +\frac{1}{1.2.3.4}\phi^0.$$

&c. &c.

That is, $\left(1 + \sqrt{-1} - \frac{1}{1.2} - \frac{\sqrt{-1}}{1.2.3} + \frac{1}{1.2.3.4} + \frac{\sqrt{-1}}{1.2.3.4.5} - \text{\&c.}\right)\phi^0 = e^{+\sqrt{-1}}\phi^0.$

Development of the negative imaginary exponential $e^{-\sqrt{-2}.x}$.

$1'_t$.	$1''_t$.
$1-1 = 1\phi^0$.	
$-\sqrt{-1} = -\sqrt{-1}\phi'$;	$\frac{(-\sqrt{-1})1}{1}\phi^0 = -\sqrt{-1}\phi^0$.
$-\sqrt{-1} = -\sqrt{-1}\phi''$;	$\frac{(-\sqrt{-1})(-\sqrt{-1})}{1}\phi'$, $\frac{(-\sqrt{-1})(-\sqrt{-1})1}{1\,.\,2}\phi^0 = -\frac{1}{1.2}\phi^0$.
$-\sqrt{-1} = -\sqrt{-1}\phi'''$;	$\frac{(-\sqrt{-1})^2}{1}\phi''$, $\frac{(-\sqrt{-1})^3}{1\,.\,2}\phi'$, $\frac{(-\sqrt{-1})^3 1}{1.2.3}\phi^0 = \frac{+\sqrt{-1}}{1.2.3}\phi^0$.
$-\sqrt{-1} = -\sqrt{-1}\phi^{\text{iv}}$;	$\frac{(-\sqrt{-1})^2}{1}\phi'''$, $\frac{(-\sqrt{-1})^3}{1\,.\,2}\phi''$, $\frac{(-\sqrt{-1})^4}{1.2.3}\phi'$, $\frac{(-\sqrt{-1})^4 1}{1.2.3.4}\phi^0 = +\frac{1}{1.2.3.4}\phi^0$.
&c.	&c.

That is, $\left(1-\sqrt{-1}-\frac{1}{1.2}+\frac{\sqrt{-1}}{1.2.3}+\frac{1}{1.2.3.4}-\frac{\sqrt{-1}}{1.2.3.4.5}-\&c.\right)\phi^0 = e^{-\sqrt{-1}}\phi^0$.

90. Other forms of circular development fall immediately under the law above explained, which is in general that of repeating or periodical functions.

We know that $\sin 0\pi = \sin 1\pi = \sin 2\pi = 0,$

and $\sin\frac{1}{2}\pi = +1$, and $\sin\frac{3}{2}\phi = -1;$

and that $\cos 0\pi = \cos 2\pi = +1$, and $\cos 1\pi = -1,$

and $\cos\frac{1}{2}\pi = \cos\frac{3}{2}\pi = 0.$

Then if the repeating operation consist in revolving the radius unity through successive right angles, and the measures be taken,

1° In sines, we will have

$$\overbrace{1-1=\sin 0}^{1'_t.}=\overbrace{0\phi^0.}^{1''_t.}$$

$$\sin\tfrac{1}{2}\pi=1\phi';\quad 1\phi^0.$$

$$\sin 1\pi=0\phi'';\quad \frac{0.1}{1}\phi',\quad \frac{0.1.1}{1.2}\phi^0=0\phi^0.$$

$$\sin\tfrac{3}{2}\pi=-1\phi''';\quad \frac{(-1)1}{1}\phi'',\quad \frac{(-1)1.1}{1.2}\phi',\quad \frac{(-1)1.1.1}{1.2.3}\phi^0=\frac{-1^3}{1.2.3}\phi^0.$$

$$\sin 2\pi=0\phi^{iv};\quad \frac{0.1}{1}\phi''',\quad \frac{0.1.1}{1.2}\phi'',\quad \frac{0.1.1.1}{1.2.3}\phi',\quad \frac{0.1.1.1.1}{1.2.3.4}\phi^0=0\phi^0.$$

$$\sin\tfrac{5}{2}\pi=1\phi^{v};\quad \frac{1.1}{1}\phi^{iv},\quad \frac{1.1.1}{1.2}\phi''',\quad \frac{1.1.1.1}{1.2.3}\phi'',\quad \frac{1.1.1.1.1}{1.2.3.4}\phi',\quad \frac{1.1.1.1.1.1}{1.2.3.4.5}\phi^0$$

$$=\frac{1^5}{1.2.3.4.5}\phi^0.$$

&c. &c.

That is, $\left(1-\frac{1^3}{1.2.3}+\frac{1^5}{1.2.3.4.5}-\text{\&c.}\right)\phi^0=\sin(0+1)\phi^0.$

2^0 In cosines, we will have

$$\overbrace{1-1}^{1'_t.}=\overbrace{\cos 0=1\phi^0.}^{1''_t.}$$

$$\cos\tfrac{1}{2}\pi=0\phi'; \quad 0\phi^0.$$

$$\cos 1\pi=-1\phi''; \quad \frac{(-1)1}{1}\phi', \quad \frac{(-1)1.1}{1.2}\phi^0=-\frac{1^2}{1.2}\phi^0.$$

$$\cos\tfrac{3}{2}\pi=0\phi'''; \quad \frac{0.1}{1}\phi'', \quad \frac{0.1.1}{1.2}\phi', \quad \frac{0.1.1.1}{1.2.3}\phi^0=0\phi^0.$$

$$\cos 2\pi=1\phi^{\text{iv}}; \quad \frac{1.1}{1}\phi''', \quad \frac{1.1.1}{1.2}\phi'', \quad \frac{1.1.1.1}{1.2.3}\phi', \quad \frac{1.1.1.1.1}{1.2.3.4}\phi^0=\frac{1^4}{1.2.3.4}\phi^0.$$

&c. &c.

That is, $\left(1-\frac{1^2}{1.2}+\frac{1^4}{1.2.3.4}-\text{\&c.}\right)\phi^0 = \cos(0+1)\phi^0.$

In these two examples, the explanation of the genesis is simple and remarkable. In circular generation, the primitive measure, the radius of the circle, is given, or exists with the commencement of the genesis; but since sines and cosines are periodical, and without any *absolutely first* origin of measurement, we may connect their origin with that of the radius. The radius being zero on the axis of x at the beginning of the time $1'_t$, its true position will be in the negative axis of y; whence, by positive revolution through 90° in $1'_t$, it comes into the position OA [fig. 22'] where it has the value $+1.1_r=\cos 2\pi.1_r=\cos 0.1_r$, and where $\sin 0\pi = 0$: this corresponds to the immediate operation of the prime circulator. The first mediate operation consists in revolving through the first right angle OAA'; the second mediate operation, through the right angle OA'A'', and so on through all the series of angles as measured by the sines and cosines in the first column of the two tablets respectively. By one single process in the first unit of time $1'_t$, the prime circulator generates the complete ascending hierarchy of powers which is divided between the two preceding tablets, namely :

Of sines, $0\phi^0$, $1\phi'$, $0\phi''$, $-1\phi'''$, $0\phi^{iv}$, $1\phi^{v}$, etc., and

Of cosines, $1\phi^0$, $0\phi'$, $-1\phi''$, $0\phi'''$, $1\phi^{iv}$, $0\phi^{v}$, etc.;

so that it takes both tablets to comprise the results of one genesis. The genetic operations of the first interval of time $1'_t$, though performed in the arc, are measured on the radius; but as the second interval of time $1''_t$ is totally independent of the first, its operations and their results may be measured on the arc itself; and therefore by what has been heretofore shown concerning the extension of the second unit of time to some greater interval $h1_t$ or $x1_t$, or as well $\theta 1_t$, we may at once extend the above developments, which are there truly written for the time 1_t (since we are at liberty to count $\sin 0=0$ and $\cos 0=1$, and of course their corresponding hierarchies of powers, as already existing at the commencement of this interval) and the arc equal to radius unity, to the time $\theta 1_t$ and arc $\theta 1_r$, when we have

$$\left(\theta - \frac{\theta^3}{1.2.3} + \frac{\theta^5}{1.2.3.4.5} - \&c.\right)\phi^0 = \sin\theta.\phi^0, \quad \text{and}$$

$$\left(1 - \frac{\theta^2}{1.2} + \frac{\theta^4}{1.2.3.4} - \&c.\right)\phi^0 = \cos\theta.\phi^0.$$

91. If, in the genesis of the first exponential form e^{+1}, we make the revolutions during the second unit of time on the radius $k1_r$ instead of 1_r, we shall construct the tablet following :

$1'_t$.	$1''_t$.		
$1-1=1\phi^0$.			
$k=k\phi'$;	$(+1)1k\phi^0=k\phi^0$.		
$k^2=k^2\phi''$;	$\frac{(+1)^2k^2}{1}\phi'$,	$\frac{(+1)^2 1k^2}{1.2}\phi^0=\frac{k^2}{1.2}\phi^0$.	
$k^3=k^3\phi'''$;	$\frac{(+1)^2k^3}{1}\phi''$,	$\frac{(+1)^3k^3}{1.2}\phi'$,	$\frac{(+1)^3 1k^3}{1.2.3}\phi^0=\frac{k^3}{1.2.3}\phi^0$.
&c.	&c.		

That is, $\left(1+k+\frac{k^2}{1.2}+\frac{k^3}{1.2.3}+\frac{k^4}{1.2.3.4}+\&c.\right)\phi^0=e^k$, or e^{kx} if the second interval of time be made $x1_t$. Then if $e^k = a$, we have $e^{kx} = a^x$; and if k be the napierian logarithm of the briggsian base, we shall have $e^{2,30258509} = 10$.

92. Under the conditions of circulative generation, we have obtained four several simultaneous series of powers, to wit :

I. $1\phi^0$, $+1\phi'$, $+1\phi''$, $+1\phi'''$, etc.;
II. $1\phi^0$, $-1\phi'$, $-1\phi''$, $-1\phi'''$, etc.;
III. $1\phi^0$, $+\sqrt{-1}\phi'$, $+\sqrt{-1}\phi''$, $+\sqrt{-1}\phi'''$, etc., and
IV. $1\phi^0$, $-\sqrt{-1}\phi'$, $-\sqrt{-1}\phi''$, $-\sqrt{-1}\phi'''$, etc., whose developments we now propose to construct geometrically.

1° With the radius unity as the given primitive measure, the development of the first real exponential $e^{+1}.1_r$ may be exhibited without going out of the first circle.

Let [fig. 69] OA $= 1_r = 1_l = 1_t = 1\phi^0$, the given primitive measure of the phenomenon generated in the time $1'_t$. The chord AB $=$ BB$'$ $=$ B$'$A$'$ of the arc $\frac{1}{3}\pi$ is equal to the radius : wherefore I place the given measure on A$'$B$'$, and have A$'$B$'=1\phi^0$ the first term of the development. The first mediate consequent $1\phi'$ transfers the material unit 1_μ from A through the arc 2π to A again, in the time $1''_t$; and I place the result $1\phi^0 = 1_r$ thus generated on B$'$B, and now have A$'$B$'$+B$'$B $= 2.1_l$. The second mediate consequent $+1\phi''$ generates the power $(+1)^2\phi'$ in $1''_t$, which power would transfer 1_μ twice through the arc 2π in $1'''_t$, and therefore through half that distance in $1''_t$, and thus gives the amount $\frac{1}{2}\phi^0=\frac{1}{2}.1_l$, which I place on Bb. The third mediate consequent $+1\phi'''$ generates the power $(+1)^2\phi''$ in $1''_t$; which will generate the power $(+1)^3\phi'$ in $1'''_t$, and therefore $\frac{1}{2}(+1)^3\phi'$ in $1''_t$; which would generate $\frac{1}{2}(+1)^3.1\phi^0$ in $1'''_t$, and therefore $\frac{1}{6}\phi^0=\frac{1}{6}.1_l$ in $1''_t$, which is to be placed on bc. Similarly we find that the fourth mediate consequent $+1\phi^{iv}$ generates the power zero $\frac{1}{2}.\frac{1}{3}.\frac{1}{4}(+1)^4 1\phi^0=\frac{1}{24}\phi^0=\frac{1}{24}.1_l$ in the time $1''_t$, to be placed from c towards A; and so on, so that the whole series which composes the number e will be comprised in the three chords, the last of which will not be filled, for $e.1_l$ $=$ 2,7182818.....$\times 1_l$.

2° The difference between the development of e^{-1} and that of the preceding example will consist only in the transfer of the material unit 1_μ, which is here made through the arc π instead of 2π in the unit of time, every thing else proceeding as before. If we wish to construct $e^{-1}.1_l = (1-1+\frac{1}{2}-\frac{1}{6}+\frac{1}{24}-\&c.)1_l$ in the circle [fig. 70], since the first two terms destroy each other, we begin at O with the third, $\frac{1}{2}\phi^0 = \frac{1}{2}.1_\iota = \text{Ob}$; from which deduct $\frac{1}{6}\phi^0 = \frac{1}{6}.1_\iota = \text{bc}$, and add $\frac{1}{24}\phi^0 = \frac{1}{24}.1_\iota$, etc.; and, finally,

$$e^{-1}.1_\iota = \frac{1}{e}.1_\iota = 0{,}3678794....\times 1_\iota.$$

3° In the development of the positive imaginary exponential $e^{+\sqrt{-1}}$, the arc of transfer becomes $\frac{1}{2}\pi$; and the first mediate consequent $+\sqrt{-1}\phi'$ transfers 1_μ [fig. 71] from A to B in the time $1''_\iota$, giving the result $+\sqrt{-1}\phi^0 = +\sqrt{-1}.1_\iota = \text{OB}$. The second mediate consequent $+\sqrt{-1}\phi''$ generates the power $(+\sqrt{-1})^2\phi'$ in $1''_\iota$, which would transfer 1_μ twice through the arc $\frac{1}{2}\pi$ in $1'''_\iota$, and therefore once in $1''_\iota$, giving the term $-\frac{1}{2}\phi^0 = -\frac{1}{2}.1_\iota$. The third mediate consequent $+\sqrt{-1}\phi'''$ generates $(+\sqrt{-1})^2\phi''$ in $1''_\iota$, which would generate $(+\sqrt{-1})^3\phi'$ in $1'''_\iota$, and therefore $\frac{1}{2}(+\sqrt{-1})^3\phi'$ in $1''_\iota$; which last power would generate in $1'''_\iota$ the result $\frac{1}{2}.\frac{1}{3}(+\sqrt{-1})^3.1\phi^0$, or $\frac{1}{6}(+\sqrt{-1})^3.1\phi^0 = \frac{1}{6}(-\sqrt{-})\phi^0$ in $1''_\iota$. The fourth mediate consequent will produce the result $+\frac{1}{24}\phi^0$; the fifth, the result $\frac{1}{120}(+\sqrt{-1})\phi^0$, and so on to infinity. We place the results in the circle thus :

The given term $1\phi^0 = 1_r = 1_\iota$ is placed in OA;
The first term $+\sqrt{-1}\phi^0 = +\sqrt{-1}.1_\iota = \text{OB}$ is placed in OB;
The second term $-\frac{1}{2}\phi^0 = \text{Ab}$, reduces OA to $\text{Ob} = \frac{1}{2}.1_\iota$;
The third term $\frac{1}{6}(-\sqrt{-1})\phi^0 = \text{Bc}$, reduces OB to Oc;
The fourth term $+\frac{1}{24}\phi^0$ increases Ob by $\frac{1}{24}.1_\iota$;
The fifth term $\frac{1}{120}(+\sqrt{-1})\phi^0$ increases Oc by $\frac{1}{120}.1_\iota$, and so on, the two series of terms continually approximating the respective points P and Q, which locate the cosine and sine of the arc AM equal to the radius unity.

4° In the development of the negative imaginary exponential $e^{-\sqrt{-1}}$, the arc of transfer [fig. 72] of the material unit 1_μ becomes $\frac{3}{2}\pi = \text{ABA}'\text{B}'$; and we substitute throughout the third fourth-root of unity $-\sqrt{-1}$, in place of the second fourth-root $+\sqrt{-1}$ in the last preceding series of operations, every thing else proceeding as in that example.

The given term $1\phi^0=1_\iota$ is placed in OA;
the first term $-\sqrt{-1}\phi^0=\mp\sqrt{-1}.1_\iota$ is placed in OB′;
the second term $-\frac{1}{2}\phi^0=$Ab, reduces OA to Ob$=\frac{1}{2}.1_\iota$;
the third term $\frac{1}{6}(+\sqrt{-1})\phi^0=$B′c′, reduces $-$OB′ to $-$Oc′;
the fourth term $+\frac{1}{24}\phi^0$ increases Ob by $\frac{1}{24}.1_\iota$;
the fifth term $\frac{1}{120}(-\sqrt{-1})\phi^0$ increases $-$Oc′ by $-\frac{1}{120}.1_\iota$,
and so on, the two series of terms continually approximating the respective points P and Q′, which locate the cosine and sine of the negative arc AM′ equal to the radius unity.

Thus in the two series
$$e^{+\sqrt{-1}}.1_\iota=(1+\sqrt{-1}-\tfrac{1}{2}-\sqrt{-1}.\tfrac{1}{6}+\tfrac{1}{24}+\sqrt{-1}.\tfrac{1}{120}-\&c.)1_\iota,$$
and
$$e^{-\sqrt{-1}}.1_\iota=(1-\sqrt{-1}-\tfrac{1}{2}+\sqrt{-1}.\tfrac{1}{6}+\tfrac{1}{24}-\sqrt{-1}.\tfrac{1}{120}-\&c.)1_\iota,$$
the real terms of each approximate to the cosine of the arc 1, and the imaginary terms of the former approximate to the sine of the same arc, and those of the latter to the sine of the equal negative arc; and therefore the first equals $(\cos 1+\sqrt{-1}.\sin 1)1_\iota$, and the second equals $(\cos 1-\sqrt{-1}.\sin 1)1_\iota$. Being true for the arc 1, they are so for any arc x; and verifications of the same might be profitably tried by making in the equations
$$e^{+\sqrt{-1}.x}.1_\iota=(1+\sqrt{-1}.x-\tfrac{1}{2}x^2-\sqrt{-1}.\tfrac{1}{6}x^3+\tfrac{1}{24}x^4+\&c.)1_\iota \text{ and}$$
$$e^{-\sqrt{-1}.x}.1_\iota=(1-\sqrt{-1}.x-\tfrac{1}{2}x^2+\sqrt{-1}.\tfrac{1}{6}x^3+\tfrac{1}{24}x^4-\&c.)1_\iota,$$
successively $x=\frac{1}{2}\pi$, and $x=2$.

93. We know that the symbols $\pm\sqrt{-1}$ have at the same time the two values 0 and 1 : by virtue of the former value, the symbols $e^{\pm\sqrt{-1}}.1_\iota$ are $e^0.1_\iota=1.1_\iota$; and further that a linear unit involved to the power x becomes a line equal to $x1_\iota$: then if $x1_\iota$ be an arc, the power $e^{+\sqrt{-1}x}.1_\iota$ is equal to that arc, and $e^{-\sqrt{-1}}.1_\iota$ is equal to the negative arc $-x1_\iota$. We conclude then that the imaginary exponentials are interpreted, both in their unitary and developed forms.

94. If we refer to n° 85, for the purpose of obtaining the four several simultaneous series of circulative powers by an analogous method, we shall find the process to consist in the successive

negative involution of each of the four fourth-roots of unity; whereby we supply the coefficients to the several powers of the respective series in the forms following :

1^0 The primitive fourth-root of unity gives the series
$1\phi^0,\ (+\sqrt{-1})^{-1}\phi',\ (+\sqrt{-1})^{-2}\phi'',\ (+\sqrt{-1})^{-3}\phi'''$, etc.;

2^0 The second fourth-root of unity gives the series
$1\phi^0,\ (-1)^{-1}\phi',\ (-1)^{-2}\phi'',\ (-1)^{-3}\phi''',\ (-1)^{-4}\phi^{iv}$, etc.;

3^0 The third fourth-root of unity gives the series
$1\phi^0,\ (-\sqrt{-1})^{-1}\phi',\ (-\sqrt{-1})^{-2}\phi'',\ (-\sqrt{-1})^{-3}\phi'''$, etc., and

4^0 The real positive root unity itself gives the series
$1\phi^0,\ (+1)^{-1}\phi',\ (+1)^{-2}\phi'',\ (+1)^{-3}\phi''',\ (+1)^{-4}\phi^{iv}$, etc.

The exponents here denote strictly nothing more than the number of genetic operations to be performed under each respective power in the unit of time, each operation in any particular series being measured by the angle expressed by the root which is its base; that is, the right angle in the first series, two right angles in the second series, three in the third, and four in the fourth. The prime circulator, with all its subordinate hierarchy of powers, operates in the negative direction during the time $1'_t$; and consequently by reaction the series of dependent primitive powers, with their subordinates, operate in the positive direction in $1''_t$. All the four forms of series are comprised in the following one :

$$(1^{\frac{1}{4}})^0,\quad (1^{\frac{1}{4}})^{-1},\quad (1^{\frac{1}{4}})^{-2},\quad (1^{\frac{1}{4}})^{-3},\quad (1^{\frac{1}{4}})^{-4},\quad \text{etc.}$$

The factorials which compose the numerators of the coefficients of the several powers of the second interval of time in positive generation, and which take the negative sign into each factor in negative generation, degenerate into numerical (circular) powers of unity in circulative generation.

95. Logarithms are the measures of ratios : then if we divide a by a, we get at once two results, namely, log$a$ the measure of the ratio, and the quotient 1. If we let the first result stand as the immediate consequent of the prime circulator, and pursue the successive division of the quotient by a, we form the series

$$1^1 \div a1^1 = \frac{1^0}{a},\quad \frac{1^0}{a} \div a1^1 = \frac{1^{-1}}{a^2} = -\frac{1}{a^2},\quad \frac{1^{-1}}{a^2} \div a1^1 = \frac{1^{-2}}{a^3} = -\frac{2}{a^3},$$

$$\frac{1^{-2}}{a^3} \div a1^1 = \frac{1^{-3}}{a^4} = -\frac{3}{a^4},\quad \&c.;$$

which we may assume as coefficients wherewith to construct the following tablet :

$$\overbrace{a \div a = \log a . \phi^0.}^{1'_t.} \qquad \overbrace{\qquad\qquad\qquad\qquad\qquad\qquad}^{x1_t.}$$

$$+\frac{1}{a} = \frac{1}{a}\phi'; \quad \frac{1.1}{a}x\phi^0 = \frac{1}{a}x\phi^0.$$

$$-\frac{1}{a^2} = -\frac{1}{a^2}\phi''; \quad \frac{(-1)(+1)x}{1}\frac{}{a^2}\phi', \quad \frac{(-1)(+1)1x^2}{1\ .\ 2}\frac{}{a^2}\phi^0 = -\tfrac{1}{2}\frac{x^2}{a^2}\phi^0.$$

$$-\frac{2}{a^3} = -\frac{2}{a^3}\phi'''; \quad \frac{(-2)(-1)x}{1}\frac{}{a^3}\phi'', \quad \frac{(-2)(-1)(+1)x^2}{1\ .\ 2}\frac{}{a^3}\phi',$$

$$\frac{(-2)(-1)(+1)1x^3}{1\ .\ 2\ .\ 3}\frac{}{a^3}\phi^0 = +\tfrac{1}{3}\frac{x^3}{a^3}\phi^0.$$

&c. &c.

That is, $\left(\log a + \frac{1}{a} - \tfrac{1}{2}.\frac{x^2}{a^2} + \tfrac{1}{3}.\frac{x^3}{a^3} - \&c.\right)\phi^0 = \log(a+x)\phi^0.$

96. Sines and arcs are each mutually measures of operations performed on the other; and in this respect, the unit of the arc corresponds to the right angle which measures the sine 1.1_t. When successive equal unit operations are performed on a sine, then [fig. 74], it is transferred uniformly through a right angle from its first position PM=sinAOM, successively into the positions P′M′=cosBOM′, P″M″=sinA′OM″, P‴M‴=cosB′OM‴, PM=sinAOM again; or $\sin\theta$, $\cos\theta$, $-\sin\theta$, $-\cos\theta$, $\sin\theta$, etc. Hence, 1°, in operating on sines, we proceed in the direction AB; and, 2°, in operating on cosines, we may proceed in the negative direction AB′, and thus find the two following simultaneous series of circulative powers for the development respectively of a sine and of a cosine in terms of sines and cosines :

I. Series of sines.	II Series of cosines
$1-1 = \sin x.1\phi^0.$	$1-1 = \cos x.1\phi^0.$
$\sin(x+\tfrac{1}{2}\pi) = \cos x.\phi',$	$\cos(x+\tfrac{1}{2}\pi) = -\sin x.\phi',$
$\sin(x+1\pi) = -\sin x.\phi'',$	$\cos(x+1\pi) = -\cos x.\phi'',$
$\sin(x+\tfrac{3}{2}\pi) = -\cos x.\phi''',$	$\cos(x+\tfrac{3}{2}\pi) = +\sin x.\phi''',$
$\sin(x+2\pi) = +\sin x.\phi^{iv}$, etc.	$\cos(x+2\pi) = +\cos x.\phi'^{v}$, etc.

These two simultaneous series furnish the following tablets :

1. *Development of the sine of an arc in sines and cosines of the same.*

$$\overbrace{1-1=\sin x.\phi^{0}.}^{1'_{t}.}\quad\overbrace{\qquad\qquad\qquad\qquad\qquad\qquad}^{h1_{t}.}$$

$$+\cos x.\phi';\quad +\cos x.h\phi^{0}.$$

$$-\sin x.\phi'';\quad -\sin x\frac{1.1}{1}h\phi',\quad -\sin x\frac{1.1.1}{1.2}h^{2}\phi^{0}.$$

$$-\cos x.\phi''',\quad -\cos x\frac{1.1}{1}h\phi'',\quad -\cos x\frac{1.1.1}{1.2}h^{2}\phi',\quad -\cos x\frac{1.1.1.1}{1.2.3}h^{3}\phi^{0}.$$

$$+\sin x.\phi^{iv};\quad +\sin x\frac{1.1}{1}h\phi''',\quad +\sin x\frac{1.1.1}{1.2}h^{2}\phi'',\quad +\sin x\frac{1.1.1.1}{1.2.3}h^{3}\phi',$$

$$+\sin x\frac{1.1.1.1.1}{1.2.3.4}h^{4}\phi^{0}.$$

&c. &c.

That is, $(\sin x+\cos x.h-\frac{1}{2}\sin x.h^{2}-\frac{1}{6}\cos x.h^{3}+\frac{1}{24}\sin x.h^{4}+\&c.)\phi^{0}$ $= \sin(x+h)\phi^{0}$.

2. *Development of the cosine of an arc in sines and cosines of the same.*

$$\overbrace{1-1=\cos x.\phi^{0}.}^{1'_{t}.}\quad\overbrace{\qquad\qquad\qquad\qquad\qquad\qquad}^{h1_{t}.}$$

$$-\sin x.\phi';\quad -\sin x.h\phi^{0}.$$

$$-\cos x.\phi'';\quad -\cos x\frac{1.1}{1}h\phi',\quad -\cos x\frac{1.1.1}{1.2}h^{2}\phi^{0}.$$

$$+\sin x.\phi''';\quad +\sin x\frac{1.1}{1}h\phi'',\quad +\sin x\frac{1.1.1}{1.2}h^{2}\phi',\quad +\sin x\frac{1.1.1.1}{1.2.3}h^{3}\phi^{0}.$$

$$+\cos x.\phi^{iv};\quad +\cos x\frac{1.1}{1}h\phi''',\quad +\cos x\frac{1.1.1}{1.2}h^{2''},\quad +\cos x\frac{1.1.1.1}{1.2.3}h^{3'},$$

$$+\cos x\frac{1.1.1.1.1}{1.2.3.4}h^{4}\phi^{0}.$$

&c. &c.

That is, $(\cos x-\sin x.h-\frac{1}{2}\cos x.h^{2}+\frac{1}{6}\sin x.h^{3}+\frac{1}{24}\cos x.h^{4}-\&c.)\phi^{0}$ $= \cos(x+h)\phi^{0}$.

97. A method of exhibiting the results of the development of the real positive exponential formula a^x by actual motion is given here, for the purpose of comparison with the method furnished by the calculus of operations.

The equation $(1+b)^n=N$, when b is given, and n is successively expounded by the numbers 0, 1, 2, 3, etc., gives for N a series of values 1, $1+b$, $(1+b)^2$, $(1+b)^3$, etc., which become each unity when $b=0$, but form an increasing geometrical progression when b has a positive value. Let $b=1$; then the series becomes

$$2^0, \quad 2^1, \quad 2^2, \quad 2^3, \quad \text{etc.},$$

that is, 1, 2, 4, 8, etc.; so that were it required to interpolate in the second series the natural numbers which are absent, it would be necessary to introduce fractional powers; for instance, the number 3 would require the base 2 to be involved to some fractional power comprised between the values 1 and 2, and the numbers 5, 6, 7 would require fractional powers comprised between 2 and 3; and in this way, any positive whole number whatever could be obtained as a power (whole or fractional) of 2, or in general of any base $(1+b)$.

We have $(1+b)^0 = (1+b)^{\frac{1}{\infty}} = 1$; that is, the power zero, or the infinite root, of any number $(1+b)$ is equal to unity; and although we cannot return from unity and obtain $1^\infty=1+b$, yet we may take ω equal to an exceedingly great number, and obtain $\left(1+\frac{1}{\omega}\right)^\omega = 1+n$; and then when n is determined by actual development of the lefthand member, the expression $(1+n)^p$ may be made to yield any positive number whatever. We can therefore obtain $(1+n)^p = 1+b$; and in its turn, the expression $(1+b)^x$ can produce any positive number. We therefore have

$$N = (1+b)^x = (1+n)^{px} = \left(1+\frac{1}{\omega}\right)^{\omega px}$$

Let the reciprocal of ω, that is, $\frac{1}{\omega} = \delta$. Let the line 1_ι be divided into ω equal parts, each being equal to $\frac{1}{\omega}.1_\iota = \delta.1_\iota$; and let this line $\delta 1_\iota$ be regarded as a new linear unit, so that the mobile unit 1_μ may describe the distance $\delta 1_\iota$ uniformly in a corresponding unit of time $\delta 1_t$, and thus achieve the whole distance $\omega.\delta.1_l = 1_l$ in the time $\omega.\delta 1_t$ by uniform motion; and at the same time let a second mobile unit $1'_\mu$ describe the successive differences of the distances $(1+\delta)^0 1_l$, $(1+\delta)^1 1_l$, $(1+\delta)^2 1_l$, $(1+\delta)^3 1_l$, etc. each in the unit of time $\delta 1_t$, so that the whole distance $(1+\delta)^{\delta} 1_l$ will be achieved in the time $\omega.\delta.1_t = 1_t$. Now

$$(1+\delta)^1 - (1+\delta)^0 = 1+\delta-1 = \delta;$$

and the successive stages of the two mobile units will be

$$\begin{array}{llllll} & \delta 1'_t. & \delta 1''_t. & \delta 1'''_t. & \delta 1^{iv}_t. & \\ 1_\mu: & \delta 1_l, & \delta 1_l \quad , & \delta 1_l \quad , & \delta 1_l \quad , & \text{etc., and} \\ 1'_\mu: & \delta 1_l, & \delta(1+\delta)1_l, & \delta(1+\delta)^2 1_l, & \delta(1+\delta)^3 1_l, & \text{etc.;} \end{array}$$

and these stages make the corresponding distances from the origin at the expiration of the times

$$\begin{array}{lllllll} 0_t. & \delta 1'_t. & \delta 1''_t. & \delta 1'''_t. & \delta 1^{(\omega)}. & & 1.1_t. \\ 1_\mu: 0.1_l, & \delta 1_l \quad , & 2\delta 1_l \quad , & 3\delta 1_l \quad , \ldots & \omega\delta 1_l & = & 1.1_l; \end{array}$$

$$1'_\mu: 1.1_l,\ (1+\delta)1_l,\ (1+\delta)^2 1_l,\ (1+\delta)^3 1_l, \ldots (1+\delta)^{\omega} 1_l = (1+n)1_l;$$

Here the distances described by the two mobiles in the first unit of time $\delta 1'_t$ are each equal to $\delta 1_l$; that is, the mobiles have both the same rate of motion or velocity at the outset, and the ratios of the terms of the second series to unity are truly expressed by the corresponding terms of the first series, that is, by the times of description.

Now $\delta = (1+n)^{\delta} - 1$; but since $1+b = (1+n)^p = (1+\delta)^{\omega p}$, we have

$$(1+b)^{\delta} = (1+\delta)^p,$$

$$(1+b)^{\delta} - 1 = p\omega + p^2\omega^2 + \text{etc.};$$

so that in this case, while the first mobile 1_μ describes the distance $\delta 1_l$ in the first unit of time $\delta 1'_t$, the second mobile $1'_\mu$ describes a greater distance equal to $p\omega 1_l$; and therefore their velocities at the outset are unequal, and each term of the series formed in generating the base $(1+b)$ will be p times greater than its corresponding term in the series for $(1+n)$, the measure of the ratio of which to unity is expressed by the time of description. Thus in generating the base $1+b$ in the time $\omega\delta 1_t = 1_t$, the velocity of the mobile $1'_\mu$ at the beginning of the time $\delta 1'_t$ is such as to generate the distance $p\delta 1_l$ uniformly in that unit of time, while the mobile 1_μ

describes the distance $\delta 1_t$ only in that time; from which it follows that we shall have, in place of the former series for 1_μ and $1'_\mu$, the following pair, to wit :

$$\begin{array}{lllllll} & '1_t. & \delta 1'_t. & \delta 1''_t. & \delta 1'''_t. & & \omega\delta 1_t = 1_t. \\ 1_\mu: & 0.1_l, & \delta 1_l\ , & 2\delta 1_l\ , & 3\delta 1_l & , \ldots\ldots & \omega\delta 1_l = 1_l. \end{array}$$

$$1'_\lambda:\quad 1.1_l,\ (1+p\delta)1_l,\ (1+p\delta)^2 1_l,\ (1+p\delta)^3 1_l \ \ldots\ldots\ (1+p\delta)^\omega 1_l$$
$$= (1+n)^p 1_l = (1+b)1_l.$$

So that in this case the distance described by the mobile $1'_\mu$ in the time 1_t has to that described in the same time by the same mobile in the former case the ratio which is measured by p to 1; that is,

$$\frac{(1+b)1_l}{(1+n)1_l} = \frac{(1+n)^p.1_l}{(1+n)1_l} = \text{the ratio whose measure is } p.$$

Now the number ω is exceedingly great, and therefore the line $\delta 1_l = \frac{1}{\omega}.1_l$ and the time $\delta 1_t$ are exceedingly small, or infinitesimal, and $\omega\delta 1_t = 1_t = 1_l$ the linear unit. We say, then, that the mobile 1_μ will describe the linear unit 1_l uniformly in time, beginning with $1'_t$; and that the mobile $1'_\mu$, having already described the distance 1_l previous to the commencement of the time $1'_t$, will describe the distance $n1_l$ in the time $1'_t$, making the whole distance $(1+n)1_l$ at the end of that time, and, its velocity continually increasing proportionally to the distance from the origin o, will complete the successive distances $(1+n)^2 1_l$, $(1+n)^3 1_l$, etc. in the successive units of time $1''_t$, $1'''_t$, etc. Therefore in the time $x1_t$, every position in the distance from zero to $(1+n)^x 1_l$ will be passed over; and this necessitates the continuous variation of the exponent from the value 0 at the distance $(1+n)^0 1_l = 1_l$, up to the distance at pleasure $(1+n)^x 1_l$; that is, the expression $(1+n)^x$ may be rendered equal to any positive number whatever. Thus we should have the two corresponding series of distances :

$$\begin{array}{lllll} & '1_t. & 1'_t. & 1''_t. & 1'''_t. \\ 1_\mu: & 0.1_l, & 1.1_l\ , & 2.1_l\ , & 3.1_l\ ,\ \text{etc. and} \end{array}$$

$1'_\mu$: 1.1_l, $(1+n)1_l$, $(1+n)^2 1_l$, $(1+n)^3 1_l$, etc., the general term of the last of which is $(1+n)^x 1_l$, which gives x as the general measure of the ratio $(1+n) : 1$; and we have similarly the two corresponding series :

$'1_{t}.$ $\quad 1'_{t}.$ $\quad 1''_{t}.$ $\quad 1'''_{t}.$

1_{μ}: 0.1_{t}, $\quad 1.1_{t}$, $\quad 2.1_{t}$, $\quad 3.1_{t}$, etc. and

$1'_{\mu}$: 1.1_{t}, $(1+b)1_{t}$, $(1+b)^{2}1_{t}$, $(1+b)^{3}1_{t}$, etc., the general term of which is $(1+b)^{x}1_{t}$, which may, as before, become equal to any positive number whatever.

The base $1+n$ must be determined by the actual development of the formula $\left(1+\frac{1}{\omega}\right)^{\omega}$, in which ω is made infinitely great, when it is found that

$(1+\delta)^{\omega}-(1+\frac{1}{\infty})^{\infty}=(1+0)^{\infty}=1+n=2,718281828 45....= e$, the base of napierian logarithms, where the properties of e^{x} are well known.

If $\delta = 0,00000043429....$, then $\omega=2302585,09299404568....$, and the above development may be exhibited thus :

$$(1,00000043429)^{2302585,09299404568} = 2,71828182845.$$

Then making $b = 9$, the equation $(2,71828182845)^{p} = 10$ gives

$$p = 2,30258509299.... = \frac{\omega}{1000000};$$

and therefore $(2,71828182845)^{2,30258509299} = 10 = a$, the base of common logarithms, 2,30258509299 being the napierian logarithm of 10.

Now $(1+b)^{x}=(1+n)^{px}$, or $a^{x}= e^{px}$; and therefore if $N = a^{x}$, x will be the logarithm of N to the base a; but to the base e, the logarithm of the same number N will be px; that is, the napierian logarithm of any number is equal to p times its common logarithm; or the napierian logarithm of a number, being divided by the napierian logarithm p of a new base $1+b$, gives the logarithm of the same number to the base $1+b$. In fact the base $1+b$, having arisen from the development of $(1+p\delta)^{\omega}$ in the unit of time 1_{t}, is greater than the base $1+n$ arising from the development of $(1+\delta)^{\omega}$ in the same time 1_{t}; and therefore the latter base must necessarily be elevated to a higher power than the former one, to produce the same number N.

Thus when the velocity of the mobile $1'_{\mu}$ increases so as to be always exactly equal to the distance from the origin o of its motion, the mobile generates the napierian base $1+n=e$ in the unit of time 1_{t}; but when the velocity is always p times the distance from the origin, some other base $1+b=a$ is generated in the unit of time. In both cases, the mobile $1'_\mu$ has described the unit of distance 1_l with an accelerated motion from rest at o, in a unit of time $'1_t$, when the mobile 1_μ commences its motion from the point 1 with a uniform velocity : in the first case, $1'_\mu$ passes the point 1 with a velocity exactly equal to the uniform velocity of 1_μ; while in the second case, $1'_\mu$ passes that point with p times the uniform velocity of 1_μ. Either base e or a, being generated in the unit of time 1_t, is, by the same law of genesis, afterwards competent to generate any positive magnitude whatever of distance $e^{px}1_l=a^x1_l$, or of number $e^{px}=a^x$, in the succeeding time $px1_t$ and $x1_t$ respectively.

98. In the preceding example, the motion of the first mobile 1_μ, being uniform, has a simple cause, a constant velocity, and the inquiry of causation terminates here with respect to the phenomenon of the motion of 1_μ; but the variation of the velocity of the second mobile $1'_\mu$ suggests the conclusion that the cause of its motion is complex, and is to be sought among the principles and laws of accelerating forces. Now it is the business of the calculus of operations to attempt to assign the origin and law of such accelerating forces, in such manner as will rationally achieve the genesis of the several exponential functions in question.

The simplest method for the construction of logarithms would consist in extracting the infinitesimal root of a number exceeding unity by a very small fraction : the subsequent involution of this infinitesimal root would generate all possible variations of number, each exponent being the logarithm of the number generated; but as this method, though simple, is nearly impracticable, more feasible ones have been substituted.

The first root of unity is obtained by dividing that number by itself; which process may be repeated indefinitely, so that we approximate to the infinite root of unity $1^{\frac{1}{\infty}} = 1^0$ in a series of divisions: $1^1\div1^1=1^0$, $1^0\div1^1=1^{-1}$, $1^{-1}\div1^1=1^{-2}$, $1^{-2}\div1^1=1^{-3}$, and so on until $1^{-\frac{1}{\infty}}=1^0$. Each term here has the same numerical value 1; and we may introduce the linear unit under the form of the radius of the circle, when each division may be regarded as expressing the result of an operation of revolution of the radius negatively through the circumference or arc of four right angles, since the results will be always positive unity in both cases, and the latter has the additional advantage of implying the measure of an operation in space and time. We may further invest the several results of these successive operations of revolution with a dynamical significance, by imagining them to consist in the winding up of so many spiral springs, perfectly elastic, and nowise interfering with each other, but so adjusted and tempered as to evolve by subsequent reaction the exact distances as generated by the corresponding powers in the tablet of development on page 145, for identical periods of time.

It is the office of the independent primitive generator (here termed the *prime circulator*) to effect the genesis of the series of powers $1\phi^0$, $(+1)^{-1}\phi'$, $(+1)^{-2}\phi''$, $(+1)^{-3}\phi'''$, etc. (or, which is just the same series, $1\phi^0$, $1\phi'$, $1\phi''$, $1\phi'''$, etc.), in the first unit of time $1'_t$. By this hierarchy of dependent primitive powers, the several terms of the series which compose the development of the function $e^{+1}.1_t$ will be generated in the second unit of time $1''_t$, as shown in n° 87; where the several accessions of velocity which the mobile $1'_\mu$ of the first case in n° 97 receives in the successive infinitesimal intervals of time $\delta 1_t$, are indicated by their proper *unit measures*, to wit, $\frac{1}{2}.1_t$, $\frac{1}{6}.1_t$, $\frac{1}{24}.1_t$, etc., these being the distances the several accessions would cause the mobile $1'_\mu$ to describe in the unit of time 1_t. Each accession, added to the previous velocity, will satisfy the general term $\delta(1+\delta)^n.1_t$ of the successive stages of the mobile $1'_\mu$ on page 159.

If the radius of the generative circle be $p1_r$ instead of 1_r, the simultaneous series generated by the prime circulator in the time $1'_t$ would be $1\phi^0$, $p\phi'$, $p^2\phi''$, $p^3\phi'''$, etc., and would give the development of $e^p.1_t = a^1.1_t$ in the time $1''_t$, as in n° 91.

Having obtained the bases e and a, the development of e^x and a^x are sufficiently explained.

There is no difficulty in accommodating the above explanation to each of the three remaining exponentials e^{-x}, $e^{+\sqrt{-1}.x}$ and $e^{-\sqrt{-1}.x}$, the several reactions being referred to the directions pointed out by the exponents.

99. An analogy may be traced between linear and circular logarithms. 1° The series of powers of a linear unit 1_λ, namely, $1^0.1_l$, $1^1.1_l$, $1^2.1_l$, $1^3.1_l$, ..., $1^n.1_l$, are the results of the action of a force of the first order ϕ' on the material unit 1_μ, during 1, 2, 3, ..., n successive units of time 1_t; in which operation, the series of natural numbers 0, 1, 2, 3, ..., n, are the ratios to unity of the successive measures of operation, that is, they express at once the number of operations and the magnitude of their measure in space. If instead of the linear unit 1.1_λ, we involve the napierian base $e.1_\lambda$, we shall obtain the geometrical series

P^0 P' P'' P''' $P^{(n)}$

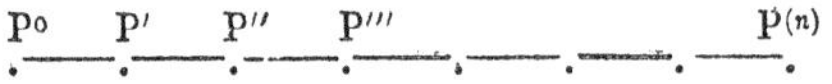

$e^0.1_l$, $e^1.1_l$, $e^2.1_l$, $e^3.1_l$, ..., $e^n.1_l$, yielding the numbers of which the terms of the linear series are the logarithms.

2° When [fig. 75] the linear unit $1_l = 1_r = OA$ the radius of a circle, it has, in any position OM, two measures, a double linear one $(\cos\theta + \sqrt{-1}\sin\theta)1_r$, and an angular or circular one $\theta.1_r$, θ being the arc AM; and it has been shown [n° 36] that the last measure is equal to $e^{+\sqrt{-1}.\theta}.1_r$. Then when the linear unit ------ $OM = (\cos\theta + \sqrt{-1}\sin\theta)1_r$ is involved to the powers 0, 1, 2, 3, etc. (the angular unit being the right angle), it becomes

$$(\cos 0 + \sqrt{-1}\sin 0)1_r = OA,$$

$$(\cos\theta + \sqrt{-1}\sin\theta)1_r = OM,$$

$$(\cos(\theta + \tfrac{1}{2}\pi) + \sqrt{-1}(\theta + \tfrac{1}{2}\pi))1_r = OM', \text{ etc.};$$

and thus is generated a series of sines and cosines, in place of the natural numbers generated in the example of linear involution. Then again if the circular unit $e^{\sqrt{-1}.\theta}.1_r$ be involved to successive powers in which the unit is also a right angle, we shall have

$$e^{\sqrt{-1}.0}.1_r = OA, \quad e^{\sqrt{-1}.\theta}.1_r = OM, \quad e^{\sqrt{-1}(\theta+\frac{1}{2}\pi)}.1_r = OM', \text{ etc.};$$

where the continued sums of the arcs generated by the involution of $e^{+\sqrt{-1}.\theta}.1_r$ correspond to the series of sines and cosines obtained from the involution of $(\cos\theta + \sqrt{-1}\sin\theta)1_r$, just as the natural numbers obtained from the involution of 1.1_λ correspond to the geometrical series generated by the involution of e^x; that is, the arcs are circular logarithms of their corresponding sines and cosines which are measures of the radius 1_r.

CHAPTER VIII.

THE CALCULUS OF OPERATIONS.

100. THE fundamental problem of the Calculus of Operations [n° 7] may now be expounded as follows :

If the power ϕ^{n} of the nth order generate power ϕ^{n-1} of the $(n-1)$th order uniformly during the unit of time $1'_t$, the quantity of ϕ^{n-1} at the expiration of $1'_t$ will be sufficient to generate twice the quantity of power ϕ^{n-2} of the $(n-2)$th order during the time $1''_t$ that ϕ^{n-1} generated during the time $1'_t$ of its own generation; so that $2\phi^{n-1}$ may be written as the measure of the quantity of power generated by ϕ^{n} in the unit of time, and therefore $1\phi^{n-1}$ was generated in each semiunit of time $\frac{1}{2}'.1'_t$ and $\frac{1}{2}''.1'_t$, or a semiunit is the interval of time consumed in the performance of one genetic operation, or ϕ^{n} performs *two operations* in the unit of time. Now ϕ^{n-1}_1 performs one operation in the semiunit $\frac{1}{2}'.1'_t$ of time during its own generation, and also one operation in the semiunit $\frac{1}{2}''.1'_t$ afterwards; and ϕ^{n-1}_2 performs one operation in the time $\frac{1}{2}''.1'_t$ during its own generation, making in all *three operations* performed by the powers ϕ^{n-1} in the time $1'_t$, which operations consist in the generation of three powers of the order $(n-2)$, that is, $3\phi^{n-2}$. Continuing this process, we find that by the powers $3\phi^{n-2}$ there will be generated, during the same time $1'_t$, four powers of the $(n-3)$d order, or $4\phi^{n-3}$; or, in other words, the three powers ϕ^{n-2} will perform *four operations* in the unit of time, and so on, the number of operations increasing always by unity. We shall therefore have the following series or hierarchy of powers generated in the time $1'_t$:

$1\phi^n$, $2\phi^{n-1}$, $3\phi^{n-2}$, $4\phi^{n-3}$, etc., which may be written thus :

$1^1\phi^n$, $1^2\phi^{n-1}$, $1^3\phi^{n-2}$, $1^4\phi^{n-3}$, etc. when the exponents of the unit coefficients are defined to signify number of operations.

Let the primitive power be of the fourth order ϕ^4; then our hierarchy becomes

$1\phi^{iv}$, $2\phi''''$, $3\phi''$, $4\phi'$, $1\phi^0$, and may be written

$$1\phi^{iv},\ \frac{1.2}{1}\phi''',\ \frac{1.2.3}{1.2}\phi'',\ \frac{1.2.3.4}{1.2.3}\phi',\ \frac{1.2.3.4}{1.2.3.4}\phi^0 = 1\phi^0;$$

in each term of which series, exclusive of the last, the complete numerical coefficient expresses the amount of the next inferior order (when the proper numerical coefficient of that inferior order is included) that would be generated in the next *succeeding* unit of time; and this amount is restored to its value in the next *preceding* unit of time, by the introduction of the next ascending factor into its denominator. Thus when the series is expressed in this complete form, at the same time that it gives the entire genesis during the time $1'_t$, it exhibits the law for the determination of all the subordinate series of genesis during the time $1''_t$. For, during the second unit of time $1''_t$, the power ϕ^{iv} will itself repeat the genesis of the first unit of time, thus :

$\frac{1.2}{1}\phi'''$, $\frac{1.2.3}{1.2}\phi''$, $\frac{1.2.3.4}{1.2.3}\phi'$, $\frac{1.2.3.4}{1.2.3.4}\phi^0 = 1\phi^0$; and the power

$2\phi'''$ will generate $\frac{2.3}{1}\phi''$, $\frac{2.3.4}{1.2}\phi'$, $\frac{2.3.4}{1.2.3}\phi^0 = 4\phi^0$; the power

$3\phi''$ will generate $\frac{3.4}{1}\phi'$, $\frac{3.4}{1.2}\phi^0 = 6\phi^0$, and the power

$4\phi'$ will generate $4\phi^0$; thus making in all the series of the order zero $(1+4+6+4+1)\phi^0 = (1+1)^4\phi^0$, being the coefficient of the entire phenomenon $2^4 . 1_l . 1_\mu$ generated in the time 2.1_t.

Here the direction of the operations was positive during both units of time; but the condition imposed may be such as to require all the operations, during the second unit of time, to be inverted, or performed in the negative direction; which condition will be fulfilled by rendering negative all the factors in the numerators of the coefficients of the powers generated in the time $1_t''$, whence we get the result $(1-4+6-4+1)\phi^0 = (1-1)^4\phi^0$.

These generations are only for two single units of time $1_t'$ and $1_t''$; but they may be extended to any two intervals $x1_t$ and $h1_t$, as follows : The power ϕ^{iv}, being a constant or uniform generator, and generating the amount of power $2\phi'''$ in the unit of time 1_t, will generate the amount $2x\phi'''$ in the time $x'1_t$. On the completion of its generation in the time $x'1_t$, the power $2x\phi'''$ has become a uniform generator, and will generate the power $2.3x^2\phi''$ in the succeeding interval of time $x''1_t$; and therefore during the time of its own generation in $x'1_t$, the power $2x\phi'''$ will generate half the preceding amount, or $3x^2\phi''$. On the completion of its generation in the time $x'1_t$, the power $3x^2\phi''$ has become a uniform generator, and will generate the power $3.4x^3\phi'$ in the succeeding time $x''1_t$; and therefore during the time of its own generation in $x'1_t$, the power $3x^2\phi''$ will (as in the case of a single unit of time) generate one-third the preceding amount, or $4x^3\phi'$. Finally at the expiration of the time $x'1_t$, the power $4x^3\phi'$ has become a constant generator, and will generate the power zero $4x^4\phi^0$ in the succeeding time $x''1_t$; and therefore during its own generation in the time $x'1_t$, the power $4x^3\phi'$ will (as in the case of a single unit of time) generate one-fourth of the preceding amount, or $x^4\phi^0$. We get thus the simultaneous series of powers $1\phi^{iv}$, $2x\phi'''$, $3x^2\phi''$, $4x^3\phi'$, $1x^4\phi^0$, for the time $x1_t$; and by applying the same law of genesis to each of these several powers during the succeeding interval of time $h1_t$, we are enabled to write the arithmetical triangle of the fourth order, as it is given in A′ on page 101, where it furnishes the development $(x^4+4x^3h+6x^2h^2+4xh^3+h^4)\phi^0$, being the coefficient of the entire phenomenon $(x+h)^4 1_t . 1_\mu$ generated in the time $(x+h)1_t$; and if all the factors in the numerators were rendered negative for the time $h1_t$, we should have $(x-h)^4 1_t . 1_\mu$ in the time $(x-h)1_t$.

This fundamental case constitutes the normal form of genesis, wherein all the genetic operations during the first unit of time are positive, and encounter no hindrance or interference other than the inertia of the material unit 1_μ which serves to realize the phenomenon. The genesis as it occurs in each separate semi-unit of the time $1_t'$ may be recalled thus :

$\frac{1}{2}'.1_t'+\frac{1}{2}''.1_t' = 1_t.$

$$1\phi^{\text{iv}} = 1^1\phi^{\text{iv}}, \text{ the primitive generator :}$$
$$1\phi'''+1\phi''' = 2\phi''' = 1^2\phi''', \text{ the first derivative;}$$
$$1\phi'' +2\phi'' = 3\phi'' = 1^3\phi'', \text{ the second derivative;}$$
$$1\phi' +3\phi' = 4\phi' = 1^4\phi', \text{ the third derivative;}$$
$$1\phi^0 = 1^0\phi^0, \text{ the phenomenon.}$$

101. Let all the genetic operations during the second semiunit of time $\frac{1}{2}''.1_t'$ be negative, those of the first being positive as before : then the immediate result in the time $1_t'$ will be

$$\phi^n-\phi^n = \phi^0 = 1;$$

because the operation is equivalent to the direct description of the linear unit 1_t in the time $\frac{1}{2}'.1_t'$, followed by the inverse description of the same line in the time $\frac{1}{2}''.1_t'$; which again is equivalent to the operation of taking the ratio $1_t : 1_t = 1$; and the process assigned by the condition or law of the genesis will be continued thus, when $n = 1$:

$\frac{1}{2}'.1_t'+\frac{1}{2}''.1_t' = 1_t'.$

$$1\phi^1 = 1\phi^1, \text{ the primitive destroyer :}$$
$$1\phi^0 -1\phi^0 = 1\phi^0, \text{ the ratio of the phenomenon;}$$
$$1\phi' -2\phi' = -1\phi', \text{ the first mediate consequent;}$$
$$1\phi'' -3\phi'' = -2\phi'', \text{ the second mediate consequent;}$$

$1\phi'''-4\phi''' = -3\phi'''$, etc., or the hierarchy called into existence is $1\phi^0$, $-1\phi'$, $-2\phi''$, $-3\phi'''$, etc., which may be written thus $1^0\phi^0$, $1^{-1}\phi'$, $1^{-2}\phi''$, $1^{-3}\phi'''$, etc. when the exponents are held to signify the number and direction of the operations to be performed.

The factors to be introduced into the numerators of the coefficients of the powers generated in the time $1_t''$ will be negative, and proceed in the order of positive increase as shown in n° 76, until reaching in each dependent series the power zero ϕ^0, where the genesis terminates.

Now reckoning by number of operations, if one operation like the preceding *one* division of the linear unit by itself require a unit of time for its performance, it will require x units of time for the performance of x divisions of the linear unit, and again x further units of time to repeat such divisions on the last result, and so on as discussed in n° 77, where is also given the deduction of the simultaneous series

$$\frac{1}{x}\phi^{0}, \quad -\frac{1}{x^{2}}\phi', \quad -\frac{2}{x^{3}}\phi'', \quad -\frac{3}{x^{4}}\phi''', \quad -\frac{4}{x^{5}}\phi^{iv}, \text{ \&c.}$$

With this series or hierarchy of powers, generated or originated in the time $x1_t$, we may enter upon the time $h1_t$ as shown in n° 70, and achieve the genesis of the phenomenon $(x+h)^{-1}1_t \cdot 1_\mu$ in the time $(x+h)1_t$ [p. 125]; and if the signs of all the factors of the numerators of the coefficients of the powers generated in the time $h1_t$ be changed, the phenomenon will be transformed into $(x-h)^{-1}1_t \cdot 1_\mu$ for the time $(x-h)1_t$ [p. 127].

An illustration of this first form of negative genesis may be in place here. The line OP $= x.1_t \cdot 1_\mu$ is given as the measurement of a phenomenon produced in the time $x1_t$ by the power of the first order ϕ', or the velocity 1_λ; and it is required to restore the material unit 1_μ to the origin O, and finally to a state of equilibrium or rest at that point by destroying all the powers generated during the time $x1_t$, and acting on the mobile during the time $h1_t$. To return 1_μ from P to O in $x1_t$, requires the negative velocity -1.1_λ, which perseveres in its negative direction, and carries 1_μ to the left of O during the time $h1_t$; so that a power of the second order ϕ'' is required to annihilate this negative velocity, and return 1_μ to O; from which point, again, it is carried to the right of O by the power of the second order: a force of the third order ϕ''' is demanded, in its turn to restore 1_μ to O, by destroying the velocity of the power of the second order in the direction OP; which force of the third order again carries 1_μ to the left of O, and so on *ad infinitum*.

O .——.——.——.——. P

102. We are now to study a case of interference. We know [n° 16] that ratios deduced from particular forms or species of existence are susceptible of general adaptation as coefficients to other species, provided they are homogeneous with the first. Such homogeneity exists between generating powers of the same or of different orders, all being existences of a similar nature. Therefore in the series of powers deduced in n° 77, namely, $1x^{-1}\phi^{0}$,

$-1x^{-2}\phi'$, $-2x^{-3}\phi''$, $-3x^{-4}\phi'''$, etc., we may reserve the ratios $1x^{-1}$, $-1x^{-2}$, $-2x^{-3}$, $-x^{-4}$, etc. to stand as the coefficients of a hierarchy whose power zero ϕ^0 may be located arbitrarily in the scale. For example, we may have

$-1x^{-2}\phi^0$, $-2x^{-3}\phi'$, $-3x^{-4}\phi''$, $-4x^{-5}\phi'''$, etc., or

$-2x^{-3}\phi^0$, $-3x^{-4}\phi'$, $-4x^{-5}\phi''$, $-5x^{-6}\phi'''$, etc., and so on.

This being premised, let all the negative generators operate during the second half only of the first interval of time, and all the positive generators operate positively during both halves of that interval.

1° Let $-5x^{-5}$ be the coefficient of the negative power of the fourth order, and bring the positive power $x^{-5}\phi^{iv}$ to its encounter during the first interval of time : we shall have the following genesis :

$\frac{1}{2}'.x1_t$, $\frac{1}{2}''.x1_t$. SIMULTANEOUS SERIES.

$x^{-5}\phi^{iv}-5x^{-5}\phi^{iv} = -4x^{-5}\phi^{iv}$,

$x^{-4}\phi'''-4x^{-4}\phi''' = -3x^{-4}\phi'''$,

$x^{-3}\phi'' -3x^{-3}\phi'' = -2x^{-3}\phi''$,

$x^{-2}\phi' -2x^{-2}\phi' = -1x^{-2}\phi'$,

$x^{-1}\phi^0 -1x^{-1}\phi^0 = 0x^{-1}\phi^0$. With this simultaneous series, we form the arithmetrical triangle after the usual manner; when, by dividing the lowest diagonal line (the hypothenuse) by 0, we find the development of $(x+h)^{-1}$.

2° Let $-6x^{-6}$ be the coefficient of the negative power of the fourth order, and bring the positive power $x^{-6}\phi^{iv}$ to the encounter : we shall have the following genesis :

$\frac{1}{2}'.x1_t$, $\frac{1}{2}''.x1_t$. SIMULTANEOUS SERIES.

$x^{-6}(1-6)\phi^{iv} = -5x^{-6}\phi^{iv}$,

$x^{-5}(1-5)\phi''' = -4x^{-5}\phi'''$,

$x^{-4}(1-4)\phi'' = -3x^{-4}\phi''$,

$x^{-3}(1-3)\phi' = -2x^{-3}\phi'$,

$x^{-2}(1-2)\phi^0 = -1x^{-2}\phi^0$. With this simultaneous series, we form the arithmetical triangle after the usual manner; when, dividing the inferior diagonal line by -1, we find the development of $(x+h)^{-2}$.

3° Let $-7x^{-7}$ be the coefficient of the negative power of the fourth order, and bring the positive power $x^{-7}\phi^{iv}$ to the encounter : we shall have the following genesis :

$\frac{1}{2}'.x1_t$, $\frac{1}{2}''.x1_t$. SIMULTANEOUS SERIES.

$x^{-7}(1-7)\phi^{iv} = -6x^{-7}\phi^{iv}$,
$x^{-6}(1-6)\phi''' = -5x^{-6}\phi'''$,
$x^{-5}(1-5)\phi'' = -4x^{-5}\phi''$,
$x^{-4}(1-4)\phi' = -3x^{-4}\phi'$,
$x^{-2}(1-3)\phi^0 = -2x^{-3}\phi^0$. Form the arithmetical triangle as usual, and divide the inferior diagonal by -2 for the development of $(x+h)^{-3}$.

For fractional development, divide the coefficients and exponents by the denominator of the fraction, and then proceed the same as with integers. Neglecting x because we cannot print the fractional exponents, we have the numerical coefficients thus :

1° Let $-\frac{7}{2}$ be the numerical coefficient of the negative power of the fourth order, to be encountered by the positive power ϕ^{iv}: we shall have the genesis :

$\frac{1}{2}'.1_t$, $\frac{1}{2}''.1_t$. SIMULTANEOUS SERIES.

$(1-\frac{7}{2})\phi^{iv} = -\frac{5}{2}\phi^{iv}$,
$(1-\frac{5}{2})\phi''' = -\frac{3}{2}\phi'''$,
$(1-\frac{3}{2})\phi'' = -\frac{1}{2}\phi''$,
$(1-\frac{1}{2})\phi' = +\frac{1}{2}\phi'$,
$(1+\frac{1}{2})\phi^0 = +\frac{3}{2}\phi^0$. In each term of this simultaneous series, introduce the power of x to the exponent equal to the coefficient *minus* 1, form the arithmetical triangle as usual, and divide the inferior diagonal or hypothenuse by $+\frac{3}{2}$, when we will find the development of $(x+h)^{\frac{1}{2}}$.

2° Let $-\frac{9}{2}$ be the numerical coefficient of the negative power of the fourth order, to be encountered by the positive power ϕ^{iv}: we shall have the genesis :

$\frac{1}{2}'.1_t$, $\frac{1}{2}''.1_t$. SIMULTANEOUS SERIES.

$(1-\frac{9}{2})\phi^{iv} = -\frac{7}{2}\phi^{iv}$,
$(1-\frac{7}{2})\phi''' = -\frac{5}{2}\phi'''$,
$(1-\frac{5}{2})\phi'' = -\frac{3}{2}\phi''$,
$(1-\frac{3}{2})\phi' = -\frac{1}{2}\phi'$,
$(1-\frac{1}{2})\phi^0 = +\frac{1}{2}\phi^0$. Introduce x with the exponents equal to the coefficients *minus* 1, form the arithmetical triangle, and divide the hypothenuse by $+\frac{1}{2}$: we shall find the development of $(x+h)^{-\frac{1}{2}}$.

Beginning with the numerical coefficient $-\frac{5}{2}$ of the negative power of the fourth order, we should get the development of $x+h$ to the power $\frac{3}{2}$, etc.

As a last example, let $-4x^{-4}$ be the coefficient of the negative power of the fourth order, to be encountered by the positive power $x^{-4}\phi^{iv}$: we obtain the genesis :

$\frac{1}{2}'.x1_t$, $\frac{1}{2}''.x1_t$. SIMULTANEOUS SERIES.

$$x^{-4}(1-4)\phi^{iv} = -3x^{-4}\phi^{iv},$$
$$x^{-3}(1-3)\phi''' = -2x^{-3}\phi''',$$
$$x^{-2}(1-2)\phi'' = -1x^{-2}\phi'',$$
$$x^{-1}(1-1)\phi' = 0x^{-1}\phi',$$
$$x^{-1}.x(1+0)\phi^0 = 1\phi^0.$$

Now in logarithmic development, the the term $x^{-1}.x$, rejected in division, is retained [p. 114]; whereby another diagonal or hypothenuse line is added to the arithmetical triangle for $(x+h)^{-1}$, which is now to be divided by 0.1, and, writing $\log x.\phi^0$ in place of $x^{-1}.x.\phi^0 = 1\phi^0$, we find the development of $\log(x+h)$.

All these developments may be obtained from Table B, which is a form of arithmetical triangle so generalized as to give the particular triangle corresponding to any exponent n. By changing the signs of the factors in the numerators of the coefficients of the terms under the time $h1_t$, we convert any development of $x+h$ into that of $x-h$.

103. In the two classes of development considered in n°s 100 and 102, the genetic operations agreed in the character of being *free* or unconstrained, and differed in the *opposite direction* of their respective actions. The generating powers being entirely free, each successive production exceeded the preceding one in extent by unity, which gave to the numerical coefficients of the successive powers in the first class the forms 1, $1^2=2$, $1^3=3$, etc., and the forms 1, $1^{-1}=-1$, $1^{-2}=-2$, $1^{-3}=-3$, etc. in the second class.

Now suppose the genetic operations are not free, but that they are confined to a resisting medium, or otherwise constrained or hindered during the first unit of time, so that each successive production (in order, not in time) just equals the preceding one :

then the numerical coefficients of the successive powers in this third class of development will take the form 1, $1_0^1=1$, $1_0^2=1$, $1_0^3=1$, $1_0^4=1$, etc., or as well $1_0^{-1}=1$, $1_0^{-2}=1$, $1_0^{-3}=1$, etc.; each power increasing from 0 at the commencement to 1 at the termination of the time 1_t. The condition of constraint may be fulfilled by compelling the genetic powers to act in an angular direction, upon the extremity A of the radius $OA = 1_r = 1_l$ [fig. 51]. Unlike the indeterminate unit of magnitude 1_l, the unit of angular magnitude 1_0 is absolute, and has the circumference for a fixed measure; a complete revolution of the radius measuring at the same time one single operation performed in the unit of time 1_t, and restoring the primitive value of the linear unit 1_l, or satisfying the equality $1_0^n.1_r.1_\mu = 1_0^{-n}.1_r.1_\mu = 1.1_r.1_\mu = OA \times 1_\mu$. More generally the point of application of the primitive power ϕ^0 may be at either of the four positions A, A′, B, B′; when, accordingly, we must replace the absolute unit 1_0 by one of its four values $+1$, -1, $+\sqrt{-1}$, $-\sqrt{-1}$, corresponding to the four angles 0°, 180°, 90°, 270°, and which are all comprised in the symbol $\sqrt[4]{1}$ of the fourth-roots of unity.

The following general triangle for this class of developments (comprising those in which the base is constant and the exponent variable) is arranged by placing the simultaneous series of the first interval of time 1_t in the first horizontal line, the interval $x1_t$ occupying all the rest of the tablet :

THE GENERAL EXPONENTIAL TRIANGLE.

$$1\phi^0;\ (\sqrt[4]{1})\phi',\ (\sqrt[4]{1})\phi'',\ (\sqrt[4]{1})\phi''',\ (\sqrt[4]{1})\phi^{iv},\ (\sqrt[4]{1})\phi^{v},$$

$$(\sqrt[4]{1})x\phi^0;\ (\sqrt[4]{1})x\phi',\ (\sqrt[4]{1})x\phi'',\ (\sqrt[4]{1})\phi''',\ (\sqrt[4]{1})x\phi^{iv},$$

$$\frac{(\sqrt[4]{1})^2}{1.1^2}x^2\phi^0;\ \frac{(\sqrt[4]{1})^2}{1.1^2}x^2\phi',\ \frac{(\sqrt[4]{1})^2}{1.1^2}x^2\phi'',\ \frac{(\sqrt[4]{1})^2}{1.1^2}x^2\phi''',$$

$$\frac{(\sqrt[4]{1})^3}{1.1^2.1^3}x^3\phi^0;\ \frac{(\sqrt[4]{1})^3}{1.1^2.1^3}x^3\phi',\ \frac{(\sqrt[4]{1})^2}{1.1^2.1^3}x^3\phi'',$$

$$\frac{(\sqrt[4]{1})^4}{1.1^2.1^3.1^4}x^4\phi^0;\ \frac{(\sqrt[4]{1})^4}{1.1^2.1^3.1^4}x^4\phi',$$

$$\frac{(\sqrt[4]{1})^5}{1.1^2.1^3.1^4.1^5}x^5\phi^0,$$

&c.; the

denominators to be expanded dynamically, and the numerators arithmetically for each fourth-root of unity.

104. The law of uniform operation, hitherto applied only to the development of successive multiplications and divisions, is readily applicable to various other direct and inverse processes, such as the taking of successive differences and differentials, of successive integrals, etc. Indeed it forms the basis of the calculus of generating functions; and it eliminates the distinction between symbols of operation and of quantity, because multiplication and division are merely operations, and express quantity only mediately through ratio.

From the exponential triangle in the preceding paragraph, for the root $\sqrt[4]{1} = 1$, we get the series

$$\left(1^0+\frac{1^1}{1}x+\frac{1^2}{1.2}x^2+\frac{1^3}{1.2.3}x^3+\frac{1^4}{1.2.3.4}x^4+\frac{1^5}{1.2.3.4.5}x^5+\&c.\right)\phi^0=e^x\phi^0.$$

Now the most general interpretation of the positive nth power of unity 1^n, is, that it is the unit measure of n operations, that is to say, the measure of n direct and equal operations performed in the unit of time 1_t. Suppose these n operations to consist of so many successive differentiations performed on the function fx, and we shall have

$$\frac{d^0fx}{dx^0}=1^0,\quad \frac{d^1fx}{dx^1}=1^1,\quad \frac{d^2fx}{dx^2}=1^2,\quad \frac{d^3fx}{dx^3}=1^3,\ \text{etc.};\qquad \text{which,}$$

being substituted in the above series, and writing h for x, gives

$$f(x+h)\phi^0 = \left(fx+\frac{dfx}{dx}h+\frac{d^2fx}{dx^2}.\frac{h^2}{1.2}+\frac{d^3fx}{dx^3}.\frac{h^3}{1.2.3}+\&c.\right)\phi^0.$$

TAYLOR'S THEOREM.

105. RESUME. All ratios are obtained from the comparison of the measures of operations performed in space and time. Assume the generative power ϕ^n of the order n, subject to the law of uniformity of action, and inquire into the operation performed and the ratio generated in the unit of time 1_t :

I. If $n = 0$, we have the power zero ϕ^0, the *infima species* or lowest category of existence, the void space itself; in which nevertheless are two fundamental forms of unity, the linear 1_l and the angular 1_θ unit, the latter having an absolute or fixed unit measure 1_0 in the circumference, while the former is indeterminate. To these two geometrical forms of unity, all phenomena, and all operations, are referred by their measures; but they correspond in themselves to the ratio 1^0, which indicates the performance of *no* operation. So much of elementary geometry, both of two and three dimensions, as consists in verifying the relations of lines and angles to each other by means of the rule and compasses, without the aid of higher operations in the way of multiplication and division, will have its results expressed under this value of the exponent n.

II. If $n = 1$, we have the power of the first order ϕ', the immediate physical cause of the phenomenon, or performer of the operation, whose measure in space is unity. This power corresponds to the unit of velocity 1_λ; and when operating angularly upon the unit radius 1_r of a circle, it may be so regulated as to generate the four fundamental algebraical ratios $+\sqrt{-1}$, -1, $-\sqrt{-1}$, $+1$, which affect all phenomena, and enter into the composition of all forms of development in space and time. It yields the direct, positive, or normal form of operation, and generates the ratio 1^1 in the unit of time. The operations of arithmetic, and of geometry by proportion, proceed under the value of the exponent $n=+1$, and also under the value $n = -1$ in its first power only; while algebraical processes take cognizance of all the four fourth-roots of unity in their place.

III. If $n = -1$, we have the power of the first negative order $\phi^{-\prime}$, which governs the performance of inverse or negative operations, and generates different ratios according to the ratio of the phenomenon to which it is opposed, as,

$1^2.1_\lambda \div 1^1.1_\lambda = 1^1$, the positive rational unit;

$1^1.1_\lambda \div 1^1.1_\lambda = 1^0$, the geometrical unit, or zero of power, which also corresponds to $\log 1$;

$1^0.1_\lambda \div 1^1.1_\lambda = 1^{-1}$, the reciprocal unit;

$1^n.1_\lambda - 1.1_\lambda = 0$, the absolute zero;

$0.1_\lambda - 1.1_\lambda = -1$, the negative rational unit.

IV. If $n > 1$, we have the general power ϕ^n, which, during a first unit of time $1'_t$, generates a hierarchy of powers expressed by the series

$$1^1\phi^n,\ 1^2\phi^{n-\prime},\ 1^3\phi^{n-\prime\prime},\ \ldots,\ 1^{n-2}\phi''',\ 1^{n-1}\phi'',\ 1^n\phi',\ 1^0\phi^0=1;$$

where the unitary coefficients will have one of three different forms, accordingly as the operations are conditioned to be, 1° free and direct, 2° free and inverse, or 3° constrained.

1° When the operations are free and direct, the coefficients will be expanded dynamically and positively, and the hierarchy becomes

$$1\phi^n,\ 2\phi^{n-\prime},\ 3\phi^{n-\prime\prime},\ \ldots,\ (n-1)\phi''',\ (n-2)\phi'',\ n\phi',\ 1\phi^0.$$

This condition leads to the development of $(x\pm h)^n$.

2° When the operations are free but inverse, the coefficients will be expanded dynamically and negatively, the order of the terms will be inverted, and the hierarchy becomes

$$1\phi^0=1,\ -n\phi',\ -(n+1)\phi'',\ -(n+2)\phi''',\ \text{etc.}$$

This condition gives the development of $(x\pm n)^{-n}$.

3° If the operations are constrained, so that all are confined to the value of the first one, the coefficients will be expanded arithmetically, and the hierarchy will be

$$1\phi^0=1,\ 1_0\phi',\ 1_0\phi'',\ 1_0\phi''',\ \text{etc.},$$

where 1_0 may have either one of the four values $+\sqrt{-1}$, -1, $-\sqrt{-1}$, $+1$, and the condition gives the development of $e^{(1)^{\frac{1}{4}}}$.

Thus when the exponent of unity 1^n is other than 0 or 1, the operations which generate that form of unity are such as yield also the differential coefficient, and have hitherto been only obscurely known through the medium of the fluxionary calculus, but are now found to constitute the most general form of synthetical and analytical calculation, and to be possessed of sufficient symmetrical compactness of comprehension and amplitude of extension to merit the title of a new calculus, to wit, THE CALCULUS OF OPERATIONS.

1° The same process that evolves the four fourth-roots of absolute unity $\sqrt[4]{1_0}$, demonstrates the properties of the four algebraical signs $+1$ and -1, $+\sqrt{-1}$ and $-\sqrt{-1}$.

2° The same process that involves dynamical unity to positive powers $1^n = +n$, yields the hierarchy of generative powers which serve to develop a variable base to a constant positive exponent.

3° The same process that involves dynamical unity to negative powers $1^{-n} = -n$, yields the hierarchy of destructive powers which serve to develop a variable base to a constant negative exponent.

4° The same process that involves the four fourth-roots of unity to entire arithmetical powers $(\sqrt[4]{1})^n = 1$, yields the hierarchy of circulative powers which serve to develop a constant base to a variable exponent.

106. Recurring to the operative triangle of n° 57, which may serve to represent either a scale of natural powers engaged in the production of phenomena, or a system of operators so arranged for the purpose of performing the measurement of such phenomena : without inquiring into its origin, we may suppose the system to be formed, and that in obedience to signals propagated from the central operator at A [fig. 64] through all the subordinates down to the lowest at D, D′, D″, D‴, each operator acts in his place and duty of measuring the appropriate angle or arc subtended by the phenomenon. These signals being unseen any where but in the line of the operators themselves, observations made from the base line EE^{iv} could discover none but the immediate operators on the line DD‴; and so in fact nothing beyond the immediate physical cause is directly inferable from the mere examination of the phenomena of nature. On the hypothesis that the operators are all isolated, and act in virtue of their own proper energy and merely in obedience to the signals, it follows that the antecedents are only *unerring signs*, and not *causes*, of their consequents; and if this conclusion is made so general as to include the lowest or physical cause, we shall have the denial of the principle of causality, and fall into the philosophical system maintained by Brown and Mill, in which the error on this point appears to have arisen from the very superficial mistake of misapprehending the *invariably antecedent phenomenon* to constitute all that is meant by the *physical cause* of the *consequent* phe-

nomenon, and thereby ignoring the notion of the noumenon, the *vera causa*, and leaving the statical interpretation of nature in the ascendant.

But when we inquire into the formation of the system either of operators or of natural powers, we are led to the conclusion that such isolation does not exist; and that just as the complex flows from the simple, so the powers of nature descend from unity to variety or multiplicity in successive dependence, according to laws which the finally resulting phenomena in each particular class of cases must assist us to find out inductively. On this hypothesis of successive dependence, then, we build our theory of generating powers; and the system, if of the powers of nature, is formed by the actual generation or production of powers in successive gradation from the primitive noumenon down to the lowest which merges into the phenomenon; and if of operators, by the furnishing and despatching of operative agents from each station to the next lower ones, in which manner the whole system would really be dependent upon the primitive actor and overseer at the centre A, and present an analogy to the system of nature. In addition to the final operations, or the phenomena, which will be the same as in the former example, we have here an account of the formation of the system, which introduces and verifies the principle of causality, and thereby renders deductive science possible, and finally crowns the result by establishing the dynamical interpretation of nature.

This is the boldest hypothesis, and constitutes the ontological method nearly as it is indicated in the philosophical system of KRAUSE, and recently taught in the University of Brussels : it is deductive, living, and fertile; while the method furnished by the hypothesis of isolation, which acknowledges no other existences, no other tenants of the universe than phenomena and their laws, is merely classificatory, and amounts to nothing better than the arranging of a collection of dead facts in a charnel-house.

An intermediate hypothesis would be one which should assign to the primitive power at A a force equal to the sum of the forces of the two powers at B and B′; to the sum of the forces of the three powers at C, C′ and C″; and finally to the sum of the forces of the four powers at D, D′, D″ and D‴. In this case, either set of operators, 1°, A; 2°, B and B′; 3°, C, C′, C‴; or, 4°, D, D′, D″, D‴, can turn the system (through the angle 60°) in the unit of time; which assumption leads immediately to the recognition of the property of the lever, because the transfer of a unit of mass through four units of distance in the unit of time, requires four times the force of the first order that is requisite to accomplish the unit of distance in that time : then four units of weight at B are required to balance one at E^{iv}. Suppose all the forces, except the primitive at A, to be solidified; that is, let the operative triangle be converted into a machine : we shall have the purely mechanical interpretation of nature, all the phenomena occurring immediately at the beck of the prime mover at the centre. This will be recognized as corresponding with the philosophical systems of MALEBRANCHE and BERKELEY.

107. An image of the gradual conversion of intension into extension, may be formed after the following model :

Suppose (on a plane) a uniform fluxion of heat (propagation of heat by conduction) from the centre O [fig. 76] to the successive circumferences A′, A″, A‴, A^{iv}; at which last circumference let the temperature zero be maintained, and the conduction cease at the circumference A‴. For the same angle ZOZ′, after the system is formed, the quantity of heat contained in each arc (up to and including that of A‴) will be the same; but for the same length of arc, the quantity decreases proportionally to the increase of the radii, and this represents the decrease of intension. The projection of heat (propagation of heat by radiation), on the contrary, increases with the extent of the radiating surface of the successive circumferences, that is, proportionally to the increase of the radii, which represents the increase of extension.

Let the several radii be

$$OA'=1.1_r,\ OA''=2.1_r,\ OA'''=3.1_r.\ OA^{iv}=4.1_r,$$

and make the angle $ZOZ' = 60°$; whence the several chords $\phi'''\phi'''$, $\phi''\phi''$, $\phi'\phi'$, $\phi^0\phi^0$, are equal to the radius, and the arcs are proportional thereto. Then if the intension at O be measured by 4, it will be 3 at A′, 2 at A″, 1 at A‴ (thus far inversely proportional to the radius), and 0 by condition at A^{iv}; and if the extension be 1 at O, it will be measured by the chord $\phi'''\phi'''$, and become 2 at A$'$, 3 at A$''$, 4 at A$'''$ (thus far directly proportional to the radius), and be reduced to 1 again at A^{iv} by condition.

Let now the first column on the left represent the series of powers simultaneously generated by the primitive power of the fourth order ϕ^{iv} in the first semiunit of time $\frac{1}{2}'.1'_t$, and the remaining columns of powers as written on the right of the first lefthand column be simultaneously generated in the second semiunit of time $\frac{1}{2}''.1'_t$; then we shall have the hierarchy of the fourth order, deduced from the philosophical triangle according to the preceding analogy, and enumerated as follows :

$$\frac{1}{2}'.1'_t,\ \frac{1}{2}''.1'_t = 1'_t.$$
$$\phi^{iv} = 1\phi^{iv};$$
$$\phi''' + \phi''' = 2\phi''';$$
$$\phi'' + 2\phi'' = 3\phi'';$$
$$\phi' + 3\phi' = 4\phi';$$
$$\phi^{0} = 1\phi^{0}.$$

This device exhibits merely the normal form of genesis during the first unit of time, or rather during four successive units rendered simultaneous by superposition. Combination during the second semiunit of time must be resorted to for the exhibition of the genesis of negative powers [n° 78], and the artifice of spirals for that of repeating powers [n° 98]. But when once the logical deduction of the hierarchy of generative powers is established, we see that the primitive power ϕ^{n} commands the entire process of development.

ADDENDA.

108. To render the demonstration of the properties of the four fundamental algebraical signs more concise and perspicuous than a first investigation would permit, I here recal the separate steps under which the same may be arranged.

1° We hold that the human mind is immediately conversant with nothing else but the relations of phenomena, under the various forms of ratio obtained by comparing together the actual measures of such phenomena in space and time; our preliminary knowledge of the nature of space being derived from our tactual and motory sensations, the repetition of which begets in us the idea of time. Any measure whatever in and of space involves in itself necessarily the measure of its concomitant time; while it is also the measure of an operation, to wit, of the very operation of measurement, as well as of the phenomenon measured. There are two, and only two, elementary standards of measurement : the straight line, which measures the direct distance between two points; and the circular line, which measures the angular deviation between two straight lines. Corresponding to these two elementary standards, arose the primitive instruments of measurement, the rule and the compasses; and all other standards and scales of measurement in use are formed by combining the two simple elements of linear and angular magnitude, and are resolvable into them.

2° The simplest kind of operation would consist in transferring a unit of burthen 1_μ through a unit of distance 1_l in a unit of time 1_t, which would give the unit of distance 1_l = OP for the measure of the phenomenon and of the operation; and this operation evidently is

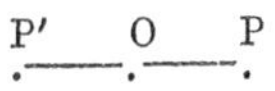

P′ O P
.——.——.

equivalent to the performance of one addition (adding 1_μ to the station P), and as well to the multiplication of 1_μ by the dynamical unit of the first order, the unit of velocity 1_λ (transferring 1_μ through the unit of distance 1_l). The expression of the measure of the operation is therefore simple and unique 1_l; but let now the equally simple operation be prescribed, of transferring 1_μ from P back to O : the measure of this operation will be equal in magnitude to that of the former, but the two measures will have a relation to each other which is necessary to be noted. To do this, we combine the idea of distance with that of direction, and distinguish the expressions for the unit measure of distance by marks suitable to denote coincidence and opposition of direction, which may be done by the characters $+1$ and -1, since the signs $+$, $-$ have already been used to direct the performance of the opposite operations of addition and subtraction. Generalizing these simple and single operations, we shall have the expression $+1.1_\lambda$ competent to direct the performance of one addition or (of its equivalent) one multiplication by unity, which will give $+1.1_l$ $=$OP as the distinctive measure of such positive operation; and the expression -1.1_λ as yet only serving to direct the performance of one subtraction, which, when regarded as a general measure of a negative operation (that is, one opposite in direction to, and of course destructive of the effect measured by, the former measure), will have $-1.1_l =$ OP′ as the proper measure of such negative operation.

3° When multiplication by linear unity 1_λ is repeated on the material unit 1_μ, we have (as has been abundantly shown in n°s 17, 18) in general $1_\lambda^n.1_\mu = n1_l.1_\mu$, and of course $1_\lambda^{\frac{1}{2}n}.1_\mu = \frac{1}{2}n1_l.1_\mu$, and consequently $1_\lambda^{\frac{1}{2}}.1_\mu = \frac{1}{2}.1_l.1_\mu$, where the results transcend the province of arithmetic, because they have no fixed geometrical measure, the unit of linear magnitude being entirely indeterminate. But angular magnitude has the circumference of a circle for its fixed measure; so that if we take an arc for multiplying unit 1_θ, and that arc be the nth part of the circumference, we shall have $1_\theta^n.1_r.1_\mu = +1.1_r.1_\mu$ provided we started from the position expressed by $+1.1_r.1_\mu$. Then if we make $\theta = 2\pi$, we have $1_{2\pi}^1.1_r.1_\mu = +1.1_r.1_\mu$, or one multiplication carries 1_μ through the circumference in the unit of time 1_t; and if $\theta = \pi$, we shall have

$1^1_\pi.1_r.1_\mu = \mathrm{OP}'\times 1_\mu$, that is, one multiplication carries 1_μ through the semicircumference, from the position in OP to that in OP′ (which last was above denoted by -1.1_l), in the unit of time; so that $1_\pi.1_r.1_\mu = -1.1_\lambda.1_\mu = -1.1_l.1_\mu$, the second expression being in the imperative mood and the last in the indicative. Obviously then we may substitute the expression -1.1_λ for $1_\pi.1_r$, to direct the revolution of 1_μ through the semicircumference in the unit of time, from the position $\mathrm{OP}\times 1_\mu = +1.1_l.1_\mu$, to the opposite position $\mathrm{OP}'\times 1_\mu = -1.1_l.1_\mu$, and this is multiplying 1_μ by -1.1_λ: whence a repetition of the operation of multiplying 1_μ by -1.1_λ will revolve the multiplicand 1_μ into the position $\mathrm{OP}\times 1_\mu$, giving the result $(-1)^2 1_\lambda.1_\mu = +1.1_l.1_\mu$; and consequently we have inversely $-1.1_\lambda.1_\mu = (+1)^{\frac{1}{2}}.1_\lambda.1_\mu$, which completes the demonstration of the properties of the negative sign.

4° If we take for multiplying unit the arc which measures one right angle, we have $1^1_{\frac{1}{2}\pi}.1_r.1_\mu$, which revolves $1_r.1_\mu$ through 90° into the position $\mathrm{OQ}\times 1_\mu$; and a repetition gives $1^2_{\frac{1}{2}\pi}.1_r.1_\mu$, and carries 1_μ into the position $\mathrm{OP}'\times 1_\mu = -1.1_r.1_\mu = -1_l.1_\mu$: then of course we have

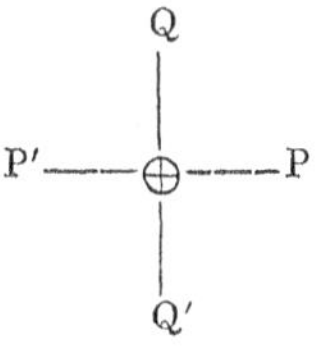

$$1_{\frac{1}{2}\pi}.1_r.1_\mu = 1^{\frac{1}{2}}_\pi.1_r.1_\mu = (-1)^{\frac{1}{2}}.1_\lambda.1_\mu = (\sqrt{-1})1_r.1_\mu = (\sqrt{-1})1_l.1_\mu$$

to express the position $\mathrm{OQ}\times 1_\mu$ perpendicular to the line PP′. A second repetition of the multiplication by $1^1_{\frac{1}{2}\pi}$ will give $1^3_{\frac{1}{2}\pi}.1_r.1_\mu$, carrying 1_μ into the position OQ′ again perpendicular to the line P′P, but opposite to the former perpendicular position OQ. We have now the same relation between OQ′ and OQ, that exists between OP′ and OP, namely, opposition of direction : we therefore indicate the relation in this instance by the same marks + and − distinctive of direction by coincidence and by opposition, and write $(+\sqrt{-1})1_l = \mathrm{OQ}$ and $(-\sqrt{-1})1_l = \mathrm{OQ}'$, so that we have

$$1^3_{\frac{1}{2}}.1_r.1_\mu = (-1)(+\sqrt{-1})1_\lambda.1_\mu = (+\sqrt{-1})^3.1_\lambda.1_\mu = (-\sqrt{-1})1_r.1_\mu = (-\sqrt{-1})1_l.1_\mu.$$

Finally the fourth multiplication of 1_μ by $1_{\frac{1}{2}\pi}$ gives $1^4_{\frac{1}{2}\pi}.1_r.1_\mu$, and restores 1_μ to its primitive position at P, with the result

$$1^4_{\frac{1}{2}\pi}.1_r.1_\mu = (+\sqrt{-1})^4 1_r.1_\mu = (+1)1_r.1_\mu = \text{OP}\times 1_\mu, \text{ and}$$

consequently
$$(+\sqrt{-1})1_r.1_\mu = (+1)^{\frac{1}{4}}.1_r.1_\mu = \text{OQ}\times 1_\mu,$$
$$(+\sqrt{-1})^2 1_r.1_\mu = (-1)1_r.1_\mu = \text{OP}'\times 1_\mu,$$
$$(+\sqrt{-1})^3 1_r.1_\mu = (-\sqrt{-1})1_r.1_\mu = \text{OQ}'\times 1_\mu,$$

which completes the demonstration of the properties of the imaginary sign.

Thus the four symbols $+\sqrt{-1}$, -1, $-\sqrt{-1}$, $+1$, are truly ratios obtained from the comparison of the linear unit placed in the four mutually rectangular directions about a point, and involving the measure of the operation of placing the unit radius in such respective positions.

109. Perhaps the principle of the superposition of time leads to quite as cogent a demonstration of the parallelogram of forces, as any of those usually given.

The forces P and Q [figs. 30, 31, 32] are such as to carry the unit of mass 1_μ through the distances OP and OQ = PR, when successively applied, in two units of time $1'_t$ and $1''_t$. The resultant is found, by superposing the second unit of time upon the first, to be that force which will carry 1_μ in a direct line from O to R in a single unit of time, since such line allows to each component force its proper proportion of effect during the whole of $1'_t$. When the angle of the components does not exceed 90° [figs. 30 and 31], each force will have its full effect in its own direction, being unopposed by the other; but when that angle is obtuse [fig. 32], the two forces will have opposing measures on one same axis X′X [fig. 42]; and since 1_μ cannot be moved in opposite directions at the same time, it is clear that an equal amount of these opposite measures will be destroyed by the opposing efforts of the components, and 1_μ will move by virtue of their difference OR′ on that axis, and of their sum OR″ on its perpendicular.

PLATE 1

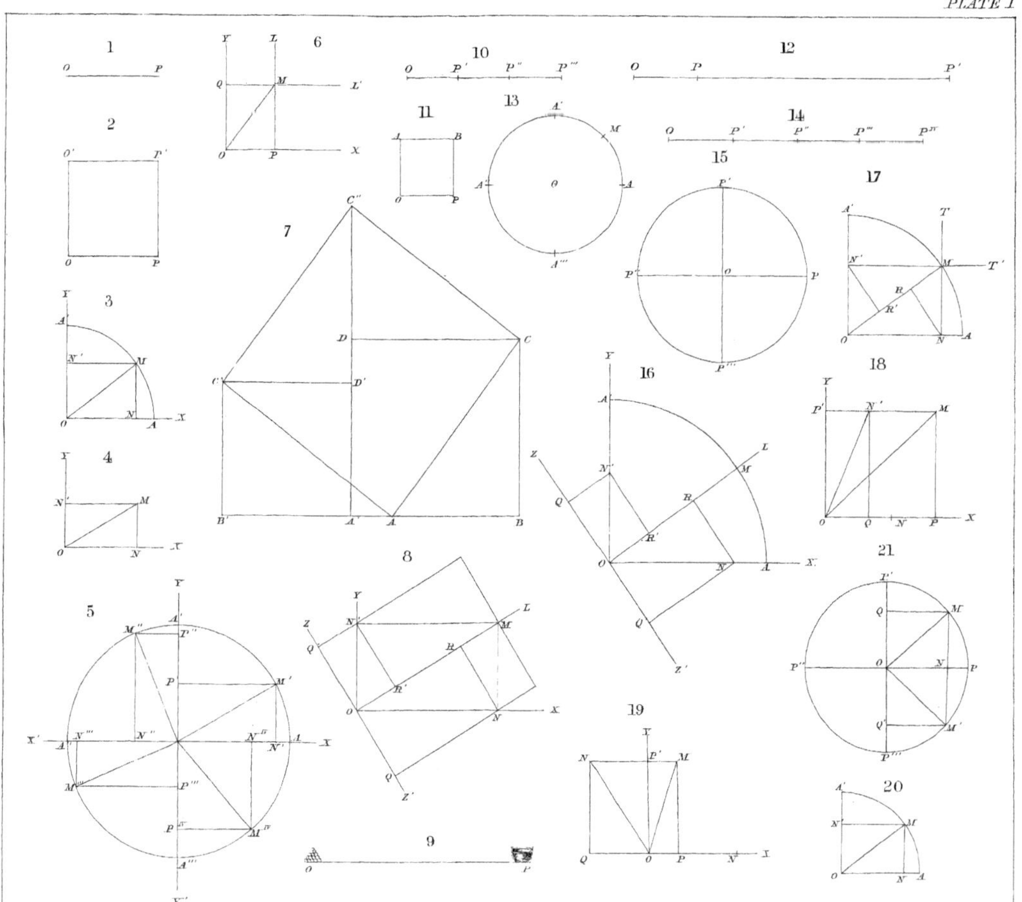

PLATE. 2.

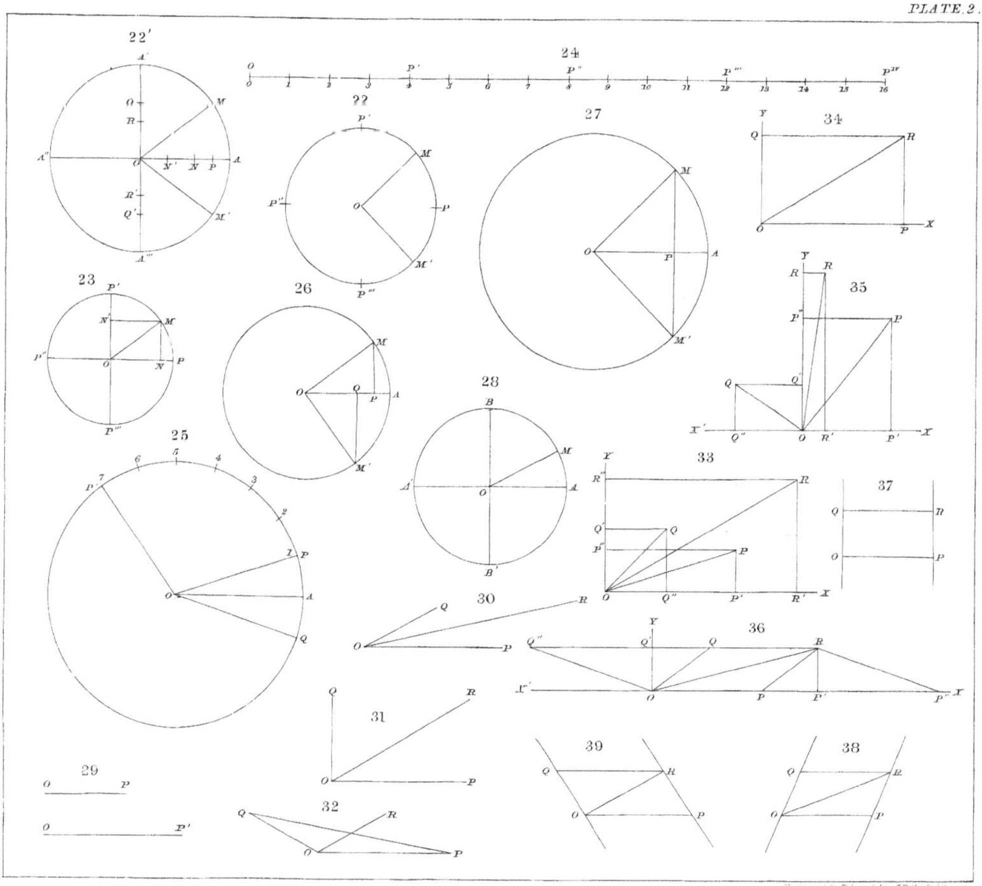

Engraved & Printed by J.E. Gavit, Albany.

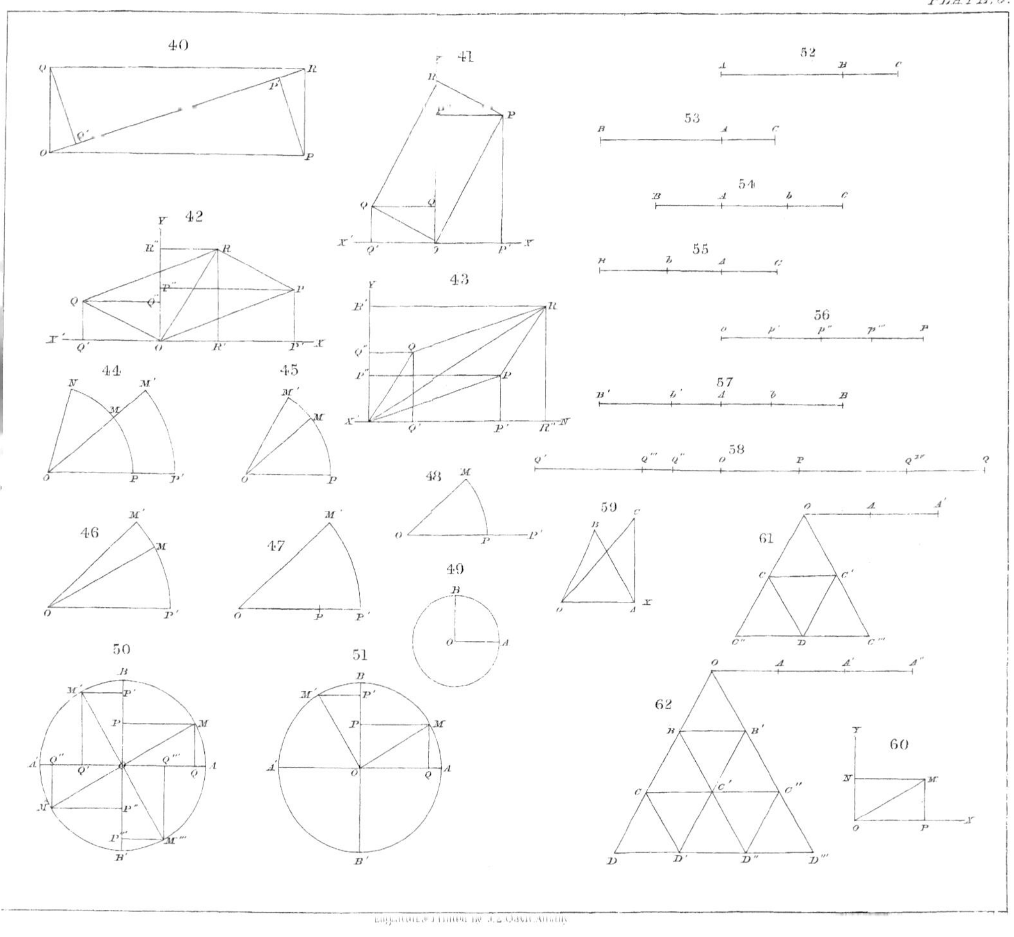
40
41
42
43
44
45
46
47
48
49
50
51
52
53
54
55
56
57
58
59
60
61
62

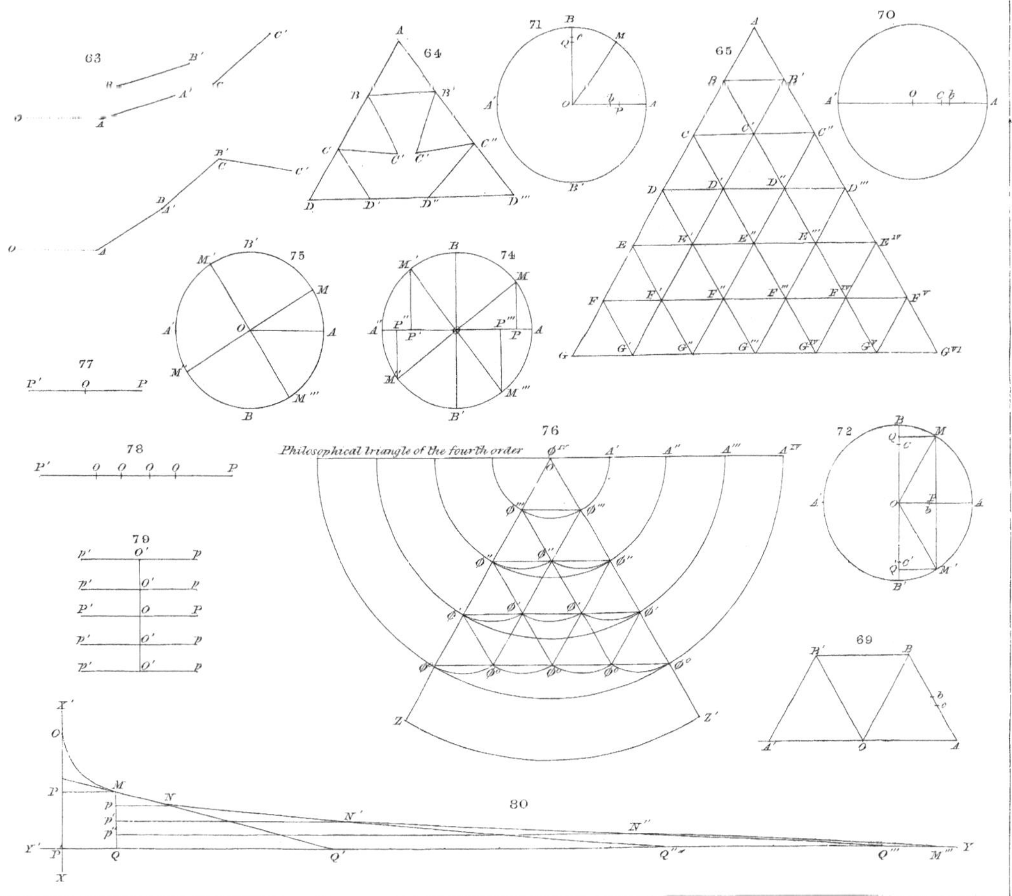

Engraved & Printed by J. E. Gavit, Albany

www.ingramcontent.com/pod-product-compliance
Lightning Source LLC
LaVergne TN
LVHW011217110826
845150LV00006B/1458

* 9 7 8 1 4 2 5 5 1 6 9 6 3 *